Praise for *Getting Rich Your Own Way*

The opportunities to create your own personal fortune have *never* been better than they are today, and *Getting Rich Your Own Way* is the ultimate how-to book for anyone who wants to achieve massive financial success. Brian Tracy takes the proven lessons and strategies from the many who have gone from rags to riches, and empowers readers with this success knowledge so that anyone can take action and create this same wealth in their own lives.

> —Joe Polish, Founder and President, Piranha
> Marketing, Inc., and
> TheGeniusNetwork.com

Financial success is not a miracle, nor is it based on luck. It is simply the law of cause and effect in action. If you initiate the causes you will get the effects. When you learn the essential principles, ideas, and concepts Brian presents in *Getting Rich Your Own Way* you will be on your way to financial independence.

> —Tony Jeary, Mr. Presentation™,
> Author, *Life Is a Series of Presentations*

This fast-moving book is full of practical, proven methods and strategies used by all financially successful people to become wealthy. By learning and applying the ideas in these pages, you will save yourself 10 to 20 years of hard work in becoming wealthy.

> —Raymond Faltinsky, CEO/
> Co-Founder, FreeLife International

An exciting, stimulating, and practical approach to proven wealth creation. By learning and applying Brian's ideas you will save yourself time and virtually guarantee your success!

> —Michael Burnett, CEO, Vision Pursuit

Financial success is not an accident! It comes to anyone who does the right things in the right way, over and over. Brian's book shows you exactly what you need to do to achieve all your financial goals.

> —Tom Hopkins, The Builder of Sales Champions

We are entering into an extended period of affluence and prosperity, and this powerful, practical book shows you how to achieve financial success beyond your dreams or imagination.

> —Lee Iacocca

GETTING RICH YOUR OWN WAY

ACHIEVE ALL YOUR FINANCIAL
GOALS FASTER THAN YOU
EVER THOUGHT POSSIBLE

BRIAN TRACY

WILEY

JOHN WILEY & SONS, INC.

Published by John Wiley & Sons, Inc., Hoboken, New Jersey.
Published simultaneously in Canada.

For general information on our other products and services please contact our Customer Care Department within the United States at (800) 762-2974, outside the United States at (317) 572-3993 or fax (317) 572-4002.

Wiley also publishes its books in a variety of electronic formats. Some content that appears in print may not be available in electronic books. For more information about Wiley products, visit our web site at www.Wiley.com.

Library of Congress Cataloging-in-Publication Data:
Tracy, Brian.
   Getting rich your own way : achieve all your financial goals faster than you ever thought possible / Brian Tracy.
     p. cm.
   ISBN 0-471-65264-4 (cloth)
   1. Finance, Personal. 2. Investments. 3. Success in business. I. Title.
   HG179.T73   2004
   650.1'2—dc22   2004005514

Printed in the United States of America.

10 9 8 7 6 5 4 3 2 1

To my four wonderful children—
Christina, Michael, David, and Catherine—
my primary reason for learning and applying
these ideas. May each of you get rich in
your own way in the years ahead.

Contents

Preface

*"The golden opportunity you are seeking is in yourself.
It is not in your environment; it is not in luck or
chance, or in the help of others; it is in yourself alone."*
—Orison Swett Marden

Immigrants to America used to think that the streets were paved with gold. They believed that fame and fortune was possible for everyone. Eventually, experience taught them this wasn't necessarily true. But what turned out to be true was that wealth came to those who knew how to look for it. Brian Tracy is one of those who knows where to look. By applying the principles he shares with you in this book, Brian Tracy went from a struggling salesman to a millionaire, and he did it in less than 10 years.

Brian has helped hundreds of businesses and thousands of individuals achieve financial success far beyond their expectations. He is constantly traveling the world, giving seminars on sales, management, entrepreneurship, business development, and personal achievement. He is the president of his own human resources company and the author/narrator of more than 300 best-selling audio and video learning programs. He is the author of 35 books, which have been translated into as many as 25 languages. In *Getting Rich Your Own Way*, Brian Tracy shows you, whoever you are and wherever you are starting from, how to become wealthy in the years ahead.

You will discover the five major sources of self-made millionaires, and the 18 principles, ideas, and concepts you need to program your mind for total success. You will learn the five rules for starting and building your own successful business. You will learn how to get the money you need, plus the 10 rules for investment success. You will learn the tried-and-true methods that have been proven over and over again by people who have gone from rags to riches in one generation. By reading about how Brian Tracy and so many others have done it, you too will learn how to get rich your own way, the way that is exactly right for you and your special talents and abilities. You will discover that there are no real limits.

—VICTOR RISLING

Introduction

"Are you in earnest? Seize this very minute—
What you can do, or dream you can, begin it,
Boldness has genius, power, and magic in it.
Only engage, and then the mind grows heated—
Begin it, and the work will be completed!"

—Prelude to Goethe's *Faust*,
translated by John Anster

The Difference between Success and Failure

Thank you for reading this book. The major difference between those who succeed and those who fail is simple: Successful people in every field are action-oriented, while failures are talk-oriented. People who achieve greatly are those who "just do it!" while those who accomplish little spend their lives hoping, wishing, dreaming, and making excuses. By opening this book, you have stepped forward into the ranks of those few people who *make* things happen, rather than the majority who continue to wait for things to happen to them.

This book is written with an American flavor, using American examples and statistics, but the principles it teaches are universal. They can be applied with some modifications in any other country with a market-based economy. Today the United States has the freest economic system and the greatest number of opportunities for a person to become wealthy of any country in the world. In 2004, according to the Organization for Economic Cooperation and Development in Paris, 19 percent of Americans between the ages of 18 and 54 were planning to start a new business—the highest percentage in the world. As a result of this entrepreneurial climate, there are more self-made millionaires and billionaires in the United States than in any other country. So we'll start here.

Starting with Nothing

When I was growing up, my family had very little money. My father was not regularly employed and my mother's work as a nurse was often the only thing that put food on the table for my three brothers and me. We were raised on macaroni and cheese, and wore clothes from the Goodwill and the Salvation Army. From the age of 10, I made my own money and paid my own bills working at gardening and odd jobs around the neighborhood.

When I was 15, I began searching for the so-called secrets of financial success. Like many young people, my goal was to be a millionaire by the time I was 30. However, when I turned 30, even though I had had spurts of success from time to time, I was just as broke as when I was 20. I had not even graduated from high school, and aside from being able to sell, I had no real skills at all.

It was about that time that I started to think seriously about my situation, and how little progress I had made in the preceding 10 years. Many of my friends were already doing quite well, married with children, living in nice homes, and making good money. But I was going nowhere financially.

My concern drove me into getting really serious about money for the first time. After trying a variety of shortcuts to get rich, I finally settled down and created a real plan for becoming wealthy. And the plan worked. I had countless setbacks and temporary failures, and I learned a lot of hard lessons over the next seven years, but I came out the other end with a net worth of more than one million dollars. And what I have done, within reason, you can do as well.

You Can Do It

My goal in writing this book is to convince you that, wherever you are in your financial life today, you, too, can become wealthy over the course of your working lifetime. If you start soon enough, work hard enough, and do some of the things I recommend, you may even become a millionaire. Thankfully, these methods, techniques, and strategies have worked for me and countless others. There is no reason why you, too, cannot achieve the American dream, if you are willing to take the time to learn how to attain it.

In the year 1900, there were about five thousand millionaires in the United States, and at that time the sum of a million dollars was worth a lot more than it is today. In 1980, when I began my research into the subject, there were about 1.5 million millionaires. By the year 2000, more than seven million Americans had a net worth of more than a million dollars. In addition, there are today decimillionaires, centimillionaires, and more than 300 billionaires. And these numbers are predicted to *double* in the years ahead.

Most of these millionaires, and even billionaires, are *first-generation*. They are self-made. They started with nothing. They earned every penny by applying their talents and abilities to the opportunities that they either discovered or created. It is estimated that someone, somewhere in the country, becomes a millionaire every four minutes. Your goal should be to become one of them.

What these self-made millionaires have done you can do as well. *Believe that no one is better than you and no one is smarter than you.* Over the years, I have had opportunities to meet with countless millionaires and multimillionaires, and even several billionaires. The remarkable thing about most of them is that they are largely unremarkable. They are invariably honest, hardworking men and women who have taken risks, developed expertise in their chosen fields, and refused to quit when the going got tough, as it always does.

The Difference between Rich and Poor

The wealthy are not very different from you and me. They have simply used more of their God-given talents and done things in a different way from the majority. The wonderful discovery is this: *If you do what other successful, wealthy people do, over and over again, you will eventually get the same results.* Financial success is not a miracle, nor is it based on luck. It is simply the law of cause and effect in action. If you initiate the causes, you will get the effects.

In this book, you will learn how to start wherever you are, even deeply in debt, and achieve financial independence. Having worked with thousands of people all over the world who have become millionaires, I firmly believe that individuals who really want to can become wealthy over the course of their working lifetimes, if they do the right things over and over until they get the results they desire.

A Real Eye Opener

I had a real eye-opening experience some years ago. I was speaking to an audience of about 1,200 people on success. I was telling them that I believed that anybody could be successful if they just did certain things in a certain way. At the break, I was surrounded by about 30 well-dressed men and women who were asking me questions and sharing their own stories. At that moment, a mentally retarded young man who had been sitting in the audience pushed his way through the crowd. He said in a very loud voice, "Mister Tracy, Mister Tracy, can I be a success, too?"

I was a bit taken back. I stood there looking at him while all these people watched me to hear how I was going to answer his question. I didn't exactly know what to tell him. My mind was racing. My credibility and my message, "Anyone can be successful," were being put to the test. Fortunately, he continued speaking. He said, "Mister Tracy, I live in a group home. Mister Tracy, we repair furniture. Every month, I buy a hundred-dollar savings bond. If I continue doing that, will I be a success, too?"

The Miracle of Compound Interest

As it happened, I had just been reading about how much someone would have to save to become financially independent. I knew that a person who saved $100 per month from the age of 21 to the age of 65 and earned an average return of 10 percent on the savings over that time period would be worth more than a million dollars at retirement. I suddenly realized that that young man, living in a group home, repairing furniture, with no advantages or opportunities, could actually become wealthy. If he just kept saving $100 every month, he would retire wealthier than 95 percent percent of the population.

He would end up better off than most doctors, dentists, lawyers, architects, engineers, salespeople, small business owners, corporate executives, and people in show business. All he had to do was to save $100 per month and he would retire financially independent. If he could discipline himself to save every month, the power of compound interest would do the rest. Anyone can do it.

You Can Learn What You Need to Learn

Making money is a basic skill. It takes knowledge and practice to master, but since hundreds of thousands, and even millions, of men and women have learned how to make money over the years, it is obviously a *learnable* skill. In fact, if you can drive a car, operate a cell phone, use a computer, or carry out many of the standard tasks that are a part of daily life, you definitely have all the intelligence and ability you need to earn all the money you want.

In the pages ahead, I will show you how to achieve financial independence, and even *get rich*, in a variety of ways. After that, it is up to you to take action, and keep on taking action until you get the results you desire. There are no real limits except the ones you place on your own imagination.

> *"See the things you want as already yours. . . .*
> *Think of them as yours, as belonging to you,*
> *as already in your possession."*
> **—Robert Collier**

1

Learn How to Become Rich

*"When your desires are strong enough, you will
appear to possess superhuman powers to achieve."*

—Napoleon Hill

If someone with limited abilities can become rich, why is it that so few
people become wealthy? Even though we live in the most affluent
country in the world, where most people earn and spend a fortune
in the course of their working lifetimes, why is it that the majority
end up dependent on Social Security, pensions and relatives when
they retire?

If a person earning $25,000 per year would just save $2,500 per
year, 10 percent of his income, and invest it carefully to earn a return of
10 percent compounded over the course of his working lifetime—the
years from age 21 to age 65 (44 years)—it would grow to $1,794,762
through the miracle of compound interest.

If a mentally retarded young man without a single advantage in the
world can become wealthy (see Introduction), and a person earning
$25,000 a year, saving 10 percent of his income, can become a million-
aire or a multimillionaire, then almost anyone can become rich who
wants it badly enough.

Why People Don't Become Rich

The question I began to ask was, "Why is it that people don't become wealthy?" In a country like ours, with the opportunities that we have, why is it that so few people retire financially independent? And I eventually found the answers. Here are what I consider to be the five reasons why people don't become wealthy.

Who, Me?

First, at the top of the list, is that it never *occurs* to them. The average person has grown up in a family where he has never met or known anyone who was wealthy. He goes to school and socializes with people who are not wealthy. He works with people who are not wealthy. He has a *reference group* or a social circle outside of work who are not wealthy. He has no role models who are wealthy. If this has happened to you throughout your formative years, up to the age of 20, you can grow up and become a fully mature adult in our society without it ever occurring to you that it's just as possible for you to become wealthy as for anyone else.

This is why people who grow up in homes where their parents are wealthy are much more likely to become wealthy as adults than people who grew up in homes where their parents are not wealthy. Wealth achievement is part of the worldview of children of wealthy parents.

Therefore, the first reason why people don't become wealthy is it never occurs to them that it is possible for them. And of course, if it never occurs to them, then they will never take any of the steps necessary to make it a reality.

Make a Decision!

Another reason that people don't become wealthy is that they never *decide* to. Even if a person reads a book, attends a seminar, or associates with people who are financially successful, nothing changes until she makes a decision to do something different. Even if it occurs to a person that she could become wealthy if she just did certain things in a specific way, if she doesn't decide to take the first step, she ends up staying as she is. *If you continue to do what you've always done, you'll continue to get what you've always got.*

The primary reason for underachievement and failure is that the great majority of people don't decide to be successful. They never make a firm, unequivocal commitment or definite decision that they are going to become wealthy. They mean to, and they intend to, and they hope to, and they're going to, *someday*. They wish and hope and pray that they will make a lot of money, but they never decide, "I am going to do it!" This decision is an essential first step to becoming financially independent.

Maybe Tomorrow

Procrastination can prevent people from becoming wealthy. People always have a good reason not to begin doing what they know they need to do to achieve financial independence. It is always the wrong month, the wrong season, or the wrong year. Business conditions in their industry are no good, or they may be too good. The market isn't right. They may have to take a risk, or give up their security. Maybe next year.

There always seems to be a reason to procrastinate. As a result, they keep putting it off, month by month, year by year, until it's too late. Even if it has occurred to a person that he can become wealthy, and he has made a decision to change, procrastination will push all his plans into the indefinite future. *Procrastination is the thief of time, and of life.*

Pay the Price

What economists refer to as the *inability to delay gratification* is another reason that people retire poor. The great majority of people have an irresistible compulsion to spend every single penny they make and whatever else they can borrow or buy on credit. If you cannot delay gratification and discipline yourself to refrain from spending everything you make, you cannot become wealthy. If you cannot practice frugality as a lifelong habit, it will be impossible for you to achieve financial independence. As W. Clement Stone, founder of Combined Insurance Company of America and one of the richest men in the world, said, "If you cannot save money, the seeds of greatness are not in you."

Take the Long View

The last reason that people retire poor is perhaps as important as, if not more important than, all the others. It is *lack of time perspective*. In a longitudinal study conducted in the 1950s and published in 1964 as

The Unheavenly City, Dr. Edward Banfield of Harvard University studied the reasons for upward socioeconomic mobility in the United States. He wanted to know how you could predict whether an individual or a family was going to move upward one or more socioeconomic groupings and be wealthier in the next generation than they were this generation.

Banfield studied and compared his findings against the most common explanations for economic success in the United States and in other countries. Was it education? No. Many people with good educations actually moved *down* economically. Was it intelligence? No. A lot of very intelligent people were poor and unable to earn a living. Was it being born into the right family? No. Many people born into affluent families did poorly as adults, while many people with poor educations became very successful. Was it being in the right part of the country? Was it being in the right industry? Was it luck? What factors were best at predicting that a person would move up economically over the years?

Project into the Future

All Banfield's research brought him to a single factor that he concluded was more accurate than any other in predicting success in the United States—*time perspective*, defined as "the amount of time that you take into consideration when planning your day-to-day activities, and when making important decisions in your life." Time perspective referred to how far you projected into the future when you decided what you were going to do or not do in the present.

An example of a long time perspective is the common habit of upper class families in England to register their children at Oxford or Cambridge as soon as the children are born, even though the youngsters will not be attending for 18 or 19 years. This long-term thinking is what causes parents to open savings accounts for their young children to assure that they will be able to attend good colleges when they graduate from high school.

Saving and planning for the future is *long time perspective in action*. The young couple who begins putting $50 a month aside in an education fund so that their newborn child can go to the college or university of his or her choice is a couple with long time perspective. They are willing to sacrifice in the short term to assure better results and outcomes in the long term. People with long time perspectives almost invariably move up economically in the course of their lifetimes.

Pay the Price in Advance

A person who graduates from high school, goes on to university, attends medical school, earns an M.D. degree, perseveres through internship and residency, and then after 10 or more years of training becomes a licensed physician, has a long time perspective. He has earned the right, through years of sacrifice and delayed gratification, to prestige, status, and a high standard of living. That 10 to 12 years of work and study is an investment in his career for the rest of his life. His long time perspective will also as-sure a higher standard of living for his children, as well as better schools, and more opportunities for them. His children will very likely marry bet-ter, have higher social and economic aspirations, and live better lives.

The time perspective of a doctor investing 10 or more years in ed-ucation at the beginning of his career may be the lifetimes of one or two generations, 50 to 70 years. We intuitively sense that a doctor, someone who has dedicated so many years to learn his craft so that he can attend to us and our families when he is most needed, is a person who has earned our respect and esteem. This appreciation for long-term think-ing may be why the family doctor is usually at the top when surveys of the most respected people in society are compiled.

Attitude Is Everything

Time perspective is an essential measure of *social class*. A wealthy family or a good education will help, but ultimately your level of status and prestige will be determined by how far you think and plan into the fu-ture as you go about your day-to-day work and life.

If an immigrant couple comes to the United States with nothing and goes to work at menial jobs, sacrificing so that their children can go to school and attend university, that immigrant couple is demonstrating class, no matter how well or poorly they are doing in the present. They are virtually guaranteeing upward social mobility for themselves and their offspring.

The opposite of a long time perspective is no time perspective at all. The average professional person has a time perspective of 10, 15, or 20 years, perhaps longer. The average laborer has a time perspective of about two pay periods. The derelict, the hopeless drug addict, or the al-coholic at the bottom of the social pyramid has a time perspective of hours, or even minutes. He does not think about the future at all, only the next drink or shot. Each person's position and direction in life, from the top to the bottom of society, are determined by the length of their time perspective.

Think about the Future

The very act of *lengthening* your time perspective, of thinking far into the future, changes your attitude and your personality. You begin the process of getting rich your own way by thinking ahead 10 or 20 years. As you do, you become more capable of setting bigger, longer-term goals and making long-term plans for their accomplishment. You become more thoughtful about your decisions, and more sensitive to the long-term consequences of the ways that you invest your time or money. You develop greater patience and perseverance. You actually become a better and more positive person.

From this day forward, practice lengthening your time perspective. Begin to see that everything that you are doing today is part of a long process that is moving you inexorably toward becoming financially independent, if not rich, over the course of your career. This is the mind-set of people who move continually upward and onward throughout their lives.

Commit to Your Career

Many people begin work or start careers and it never occurs to them they may be doing the same job for 20 or 25 years. It doesn't occur to them that they should invest any amount of time, money, and energy to learn how to do their jobs very, very well.

You should be prepared to make any sacrifice to excel at what you do. This enables you to earn the very most that it is possible to earn in that field. Even if it takes years of hard work to get to the top, with a long time perspective you will persevere. You will realize that *the time is going to pass anyway*. The only question is, how much will you be earning five years from today?

Five Ways to Stay Poor

Once again, here are the five reasons why people retire poor: One, it never occurs to them that they, too, can become wealthy. Two, if it does occur to them, they never *decide* to become wealthy. Three, if they do decide to do something to improve their financial lives, they *procrastinate*, sometimes all their lives. Four, they cannot discipline themselves to *delay gratification*, to resist spending everything they earn and a little bit more besides. Five, they operate with a *short time perspective*. They think and act day to day and month to month instead of planning 10 and 20 years into the future.

Five Ways to Become Rich

If you are really serious about becoming wealthy, there are five primary ways that fortunes are made.

Become an Entrepreneur

The number one road to riches, at the head of the list and on the top of the hit parade throughout U.S. history, is *entrepreneurship*, starting and building a successful business. Entrepreneurship includes every kind of business, from farming and trucking to real estate and computers.

Seventy-four percent of self-made millionaires in the United States, going back 200 years, come from self-owned businesses. An individual starts with an idea for a product or service, turns it into a business, builds it up from the ground floor, and as a result becomes wealthy. Henry Ford, Andrew Carnegie, John Jacob Astor, Cornelius Vanderbilt, Ross Perot, Sam Walton, Bill Gates, Michael Dell, and Larry Ellison are all people who started with little or nothing and built their own successful businesses. And there are millions of others.

Work Your Way Up

Another way to become rich is as a highly paid *executive* of a successful company, or as an employee of a company that awards stock options that become valuable. Ten percent of self-made millionaires in the United States are men or women who have joined large corporations, or companies that became large, and worked for these companies for many years. They usually worked hard; were promoted and paid well; earned stock options, bonuses, and profit sharing; and as a result of holding on to that money, became millionaires and multimillionaires.

Paul Allen started Microsoft with Bill Gates, sold out when he became ill, took much of his share of the company in stock, and is now a multibillionaire. The Seattle area is famous for having so many "Microsoft millionaires," people who went to work for Microsoft in the 1970s and 1980s, sometimes as secretaries and programmers, received stock options, and became wealthy when they exercised them. Many senior executives receive bonuses and profit sharing worth many millions in a single year. Working for a large company that grows, pays well, and shares its profits is a major source of wealth.

Many executives have stayed with their corporations for many years; have risen to positions of seniority; are paid extremely well; are given stock options, profit sharing, and bonuses; and as a result of holding on to the money, they became millionaires. Not so long ago, Lee Iacocca, the chairman of Chrysler Corporation, was paid $26.7 million for one year. Michael Eisner of Disney earned a $150 million bonus. It's not too hard to become a self-made millionaire if you're making that kind of money in a year.

Become a Professional

A major source of self-made millionaires consists of *professional people*—doctors, dentists, lawyers, architects, engineers, and others with advanced degrees who can charge high fees for their services. These people earn their degrees, dedicate themselves to becoming very good at what they do, rise to the top of their professions, earn high incomes, and then hold on to the money. Ten percent of self-made millionaires in the United States fall into this category.

Get into Sales

An important source of self-made millionaires is *salespeople* and sales consultants. Five percent of self-made millionaires in the United States are men and women who are experts and at the top of their fields in selling. They never started their own businesses. Few of them went to college or earned professional degrees. Instead, they became very good at selling a product or service, and were paid well for doing it. In addition, they managed their money well, invested it intelligently, and made it grow until they were millionaires or better.

Fully 99 percent of self-made millionaires in America come from these four categories:

1. Self-owned businesses	74%
2. Senior executive positions	10%
3. Doctors, lawyers, and other professionals	10%
4. Salespeople and sales consultants	5%
Total	99%

All the Others

The final 1 percent of self-made millionaires includes all the people who have made their money in the stock market, with inventions, in show business, through the authorship of books and songs, as lottery winners, and all other sources. Unfortunately, because this group gets so much publicity, many people think that they are typical of the people who get rich. The fact is that they are quite rare.

In this book, we'll concentrate on teaching you how to become a *money magnet* and how to achieve financial independence by starting your own business, investing intelligently, getting onto the fast track in your current job, moving to the top of your field, and a combination of two or more of these. You'll learn how to spot opportunities and how to get started. You will learn how to get the money you need, how to maximize your talents and abilities, and how to gain the knowledge you need in order to succeed financially in whatever field you choose.

Definition of Wealth

Let's start off with the best definition of wealth. Wealth is *cash flow from other sources*. You may earn a lot of money, but you are wealthy only when your money works for you. To become wealthy, your job is to acquire money and then put it to work making more money. The key to wealth building is simple. It is called *adding value*. Successful people are those who find ways to add value in some way to a person or business, a product, or a service.

Here is an example of adding value: Domino's Pizza. Domino's added value to pizza by rapid delivery and as a result created a multimillion-dollar success story. Delivering something faster increases the perceived value of the product and lowers the price sensitivity.

You can add value by buying something in one place at one price and making it available in another place at a higher price. For example, buying a product or service manufactured in Hong Kong, Taiwan, Japan, or Germany, importing it and selling it at a higher price in the United States is a way of adding value. All importation and distribution is based on this principle.

You can add value with services. You can perform a service that enhances the life or work of another person or that enables someone to achieve a goal faster, more easily, more cheaply, or more conveniently. This is another way to add value. A dentist who takes away pain is adding value. An accountant who saves a client money on taxes is adding value. A salesperson who introduces a new product or service to a customer is adding value. Most fortunes in the United States begin with the sale of personal services.

Find a Need and Fill It

All financial success, especially business success, is based on the old adage *find a need and fill it*. The subjective theory of value says that all value is in the eye of the beholder. Something is worth only what someone else will pay for it. People decide what price they will pay based on their feeling of need for the product or service, and the alternatives available.

Successful business is based on someone bringing together the factors of production—land, labor, capital, raw materials, and management—and creating a product or service that a customer will pay for at a price that is greater than the total cost of producing it. This is how the entrepreneur adds value to the combination of ingredients that go into creating a product or service. This difference between what it costs to produce and deliver and the price a customer is willing to pay for it is called profit, or added value.

Profit is the stuff out of which fortunes are made. Whenever you see an opportunity to give people what they want at a price greater than it costs you to produce it, you see an opportunity to make a profit. If you can create a way of making profits, you can build a business and begin moving toward financial success. Almost any profitable business or occupation can make you financially independent if you manage it intelligently.

Big Fortunes from Small Ideas

Surprisingly enough, the businesses owned by self-made millionaires are usually quite ordinary. People become rich in construction and in subtrades like drywalling and roofing. They become rich running dry cleaning establishments and cafés. Some of them are truck drivers and auctioneers, farmers and crane operators, computer software designers, and machine tool manufacturers. Virtually any field that offers an opportunity to excel and earn profits can serve as a springboard to riches. The key is for you to do the work better and more efficiently than others, and then to hold on to the profits and excess cash that you earn as a result.

People often ask me what field they should go into if they want to make a lot of money. The answer to this question is constantly changing, just as the wants, needs, demands, and desires of consumers are constantly changing. During the 1990s boom in technology and the explosion of the Internet-based companies, millionaires were being created at the rate of 10,000 per week! When these stock option–fueled companies collapsed, most of this new wealth disappeared, only to reemerge in the booming home and real estate markets nationwide. No one knows for sure where the rapid growth opportunities of tomorrow will occur, but they will continue to rise and fall as long as customer wants continue to change, creating opportunities for ambitious, entrepreneurial-minded people.

One Idea Is All You Need

Tom Fatjo, who built Browning Ferris Industries, is a famous success story. He started off as an accountant. Because no one else would haul the weekly trash for his family and his neighbors, he bought a truck and started hauling the trash himself after work. Soon other unserviced neighborhoods and municipalities asked him if he would haul their trash as well.

He became wealthy by standardizing the trash hauling industry locally, and then nationwide, something that had never been done before. By introducing mass-production methods and new efficiencies, he made trash hauling an extremely profitable business and became one of the richest entrepreneurs in the country.

Colonel Harland Sanders, starting at age 65, became wealthy selling a fried chicken recipe. Debbie Fields, with four children at home, started with a small shop and became wealthy selling cookies, as did Famous Amos. In each case, the entrepreneur took an existing need or desire and figured out a way to offer the product or service at high quality, combined with efficient operations that enabled the company to generate high profits.

Maximize Your Assets

The logical question then comes up: "What do wealthy people do or have that enables them to accomplish so much more than the average?" I believe that people become rich as a result of developing what I call *leverage*. Leverage is the key to maximizing and multiplying your potential for success and financial achievement. Leverage enables you to accomplish vastly more than you could if you just relied on your own physical and mental efforts, as most people do. Leverage is the key to getting rich.

Here are 10 examples of leverage that you can develop and use to achieve financial independence.

Specialized Knowledge

The first type of leverage is *knowledge*. Specialized knowledge gives you leverage because it makes you worth more, and makes your contribution more valuable. Doctors, lawyers, accountants, experienced salespeople, all have practical knowledge that is of value to others. This superior knowledge enables them to get better results faster. As a result, people prefer to use their services and are willing to pay them more.

There are three ways to develop leverage through knowledge: become an expert, specialize in high-value activities, and know your product well.

Become an Expert

Resolve to become an expert in your chosen field. Make a decision today to join the top 10 percent. Set it as a goal, make a plan, and work on becoming better every day. Read the best books in your field, and take every course and seminar you can find that will help you, even if you have to travel to attend. Listen to audio programs in your car. Become an ongoing do-it-yourself project.

Specialize in High-Value Activities

Specialize in those areas that are of greatest importance and value to your company or to your customers. Apply the 80/20 Rule, which says that 80 percent of your results come from 20 percent of your activities. Focus on the 20 percent of activities in your work that contribute the most value to yourself and to other people. Specialize in excelling at those areas of specialized knowledge that customers care about the most.

Know Your Product Well

Know your product or service inside out. Aim to be recognized as the industry expert in your field. Remember that the person who has expert knowledge can make a far more valuable contribution than the person whose knowledge is just average. As a result, experts are paid much more for what they do.

Master Your Craft

Skill is a type of leverage. The better you are at your job, the more you will be paid. The top 20 percent of salespeople earn as much as 15 times the average earnings of the bottom 80 percent. The top doctors, mechanics, lawyers, technical specialists, and leaders in every field earn vastly more than the average performer.

The keys to developing the leverage of skill are: be the best, never stop learning, and exceed expectations.

Be the Best

First, make a decision to be the best at what you do. Pay any price. Make any sacrifice. Go any distance to become excellent in your field. Even if it takes you several years to master your craft, the time is going to pass anyway.

Never Stop Learning

Dedicate yourself to continuous personal and professional improvement. Never allow yourself to become satisfied or complacent at your current level of skill. As Pat Riley, the basketball coach, once said, "If you're not getting better, you're getting worse!" There is a race on and you are in it. Resolve to win by learning and applying more and faster than your competitors.

Exceed Expectations

Always strive to exceed the expectations of your customers, your boss, and the people you serve. Make it a habit to always do more than you are paid for and do it better. If you commit yourself to doing more than you're paid for, you will always end up being paid more than you're getting today.

Money Is Power

The third type of leverage you can develop is *money*. Money is a powerful source of leverage and usually follows naturally from the development of knowledge and skill in your field.

You have heard the saying, "It takes money to make money." The main reason that it takes money to make money is that your ability to save and accumulate funds is an essential step in the development of the personal qualities and character that you must possess if you sincerely want to achieve financial independence. In other words, you become a person capable of becoming wealthy by disciplining yourself to save the money that is necessary for you to achieve wealth.

There are three things you can do to develop the leverage of money: save regularly, get out of debt, and build a cash reserve.

Save Regularly

Begin a systematic savings plan, putting away at least 10 percent of your gross income each month. This is the starting point of riches. Ideally, you should have a specific amount automatically deducted and invested from your pay before you get it.

Get out of Debt

Pay off your debts, starting with those carrying the highest interest rates such as credit cards and finance companies. Set a goal to live largely debt free aside from your home mortgage and your car payments.

Build a Cash Reserve

Resolve to build up a cash reserve so that you are ready when the opportunity arises. Most people stay broke all their lives because even if a wonderful moneymaking idea comes their way, they have no money to invest. As Earl Nightingale, the motivational radio personality, once said, "If a man is not prepared when his opportunity comes, it will only make him appear foolish."

The People You Know

The fourth form of leverage is *contacts*. Knowing the right people, and being known by them, can open doors for you that will save you years of hard work. The quality and quantity of your contacts and your relationships will have more to do with your success than perhaps any other factor. Knowing one person at the right time and place can change the course of your life.

Here are three things you can do to expand your list of contacts: make a list, network regularly, and get involved in your community.

Make a List

First, make a list of the best 25 people, locally or nationally, you feel it would be most useful for you to get to know. Develop a strategy to meet each one of them over the next 12 months. Then make a list of 25 more.

List the people who head up the major corporations who would be useful for you to know. List the mayor, your congressperson, and your senator. List the important people that it would be helpful for you to know and then make a plan to get to meet them.

Network Regularly

Network at every opportunity. Join your business and trade associations. Attend meetings. Get involved. Volunteer for service on a key committee. This action alone has cut years off the career path of many people, including myself.

Once when I was giving a presentation for the chamber of commerce, I was noticed by a senior executive who sat on one of the key committees. He approached me later and hired me away from the company I was working for at triple the salary. As a result, I jumped ahead in my career by five years. It is very important that you network at every opportunity.

Get Involved in Your Community

Another way to expand your contacts is to get involved in community service organizations. The best people in every community, the people you should know and who should know you, are usually involved in public service in some way. Start with the United Way in your own city, or get involved in any charity that you care about or that you're interested in. Get involved with your church or your political party. You'll be amazed at the quality of people whom you'll meet doing volunteer work.

You Are a Genius

Creativity is a form of leverage. Remember, one new idea is all you need to start a fortune. Everyone has the ability to come up with creative ideas and solutions if they look for them. All great fortunes begin with an idea. This aspect of getting rich is so important that we'll devote a whole chapter (Chapter 8) to showing you how to unlock your inborn creativity.

Get the Job Done

Good work habits are a form of leverage that can help you. Good work habits give you an edge over others in your field. They help you stand out and bring you to the attention of people who can help you.

In every study, it appears that good work habits will open more doors for you faster than almost any other qualities you can develop. In the final analysis, you will always be paid in direct proportion to the results you get for your employer. If you develop a reputation for being the person who gets the job done fast, the one who consistently and predictably gets the results required, that alone can put you onto the fast track in your career.

A Positive Mental Attitude

Another form of leverage you can develop is a *positive personality*. Every study of successful people shows that the more people there are who like you, the more doors they will open for you, and the more opportunities you will have to get ahead. If they like you, people will do everything possible to help you succeed. Your ability to get along with others, to communicate effectively, to be a positive and cheerful person, will cause people to want to help you wherever you go.

Writer and researcher Daniel Goleman has become famous for his work on "emotional intelligence." He concludes that your ability to get along well with others is more central to your success than IQ or graduation from a top university. He concludes that most successful people reach the top by developing their ability to influence, communicate, persuade, and sell people on their ideas.

Peter Drucker says that the three key tools of the executive are the meeting, the presentation, and the written work. Excellence in each of these areas is learnable through practice and application. Resolve today to become an excellent communicator. Take a course in public speaking. Study and practice the art of negotiating. As much as 85 percent of your success will be determined by how well you communicate with others, so resolve today to become an expert in human relations.

The Luck Factor

Another element of success that is mentioned repeatedly in the stories of wealthy men and women is the factor of *luck*. Luck is a form of leverage and it is part of every great success. Fortunately, luck is largely predictable and happens to people for specific reasons. In many respects, you actually create your own luck by the things you do, or fail to do.

Luck is largely a matter of *probabilities*. There is a probability that virtually anything can happen, and these probabilities can be calculated with considerable accuracy. In almost every case, you can increase or decrease the likelihood of something happening or not happening. This is the central theme of my book *Create Your Own Future* (John Wiley & Sons, 2003).

For example, there is a certain probability that you will be killed in a traffic accident. But you can reduce this probability by staying sober, driving more carefully, and wearing a seatbelt. Some people drive all their lives and never have an accident or a speeding ticket.

Make a Million?

There is a 5 percent probability that you will become a millionaire in the course of your working lifetime. This also means that there is a 95 percent probability that you will not save a million dollars. You may even work all your life and retire poor or dependent on others. One of the main purposes of this book is to help you increase the likelihood of achieving financial independence by giving you the knowledge and tools practiced by the top 5 percent.

One thing we know, for example, is that luck is a function of *activity*. The more things you try and the faster you try them, the more likely it is that you will try the right thing at the right time that will bring you the success you desire. Bill Gates is the richest man in the world, but Microsoft has about 1,600 different projects in various stages of development at any given time. He is continually working to increase the probability that his company will come up with something new and highly profitable.

Many of the things Bill Gates attempts will fail. The fact is that most things don't work the first time, and often they don't work the first 10 times. Nonetheless, if you keep trying new things and learning from every setback, you will inevitably develop the skills and experience you need to succeed.

Continually Study and Prepare

There is a saying, "Luck is when preparation meets opportunity." The more time you take to learn, study, and prepare yourself in your chosen field, the more luck you will seem to have. The better prepared you are, the more often you will both recognize opportunity and be capable of taking advantage of opportunity when it arises.

Most importantly, luck seems to happen to people with clear goals and detailed plans of action. When you know exactly what you want and you are working diligently to achieve it every day, all kinds of wonderful things happen to you to move you more rapidly toward your goals, and your goals toward you.

When you are clear about your goals, you trigger the *law of attraction* and begin to attract into your life people, ideas, circumstances, and resources that help you to achieve them. Happy coincidences and serendipitous events occur that help you in ways that you cannot now explain. I will say more about becoming a money magnet and attracting luck in the next chapter.

Developing Personal Power

Energy is a form of leverage you can develop to get rich your own way. Most successful people have higher energy levels than the average. Because of this, they can work longer, harder hours with greater enthusiasm and persistence. They are more resilient and can bounce back from the inevitable problems and difficulties that occur on the road to success.

It is therefore essential for great success that you organize your lifestyle around proper diet, proper exercise and proper rest. For example, one common habit of virtually all successful people is that they watch very little television and they go to bed early. "Early to bed, early to rise" does seem to make people "healthy, wealthy, and wise." Successful people organize their time and lifestyle so that they can get up early and plan their days while the average person is still sleeping. This habit alone can give you an edge over the competition.

Choose the Right Job

Another form of leverage you can develop on your quest for riches is the correct choice of occupation. Choosing the right job is perhaps the most important form of leverage. The one common denominator of successful, wealthy men and women, aside from self-discipline, is that *they do what they love to do*. The most important decision you ever make in your career is choosing the right kind of work for you.

It is possible to work hard, overcome obstacles, and persist through to success only when you are working at something that you care about, something that interests you and absorbs you completely. In fact, if you don't love your job enough to want to be the very best at it, you should find something else that you can become passionate about. If you stay at a job that doesn't excite you, you are in danger of wasting your time and your life.

The Million-Dollar Question

Here is a question for you: *If you won a million dollars in the lottery tomorrow, would you continue to work at your current job?* If the answer is "no," then your first responsibility to yourself is to admit that you are on the wrong road. Your goal must be to begin seeking your ideal job or position. You must dedicate yourself to finding something you love to do, where you have the potential to excel, no matter what that may require in terms of change or sacrifice.

Once you have found the right job, the work that is perfectly suited for your unique combination of talents, interests, abilities, and temperament, then you are ready to start getting rich your own way.

Become a No-Limit Person

If you sincerely desire to be rich, there is nothing *outside* of you that can stop you. Every type of person with every imaginable handicap, limitation, and obstacle has found a way to overcome their difficulties and go on to great success.

No matter how many obstacles you face, someone else has faced 10 times as many and been successful in spite of it. If you sincerely desire to be rich, there is no miracle to it. Becoming wealthy requires a goal, a plan, self-discipline, and hard, hard work for a long, long time. These are all qualities that you can learn and develop.

If you are willing to pay the price of success in advance and keep on paying it over and over until you achieve your goals, you will surely succeed. The only real question you have to answer is, *how badly do you want it?*

Action Exercises

1. Make a decision today that you are going to achieve financial independence in the years ahead. Determine a specific financial goal, set a deadline, make a plan, and take action on it today.

2. Go to the bank and open a "financial accumulation" account where you are going to begin building your "financial fortress" in the months and years ahead.

3. Project forward 10 to 20 years and begin imagining your perfect life. What would it look like? What steps could you take immediately to begin making it a reality?

4. Commit to excellence in your chosen field. Identify the one skill that, if you did it excellently all the time, would help you the most to make a more valuable contribution.

5. Pick up the pace. Resolve to do more than you are paid for each day, do it fast, and do it dependably. Become action-oriented.

6. Refuse to play it safe. Don't worry about temporary failure. Concentrate on increasing the probabilities of success by trying more things and persisting longer.

7. Resolve to remain positive and optimistic no matter what happens. Look for the good in every situation, and in every person. Enjoy the process of getting rich your own way.

"The way to wealth, if you desire it, is as plain as the way to market. It depends chiefly on two words, industry and frugality. Waste neither time nor money but make the best use of both."

—Benjamin Franklin

2

Become a Money Magnet

*"The big challenge is to become all that you have
the possibility of becoming. You cannot believe
what it does to the human spirit to maximize
your potential and stretch it to the limit."*

—Jim Rohn

The starting point of all riches is the development of what Napoleon Hill called a *prosperity consciousness*. You must become a financial success in your thinking long before you achieve it in your reality. Both poverty and riches are the result of a state of mind. The most important single step you take on the road to wealth and financial independence is the decision to change your thinking, and to impress into your mind an unshakable belief that you can and will achieve your financial goals. This must happen before anything else happens.

When I was growing up, I was fascinated by stories of successful men and women and how they made and lost their fortunes, and then made them over again. I read about the importance of a prosperity consciousness several times. But I never fully understood what it meant until a few years ago. Then suddenly it hit me and I've never been quite the same since. Every aspect of my life improved dramatically, especially in the area of accumulating wealth, when I finally understood what was meant by the words *prosperity consciousness*.

Change Your Thinking, Change Your Life

In this chapter, you will learn some of the most exciting principles ever discovered by mankind in the search for the secrets of the ages—the secrets of health, happiness, and great personal wealth. Once you understand these key principles or laws, everything your mind can conceive and believe will become possible for you. There will be no limitations except the ones you accept in your own mind.

All Causation Is Mental

How you use your mind determines everything that you are or ever will be will be. Put another way, you are merely a *mind* with a body that you use to carry it around. Everything in the man-made world began with an idea. Everything you see around you is simply an expression of thought. Your entire life is an expression of your own thinking. And since the quality of your thinking determines the quality of your life, if you improve the quality of your thinking, you must inevitably improve the quality of your life.

When you begin to think about yourself as capable of achieving all your financial and personal goals, and constantly seek ways to make them into realities, your whole attitude toward yourself and your possibilities will change for the better.

Expect the Best

The *law of expectations* says that *whatever you expect with confidence, positive or negative, becomes your reality*. If you confidently expect to succeed and hold to that belief, and if you act as if your success was inevitable, you will eventually achieve that success.

If you confidently expect to learn something from every experience, you will become wiser and smarter from every setback or difficulty. If you confidently expect to become wealthy as a result of applying your talents and abilities to your opportunities, and you maintain that attitude of confident expectations long enough, it will become your reality. An attitude of positive expectations will give you a positive, optimistic, cheerful attitude that will attract helpful people into your life, and will cause things to happen exactly the way you expected them to happen.

Successful people expect to succeed, in advance. They expect to be popular and liked by others, in advance. They expect to learn and grow from every experience, in advance. And the wonderful truth about your expectations is that they are completely under your control. You decide for yourself what they are going to be. You manufacture them by the way you think things are going to turn out. Always expect the best and you will seldom be disappointed.

Become a Living Magnet

One of the most powerful principles in the universe is the *law of attraction*. The law of attraction says that *you are a living magnet*. This law says that your thoughts create a force field of energy that radiates out from you and attracts back into your life people and circumstances in harmony with those thoughts. Every thought you have is emotionalized in one way or another, positive or negative. Like iron filings to a magnet, whether you have thoughts of *desire* or thoughts of *fear*, you attract people, circumstances, and events into your life that are in harmony with those thoughts.

This is perhaps the most important of all mental laws in explaining success and failure, good luck and bad luck. It says if you have a very clear picture in your mind of your desired goal, and you can hold that idea in your mind on a continuing basis, you will inevitably draw into your life the resources that you need in order to achieve it.

People who have become wealthy or successful have become wealthy and successful as a result of holding the idea of wealth and success in their minds long enough and hard enough, until they drew into their lives the resources they needed to accomplish it. Your main job is to keep your mind fixed on what you really *want*, and keep your mind off of the things you *don't want*, until your true desires begin to materialize in the world around you.

As Within, So Without

The *law of correspondence* is very powerful. This law says, *as within, so without*. This law explains that your outer world is like a mirror that reflects back to you what is going on in your inner world. The law of correspondence says that everything that happens outside of you corresponds to something that is going on inside of you. This is true on both a conscious and unconscious level. Nothing can either come into your life or stay in your life unless it finds something in your own thinking that corresponds to it.

Whatever you can hold in your mind on a continuing basis you can have. If you consciously believe that you have the ability to achieve a particular goal, and you can hold a clear picture of that goal in your mind long enough, eventually your outer world will correspond with that picture. Your ability to create and hold on to that mental picture is the true test of whether you really want the goal and that you believe it is possible for you.

Three Areas of Demonstration

There are three places where you see this law of correspondence demonstrated continually: in the faces of others, in your rleationships, and in your wealth.

The Faces of Others

Your outer world of experiences with *others* will correspond exactly to your own attitude. You will always see your attitude reflected back to you in the faces and the behaviors of the people around you. If you have a positive, optimistic attitude, people will respond to you in a positive and cheerful way almost instantly, even before you open your mouth.

Your Relationships

Your relationships will mirror back to you exactly the kind of a person you are *inside*. When you feel happy, kind, and loving, your relationships will be happy, harmonious, and loving as well. But if you become angry, impatient, or fearful for any reason, consciously or unconsciously, you will immediately see this reflected in your relationships, especially at home and at work.

Your Wealth

The third area where the law of correspondence manifests itself is with regard to your *wealth*. Your external world of wealth and financial accomplishment will be a mirror image of your inner world of preparation for financial success. The more you feed your mind with thoughts, words, pictures, images, and goals of making and accumulating money, the more rapidly these will appear in the world around you.

The Laws Are Neutral

The laws of expectation, attraction, and correspondence are neutral. These laws can work for you or against you, depending on the thoughts you choose to think. These laws will make you happy or unhappy, healthy or unhealthy, rich or poor. They will help you or hurt, depending on your use of them.

The only part of the mental equation that you can control is the thoughts you choose to think. When you discipline yourself to keep your conscious thoughts on the things you want and on your images of wealth and affluence, these laws will eventually shape your external world of reality to reflect them in every detail. If you *think rich* long enough, you will eventually become rich.

What You Put In
Determines What You Get Back

One of the most important principles taught in the New Testament is the *law of sowing and reaping*. This law says, "Whatsoever a man soweth, that also shall he reap." To put it another way, whatever you put in, you get out. Some people feel that this is not fair, but this is because they do not understand true meaning of this statement.

In the modern world, you have heard it said that *the rich get richer and the poor get poorer*. Why should this happen? The reason is simple. Based on the laws of correspondence, attraction, and expectations and the fact that all causation is mental, people who become and remain wealthy deliberately cultivate and maintain a wealthy mind-set, a *million-dollar mind*. They sow good thoughts and they reap a good life. And the more they think in terms of wealth creation and prosperity, the more money they make and the richer they become.

Negative Thinking Drives Money Away

Meanwhile, people who continually worry about money create a negative force field of mental energy around them that drives money away from them, and increases their financial problems. They end up earning far less than they desire, or less than they are capable of, and are often overwhelmed by bills and debts. They reap what they sow. They become what they think about.

Some people fill their minds with thoughts of scarcity, lack, poverty, and being unable to afford the good things of life. They think continually about how much everything costs and how little money they have. They think and worry more about failure than success. As a result, they develop and maintain a *poverty consciousness*. They sow thoughts of lack and they reap lives of financial failure.

Think Like the Rich Think

What do rich people think about most of the time, and what did they think about long before they became rich? Based on thousands of interviews, we find that rich people fill their minds with thoughts, words, pictures, and images of wealth, affluence, success, productivity, and solutions to problems in the marketplace. They read books and magazines that describe other wealthy people and illustrate the rewards of wealth creation. They think in terms of beautiful homes, cars, clothes, and vacations. They continually expect to enjoy these beautiful things as the result of their efforts.

One of the rules for getting rich is that if you want to be successful, find out what people who don't get ahead think, and refuse to think in that way. Instead, find out how wealthy people think. Find out what they read. Find out how they spend their time. Find out what they talk about and think about and write about, and then do the same things that wealthy people do. Sow only the seeds in your mental garden that you want to see grow in the world around you.

Settle In for the Long Haul

A key principle that explains how people get rich starting from nothing is called the *law of accumulation*. This law says that *everything great and worthwhile in human life is an accumulation of hundreds, if not thousands, of tiny efforts and sacrifices* that few people ever see or appreciate. This law explains that great success seldom comes overnight or as the result of a single experience or breakthrough. Instead, enduring success gathers and accumulates over time.

You have to put in countless tiny efforts that nobody sees or appreciates before you achieve anything worthwhile. In some ways, financial success grows like a snowball. A snowball starts very small, but as it rolls forward, it grows and accumulates as it adds millions of tiny snowflakes to its mass. Soon it becomes unstoppable and sweeps everything before it.

Learn What You Need to Learn

There are three areas where the law of accumulation is important to financial success: knowledge, money, and experience. These are discussed repeatedly in this book because they are so important.

Knowledge Is Power

Knowledge is power, and is a key factor in giving you the leverage you need to multiply yourself times your opportunities. Your body of knowledge is a result of hundreds, perhaps thousands, of small pieces of information that you have gathered and accumulated over time.

Any person with a large knowledge base has invested thousands of hours building that mental library one idea at a time. As the cumulative result of those years of study and growth, the individual becomes an expert in a field who can command huge fees and income in comparison with someone who has not done the same amount of work and preparation. This is the primary reason why the top 20 percent in any field earn 80 percent of the money in that field. They know more than their competitors, and therefore command vastly higher payment for their services.

Save Your Money

Another area where the law of accumulation is vital to your success is with regard to *money*. Every large fortune is an accumulation of hundreds and thousands of small amounts of money. Riches seldom start with great financial breakthroughs or jackpots, even though that is what many people believe and strive for in their 20s and 30s. Instead, riches and wealth grow and accumulate slowly at first, one step at a time, and go only to those special people who demonstrate an ability to earn the money and then hold onto it.

The place to start on your road to wealth is right where you are, right now. If you cannot discipline yourself to practice frugality and begin saving your money in your current circumstances, you cannot expect to develop these qualities later on.

If you were looking for a simple formula for financial success, it would be contained in the five words: *Spend less than you earn*. The place to start is for you to take any amount of money that you can right now, open a special bank account for "financial independence" and begin to save. When you save money, you set up a force field of energy around that money that begins to attract more and more money into your life. As you add these additional amounts to your wealth account, you create an even greater magnetic force that attracts even more money into your life.

Put It Aside

Some years ago, I started a new business, made every conceivable mistake that a new entrepreneur can make, and lost all my money. As a result, to survive financially, we had to sell our house to raise cash. At this point, my wife put her foot down. She decided that she was tired of worrying about money all the time. She insisted on taking $10,000 out of the proceeds of the house sale and putting it into a separate bank account where I couldn't get my hands on it. Because she was so adamant, I agreed and allowed her to do it. And you know what happened? From the time she put that money into a separate bank account, we were never out of money again.

No matter what happened in the following months and years, with the economy and the business going up and down, enough money continued to materialize so that we never had to touch the special savings account. In a couple of years, we were out of debt and able to buy a beautiful new home in one of the best neighborhoods in the city.

I have spoken to many successful people over the years and they have told me the same story. They said that as soon as they started to save their money and put it aside, this money seemed to attract more money and opportunities into their lives. As their savings grew, they began to attract people and information that enable them to invest their funds intelligently, which caused their investments to grow more rapidly. Probably the main reason why most people retire poor is they never put the initial savings aside to start with. *It takes money to make money.*

Get Your Hands Dirty

The law of accumulation is vital to success in the area of *experience*. Successful people in any field are almost invariably those who have far more experience in that field than the average person. And there is nothing that replaces experience. Whether it is in business, or entrepreneurship, or management, or selling, or investing, or speaking, or writing, or anything else, experience is what makes the critical difference.

There are many studies and opinions on the subject of mastery. The consensus of the experts is that the foundation of mastery in any field is based on pattern recognition. This is the ability of the individual to "connect the dots" when confronted with a situation that bears a resemblance to a previous situation. The more different situations that a person has experienced, the more patterns he has recorded and the faster he can make an informed decision when something new or different occurs.

Be Willing to Fail

This quality of pattern recognition applies to every field, from law and medicine to negotiating, selling, and entrepreneurship. Experts agree that you require five to seven years and 10,000 hours of experience to master your craft, whatever it is. And the only way to acquire this experience is to be willing to fail, to use the trial and error method, and then learn from every experience.

The great enemy of mastery, and of the big rewards that go along with being the best in your field, is the "comfort zone." Most people are so comfortable at a lower level of performance and accomplishment that the very thought of trying something new and different causes them extreme anxiety. Many people do not take the risks that are necessary to move out of their comfort zones because they are afraid that they will fail.

But the fact is that until you move out of your comfort zone and make the mistakes that give you the experience you need to succeed, it is not possible for you to grow and become capable of earning the kind of money you desire. To put it another way, you learn how to succeed only by failing. You become successful only by taking risks where there is no guarantee of success. If you do not fail regularly, you can never succeed greatly.

The Great Truth

Here is the key to the law of accumulation. *Everything counts!* Everything that you do, or fail to do, counts in some way. Once you have set a goal for yourself, everything you do helps or hurts. Nothing is neutral. The biggest mistake that people make is they think that something counts only if they decide that it counts, or that they are going to count it. But the rule is that if it doesn't help, it hurts. If it is not adding, it is probably taking away.

When you set a goal to become wealthy, you place yourself under a new set of rules, and everything from that day forward counts in some way. When you read a book, listen to an audio program, take an additional seminar or course to upgrade your moneymaking abilities, go to bed early, and get up early, it all *counts*. When you plan each day in advance and work on your most important tasks before you do anything else, it all counts. Every positive, helpful action is going on the plus side of your ledger.

Don't Waste Time

But if you spend your evenings watching television, socializing with your friends, killing time on low-value, no-value activities, it all counts as well, and it is going on the *negative* side of the ledger. Just as a successful company has a positive balance sheet, you have a balance sheet as well. You create a great life for yourself when you accumulate far more points on the credit side than on the debit side. And just as in financial accounting, everything counts.

Here is an important point. If what you are doing is not moving you *toward* your goals, then it is probably moving you *away* from your goals. *Nothing is neutral.* What you do either moves you toward the things that you want to accomplish in life, the person you want to be, the wealth you want to accumulate, or it moves you away. Everything counts. This is one of the most important applications of the law of accumulation in your life.

You Will See It When You Believe It

The *law of belief* has an inordinate impact on your life. This law says that *whatever you believe, with feeling, becomes your reality*. You do not believe what you see; instead, you see what you already believe. Your beliefs predispose you to see yourself and your world in a certain way. If you intensely believe something to be true, you will think, feel, and act in a certain way, and your behaviors will determine your results. Your beliefs will become your reality.

Your mind is so designed that you have a tendency to ignore or block out any information coming to you that is inconsistent with what you already believe to be true, whether your beliefs are based on fact or on fiction.

The Mind-Set of Millionaires

Here is an important discovery: People destined for success absolutely believe that they are going to be successful, sooner or later. They believe that everything that happens to them, positive or negative, is part of a great plan to ultimately make them successful. They refuse to entertain, think about, or discuss the likelihood of failure. The concept of *not* succeeding never occurs to them. They do not even consider the possibility of failure.

You will always act in a matter on the outside consistent with your true beliefs on the inside. When you have convinced yourself totally that *you are a successful person just waiting for a place to happen,* you will become completely different from a person who still doubts his ability to succeed. When you develop a prosperity consciousness, you will become convinced that there is a universal plan to make you successful, and that everything that happens to you is a part of the plan.

You will start to see good things in every setback or difficulty. You will derive valuable lessons from every temporary failure or problem. Like Henry Ford, you will confidently say, "Failure is merely an opportunity to more intelligently begin again." You will develop a consciousness where you absolutely believe that your financial success is inevitable.

You will make the great leap from positive *thinking* to positive knowing. Positive thinking can sometimes be wishing or hoping, a cover-up for fear and doubt. But positive knowing occurs when you have reached the state of belief where you are absolutely confident that no matter what, you will be successful. From this point on, you are unstoppable.

Resolve to Pay the Price

A key personality quality that underlies all great success is *willpower*. Willpower is essential to the accomplishment of anything worthwhile. Willpower is based on confidence. It is based on conviction. It is based on faith. It is based on your belief in your ability to triumph over all obstacles. And like all qualities, you can develop willpower by practicing it whenever willpower is called for.

You can develop greater willpower and strength of character by persisting whenever you feel like quitting. You develop greater willpower by disciplining yourself to work toward your most important goals every day, even when there are a thousand other things you could be doing. You develop willpower by reading the biographies of successful people whose victories were the result of the triumph of willpower.

The more ideas and information you feed into your mind that are consistent with success, the more likely it is that you will develop the willpower you need to push you over the obstacles and through the difficulties that you will have to face on the path to your success.

Not for Everyone

"Many are called, but few are chosen." Everyone starts off in life with dreams, hopes, and fantasies of somehow becoming wealthy. Today we in the United States live in the most affluent country at perhaps the very best time in all of human history. It has never been more possible for more people to achieve their financial goals than it is today. Nonetheless, the fact is that *success is rare*.

Only one person in one hundred becomes wealthy in the course of their lifetime. Only 5 percent achieve financial independence, in that they have enough money to support their lifestyles without ever having to work again. This means that the odds against you ending your financial life successfully are 19 to 1.

Get Serious

The fact is that the only way that you are going to achieve your financial goals is when you quit fooling around and get really *serious*. Financial success cannot be something you are going to achieve someday, when everything is just right. The situation will never be just right. There will always be reasons to procrastinate, but the stakes are too high. You must get serious, and you must get serious *today*. Remember, everything counts.

Each time I meet someone who after drifting financially for many years had become successful and made a lot of money, I ask, "What was the turning point for you?" They almost invariably give me a funny look and say, "Well, I finally decided to get serious."

Sometimes they became angry, either at themselves or at seeing someone else who they felt was less talented than they were who was doing better than they were. Sometimes they saw an opportunity and decided to go for it. In every case, to break out of their comfort zones, they had to commit themselves and take a risk. To break out of the pack, you will have to do the same.

Take Charge of Yourself

One of Murphy's Laws is, "Before you do anything, you have to do something else first." Because success is so rare, there are many principles you must learn if you want to achieve it and keep it, but the one thing you have to do first is to take complete control of yourself and your life.

Becoming a money magnet requires the development of self-mastery, self-control, and self-discipline. Taking charge of yourself, your appetites and your behaviors is essential for anyone who wants to achieve greatly. And control over your *thoughts* is the hardest exercise in self-mastery that you will ever engage in.

The Quick List Method

Here is an exercise for you. Answer the question, "What are your three most important goals in life, right now?" You should be able to write the answers to this "quick list" in about 30 seconds.

Here is the test: Resolve to think and talk about only these three goals, and how you might attain them, for the next 24 hours. Refuse to think or talk about things you don't want. Keep bringing your mind back to your goals whenever it starts to drift.

This exercise will be very revealing. Far from keeping your mind on what you want and off of what you don't want for 24 hours, you will not be able to do it for 24 *minutes*. This exercise will demonstrate to you how hard it is to control your thinking and keep it focused. It will show you what you are really made of. It will make it clear to you why so few people succeed or fulfill their potential at anything. You will find, at least initially, that keeping your mind on what you want is like trying to control a car on a winding road with no steering wheel.

Focus and Concentrate

The good news is that *focus* and *concentration* are learnable skills. They are habits you can develop with willpower and practice, and they enable you to develop even greater willpower in the future. Self-mastery is hard at first, but with practice you can reach the point where you can keep your thinking on your goals and desires most of the time.

Once you have taken control of your *thinking*, you can then take control of your *actions*. If you can master yourself and discipline yourself to pay the price of success in advance, you must eventually succeed. As Zig Ziglar says, "If you are hard on yourself, life will be easy on you. But if you insist on being easy on yourself, life is going to be very hard on you." Everything counts. You must resolve, here and now, to fill your mind only with thoughts consistent with your desires, and simultaneously keep your mind off your doubts and fears.

You Must Want It Badly Enough

Financial success begins with an intense desire for wealth—not a lukewarm desire, but a burning, all-consuming desire to become a millionaire. This intensity of emotion, commitment, and determination is absolutely essential for you to keep driving forward in the face of the unending adversity and disappointment that will confront you and attack you from all sides when you resolve to become wealthy.

There is a Japanese proverb: "Making money is like digging with a pin; losing money is like pouring water on the sand." The fact is that we live in a increasingly competitive world, full of people who are absolutely determined to make as much money as they possibly can. These people will do anything to take away our customers, to overcharge us and underdeliver, and will even engage in deceit, embezzlement, fraud, shoddy dealing, cheating, and incompetence that you cannot even imagine at the outset.

To become wealthy, you must become as sharp as a fox, continually alert and aware of the possibility that, as Murphy's Law states, "anything that can go wrong will go wrong." You will experience never-ending reversals of fortune and unexpected setbacks. Murphy's second law says, "Of all the things that can go wrong, it will always be the worst possible thing, at the worst possible time, and cost the greatest amount of money."

A Wealthy Adviser

The financier Bernard Baruch began his career as a messenger boy on Wall Street when he was 15 years old. His starting salary was $3.50 per week. By practicing some of the principles we are discussing here, especially by becoming an expert in the field of investing, he eventually became one of the wealthiest men in the country and an adviser to six presidents, including Franklin D. Roosevelt.

Baruch's approach to value and investing was simple and direct. He once said, "The first requisite for making a lot of money is to want to make a lot of money." The first requirement was to make a clear decision and then to back that decision with will and determination. An enormous number of people have never sat down and thought through whether they want to make a lot of money. They may wish and hope and pray about making a lot of money, but they have never *decided* to do so. The truth is that you must really, really want it if you're going to achieve it.

Your Reasons Why

"Reasons are the fuel in the furnace of motivation." The more reasons you have for wanting to become wealthy, the more intensely you will desire financial success, and the more determined you will become to achieve it. All motivation requires incentives of some kind. What are yours?

If you have one or two reasons for making a lot of money, you will have a little motivation, but you will give up easily when you meet the inevitable obstacles along the way. But if you have 100 reasons for becoming wealthy, you will become like a runaway locomotive on a downgrade. Nothing will stop you.

Here is an exercise for you: Take a clean sheet of paper and write out 100 things you will do, buy, have, or achieve when you have all the money you want. Don't worry about what you write down at first. You can always go back and add or subtract. But write out at least 100 answers.

This exercise will transform your thinking and your life. It will open your mind to all the vast possibilities surrounding you. It will motivate and stimulate you, activating the law of attraction. By writing out 100 goals, you will trigger your subconscious mind into giving you ideas you can apply immediately to achieve those goals. You may never be the same again.

Make Your Goals Specific

One of the most important principles for wealth attainment is that you must set a series of specific goals for financial achievement. You must write them down. You must set deadlines and subdeadlines for their accomplishment, and then make a thorough, detailed plan of action to attain those goals. You can't hit a target you can't see.

Begin creating your financial blueprint by analyzing your current financial situation. Draw up a balance sheet on yourself, listing all your assets and liabilities. Get a loan application from your bank and use its categories as a guide. Especially, determine exactly how much you are worth today, just as if you were going to convert all your assets into cash and move to a foreign country. This is a very revealing exercise that may surprise you.

Think Long-Term

Once you know what you are really worth today, you then set a goal to be worth a million dollars at some time in the future. People who become millionaires after starting with nothing take an average of about 22 years. It takes less time if you have already built up a substantial net worth. Once you know where you are starting from and you have set your financial goal some years in the future, divide your long-term goal into separate years, and then into three-month periods for each year.

With these numbers, which may shock you, you will have a clear picture of how much you are worth and how much you intend to be worth year by year into the future, and an idea of how much you will have to save and accumulate quarter by quarter and year by year to become wealthy.

What are you going to do to achieve your financial goals? How much more will you have to earn and save to hit your financial targets? How much do you want to be earning 12 months from today? Here is a suggestion: Set your income goal for the next 12 months 50 percent higher than your very highest income year-to-date. This is a great place to start.

Give Yourself a Raise

If your highest annual income to date has been $50,000, you would set your income goal for the next 12 months at $75,000. Write it down and then make a list of every single thing you could do to increase your income by 50 percent over the coming year. Organize your list into a plan for its accomplishment. Then take action immediately. Do something. Do anything. Take the first step that lies open to you. Begin today to move toward your goal. In the weeks and months ahead, as your income increases, reset your goal at a higher level. Simply move it up like you would raise a bar in high-jumping. Keep raising it higher and higher each time you get close to it.

A definite goal, backed by burning desire, begins the process of magnetizing your mind and triggering the law of attraction. Almost immediately you will begin to attract people, ideas, opportunities, and sources of information into your life consistent with your goal. You will find books, audiotapes, magazines, and courses that will help you move toward your goal.

One important point: Be clear about the results you desire, but be flexible about the process. As you get new information and experience, be prepared to make midcourse corrections. Most goals are achieved in ways that were never anticipated when you started out toward them. Keep an open mind.

The Magic of Visualization

Once you are clear about your goals, and you have written plans to achieve them, you begin the practice of *visualization*, the process of creating clear mental pictures of the things you want. Visualization activates your creative mind, triggers the law of attraction, and gives you clarity and focus in attaining your goals. It is perhaps the most powerful faculty you can develop to accelerate the process of goal achievement.

Create a clear mental picture of your goal as if it were already realized. This is important. There is a direct relationship between the clarity of the picture you see in your mind and how rapidly your goal comes into reality in your outer world. The law of correspondence says, *as within, so without.*

Create clear mental pictures of your ideal lifestyle. Practice "back from the future" thinking. Project forward into the future in your mind and see yourself enjoying the life you desire. From the vantage point of the future, look back to the present day. Ask yourself what steps you would have taken to get from where you are today to where you want to be in two to three years. As motivational speaker Denis Waitley says, "Your imagination is your preview of life's coming attractions."

See Yourself in Action

Use your powers of visualization to see yourself actually doing the things you would be doing to achieve your goal. This is called "causative thinking." Close your eyes and imagine the various actions you could take, step-by-step, to achieve your goals. Your subconscious mind is activated by your mental pictures. It then takes over and makes all your words and actions fit a pattern consistent with your mental images. By visualizing, you actually preprogram yourself for success.

Visualization also activates your *conscious* mind and releases more of your mental potential. As you visualize, you will begin to receive a continuous flow of ideas and energy to achieve those goals. The clearer the picture is in your mind, the more rapidly your subconscious and conscious mind go to work to bring it into your reality.

Four Factors to Multiply Your Powers

There are four factors that determine how rapidly your visualization turns into realization. The first is the *length* of the visualization. How long can you hold the picture in your mind? The second is the *frequency* of the visualization. How often do you hold that picture in your mind throughout the day? The third is the *intensity* of the visualization. How much emotion is connected to the picture that you are holding in your mind? And the fourth is the *vividness* of the visualization. How clear is your mental picture?

You will find that you can increase the speed at which you realize your goal by applying these factors to your visualizing. You can either increase the length of the visualization, holding the picture longer, or you can increase the frequency by visualizing your goal more often during the day. You can increase the intensity of the mental picture by generating more emotion to go with it, or you can increase the clarity and the vividness of the picture.

The best way is to practice all four. Play and replay the picture of your goals on the screen of your mind. The more you visualize and see your goal as a reality, the more intensely you will desire your goal. The more you want it, the less you will fear failure and rejection, and the possible losses that may go along with it.

Creative visualization deepens your belief that your goals are attainable. It increases your self-confidence. It strengthens your courage and builds your faith in yourself. The more often you replay the picture of your desired future in your mind, the more unstoppable you become.

Create a Treasure Map

There is a technique you can use to increase the power of visualization called a *treasure map*. This is where you create a poster, and you put your goal, or even a picture of yourself, in the middle of the poster. You then surround the central image with pictures and clippings from magazines and newspapers that support and remind you of your goal.

Take time each day to sit and look at that poster. Feed your mind with the positive, exciting words and pictures it contains. Let your mind *photograph* those words, pictures, and images that represent what you want to be, do, or have. Include images of affluence. Include pictures of the car that you want to drive and the home that you want to live in. Add pictures with amounts of money cut out from magazines and newspapers written on them. Paste anything onto the poster that can stimulate your subconscious mind by imprinting on it a picture of something you desire. The more often you study your treasure map, the faster you will move toward the accomplishment of your goal, and the faster your goal will move toward you.

Control Your Inner Dialogue

You become what you think about most of the time. Ralph Waldo Emerson echoed this theme when he wrote, "A man becomes what he thinks about all day long." In addition, you become what you *say to yourself* throughout the day. You can exert an inordinate influence on your thoughts, emotions, and behaviors with the use of positive self-talk or positive affirmations. This technique requires that you be your own cheerleader and talk to yourself positively most of the time.

The fact is that words are very powerful in determining success or failure. Words have the power to raise or lower heart rate and blood pressure, increase your breathing, and even change the chemistry of your blood. They can make you happy or sad in a matter of moments. Your choice of the words you use when you talk to yourself can make the difference between your becoming an unshakable optimist and your being fearful and afraid. And the choice of the words you use is largely up to you.

Resist Your Fears

People tend to talk to themselves in a negative way. As much as 95 percent of your inner dialogue tends to be about the things you fear, your worries, your problems, the people you're angry at, your concerns, and so on. The more you explain and interpret your world to yourself in a negative way, the more negative you become. Psychologists and doctors today agree that negative thinking, continually dwelling on and talking about things that make you unhappy, is the primary cause of depression and psychosomatic illness. And it is largely unnecessary.

You can't afford the luxury of a negative thought. If you knew how destructive your thinking can be on your health and relationships, you would resolve to think and talk about only what you want for the rest of your life. You would not allow yourself to do or say anything that could negatively affect your subconscious mind. And everything counts.

Practice Affirmations

To succeed greatly, you must discipline yourself to keep the words you say to yourself, your inner dialogue, consistent with the very best person you could be and the most important goals that you wish to accomplish. Since everything you say is preprogramming you for the future, it is essential that you talk in terms of what you *want* to happen, rather than what might be happening at the moment.

You Can Do It

The fear of failure is the number one reason for failure in adult life. It is not the failure experience itself that holds us back. Everyone has failed countless times. As Friedrich Nietzsche said, "What doesn't kill me makes me stronger." It is the thought or anticipation of potential failure that paralyzes us and causes us to quit before we even start.

The fear of failure is expressed in the words, "I can't! I can't! I can't!" Whenever we think of doing something that entails risk and possible loss of some kind, we usually respond by saying, "I can't!" These words trigger feelings of fear, stress, and anxiety that are experienced in the body in the form of rapid heart rate, churning stomach, and even headaches.

But a positive command can override a negative message. Psychologists have discovered that the words "I can do it" actually neutralize the feelings of "I can't!," especially when these words are repeated emphatically enough. The words "I can do it!" are the antidote to the fear of failure that often holds us back from trying.

From now on, whenever you think of something big and exciting that you would like to be or do, become your own cheerleader and say over and over to yourself, "I can do it!" Repeat these words whenever you feel fearful or doubtful about anything that you want to attempt.

Just say very enthusiastically, "I can do it! I can do it! I can do it!" When you start saying, "I can do it! I can do it!," you drive that message into your subconscious mind, where it instantly cancels out the negative emotions that can hold you back.

Make a Million

Another positive affirmation you can use is, "I make a million! I make a million! I make a million!" Repeat this over and over, hundreds of times, as you go about your daily business. Impress this message deep into your subconscious mind until it "locks in." From that point forward, all your mental powers will be working day and night to make this command a reality for you.

You Are the Best

Whenever you think about your work, repeat over and over again, "I'm the best! I'm the best! I'm the best!" Combine these positive words with a mental image of yourself performing the task in an excellent way. Imagine yourself as relaxed, calm, confident, and capable. What you *see* is what you will *be*.

Reprogram Yourself for Success

When you first say these positive words to yourself, you might feel a little strange or uncomfortable inside. This feeling is perfectly normal. It is called "cognitive dissonance," and it occurs whenever your new message clashes with your old programming. But when you repeat these new commands over and over with complete confidence, eventually the new message will override your previous programming and become the new "operating instructions" for your subconscious mind.

Talking to yourself in a positive way by repeating any of these three affirmations, or by saying anything else that empowers and motivates you, changes the chemical composition of your mind. These positive messages make you feel good about yourself. They release energy and give you greater self-confidence.

Positive self-talk enables you to take complete control over your conscious mind. These words make you feel more focused and aware. They give you a greater sense of personal power. This is why most successful, happy people discipline themselves to maintain a positive inner dialogue. The payoff is tremendous.

Feed Your Mind with Mental Protein

You have heard it said that "You become what you eat." In the same way, you become what you feed into your mind on a regular basis. The key to mental programming, to assuring that your outer world of results will gradually reflect your inner world of goals and ambitions, is to feed your mind with mental protein from morning to night. To perform at your best, you must continually take in words, pictures, information, and ideas consistent with your goals for financial success.

Make it a habit to think positively and confidently about wealth accumulation. Here are four ways to do it.

Read about Successful People

Make it a practice to read stories, books, and articles about other successful people. As you do, think about how you could be like them. Visualize yourself, imagine, fantasize, and pretend in your mind that you are already like the kind of people you most admire and respect and want to be like. Remember, everyone who is at the top of their field started at the bottom. And what others have accomplished, you can accomplish as well. There are few limits.

Psychologists have demonstrated that *role models* are essential for magnetizing your mind with the qualities and characteristics that you wish to develop. Pick a person whom you admire. Whenever you face any kind of difficult situation, ask yourself, *how would this person behave in this situation?* How would this person think? What would this person do? What actions would he or she take? You will find that when you think about how another person might behave, your own thinking improves and you tend to perform at your best.

Study Your Business and Industry

Read everything you can find on your business and industry. Become an expert in your field. The more you learn about your profession, your trade and your craft, the more confident you will become in your ability to do it well.

Attend University on Wheels

Listen to educational audio programs in your car. People typically drive 12,000 to 25,000 miles each year. This is the equivalent of 500 to 1,000 hours per year that the average person spends behind the wheel. The University of Southern California estimated that you can get the equivalent of full-time university attendance just by listening to audio programs in your car as you go about your daily business. You can become an expert in your field simply by listening to audio programs by other experts in your field as you drive around.

Take Seminars and Courses

Attend seminars given by experts in your field. Take additional courses that can help you. Learn everything you possibly can, especially from the experts in your business. Ask them questions at the breaks. Write them letters or e-mails. Read their books and articles. One good seminar given by an expert can save you months and even years in learning the same things on your own.

Get Around the Right People

Ninety percent or more of your success in your field, and in life, is going to be determined by your "reference group." These are defined as the people you associate with, work with, live with and spend time with. Dr. David McClelland of Harvard, in his classic, *The Achieving Society* (Van Nostrand, 1961), wrote that people adopt the attitudes, opinions, manners of speaking and dress, goals, ambitions, and worldviews of their reference groups. He found that a dramatic change in a person's life and performance was preceded by the formation of a new reference group. Whenever a person failed to change or fell back into old, ineffective ways of acting, it was invariably because he or she continued to associate with the same old crowd.

Decide today that from now on you are going to associate only with positive, successful people. You are going to spend time only with people who are ambitious and determined, and who are definitely going somewhere with their lives. Get around winners, and avoid the company of people whom you neither admire nor respect. *You can't fly with the eagles if you continue to scratch with the turkeys.*

Meanwhile, get away from negative people, especially negative coworkers. Don't drink coffee with whoever happens to be sitting there. Don't go out to lunch with whoever is standing at the door. Don't socialize after work with the first person who invites you. If you are working for a negative boss, seriously consider changing jobs. Working in a negative environment, or with difficult people, drags you down and tires you out. Staying in a bad job with negative bosses or coworkers is enough in itself to condemn you to a life of underachievement, frustration, and failure. Your life is too precious for that.

Sleep On It

Here is a powerful way to activate your subconscious mind and become a money magnet. Your subconscious mind is most receptive to new messages and programming in the final minutes before you fall asleep, and during the first hour of the morning. When you take advantage of these two time periods, you dramatically accelerate the speed at which you magnetize your mind with the commands that attract everything you need into your life.

Each night, before you fall asleep, visualize your goals as realities. See your goals as if they already exist. Imagine yourself being the person you want to be, and doing the things you want to do. See yourself enjoying the success you desire. Feed these happy pictures into your mind just before you doze off, and then just relax and let go of them while you fall asleep.

When you wake up in the morning, immediately think about your most important goal. Imagine that there is a secret plan in the universe to make your dreams come true. Start off by saying, "I believe that something wonderful is going to happen to me today!"

Imagine Your Ideal Life

The key to visualization is to see your goal as though it already existed. The subconscious mind is activated only by affirmations and pictures that are repeated in the present tense. Imagine your goal just before you go to sleep, and see yourself performing at your best. See the events of the coming day working out exactly the way you want them to. See yourself living the kind of life that you want to live.

See yourself with the kind of relationships you want to enjoy. Imagine that your health is perfect in every way. See yourself driving your ideal car, living in your dream home, doing the kind of work you love. The more often you feed these positive, exciting pictures of happiness, health, and prosperity, the faster they become your reality.

The Golden Hour

The final principle, and perhaps the most powerful of all in becoming a money magnet and achieving lifelong success, has to do with the way you begin each day. As mentioned earlier, you become what you think about most of the time. You become the sum total result of the ideas, information, and impressions you feed into your mind, from the time you get up in the morning until you go to bed at night.

Everything counts, but some impressions count more than others. The thoughts with which you flood your mind in the first hour of the morning have a strong influence on how you think, feel, and act for the rest of the day. As the saying goes, "Well begun is half done." This applies to what you read, write, see, listen to, and say during those first and most impressionable 60 minutes.

Million-Dollar Habits

Fully 95 percent of everything you do or say is determined by your habits, either good or bad. Successful people have good habits that lead them to engage in positive, productive behaviors. Unsuccessful people have inadvertently developed bad habits that cause them to act, or fail to act, in ways that lead to underachievement and failure.

Perhaps the best habit you can develop is to start every day in a thoughtful, productive way that sets you up for greater success in the hours ahead. Here is a formula that has worked for me, and for thousands of others, in going from rags to riches. Resolve to try it yourself for 21 days before you pass judgment on whether it is helping you. My promise to you is that, by the time you have practiced these behaviors for 21 days, your whole world will have changed in wonderful ways that you cannot even imagine today.

The 21-Day Positive Mental Attitude Diet

1. Starting tomorrow, arise each morning at least two hours before you have to be somewhere, and invest the first hour in yourself and in your mind. If you exercise physically each morning, do this before you begin to exercise mentally.

2. Before you turn on the television or radio or read the newspaper, take 30 to 60 minutes and read something motivational, inspirational, or educational. Be sure that the first thing you put into your mind in the morning is positive, healthy, and consistent with the kind of day you want to have and the kind of life you want to lead.

3. After you have completed your morning reading, take a spiral notebook and write out your top 10 to 15 goals in the *present tense*, exactly as if you have already achieved them. Write goals such as: "I earn $100,000 per year." "I weigh 165 pounds and am superbly fit." "I drive a brand-new four-door, dolphin grey BMW." "I live in a beautiful 3,500-square-foot home." And so on. Rewrite your list of goals every morning *without* referring back to the goals you wrote the day before. This is very important.

4. Plan every day in advance. After you have rewritten your goals, make a list of everything you have to do that day, and then organize the list by priority, value, and importance.

5. Begin immediately to work on your most valuable and important task before you do anything else. Resolve to focus single-mindedly on that one task until it is complete. When you start and finish your major task first thing in the morning, you will experience a surge of energy, elation, and confidence that will propel you into your other tasks and dramatically increase your overall productivity for the rest of the day.

6. Listen to educational audio programs as you drive to and from work. Turn your car into a university on wheels, a mobile classroom. Leave the radio off. Continually feed your mind with high-quality mental nutrition that educates you and inspires you to do your best.

7. Finally, develop a sense of urgency. Pick up the pace. Move quickly from one task to the other. Don't waste time. The faster you move, the more energy you will have. The faster you move, the more you will get done and the better you will feel. The faster you move, the more in control of your life you will feel and the more you will like and respect yourself.

The Rudder of the Day

The golden hour is the rudder of the day. When you begin to arise early and invest the first hour in yourself, you will be amazed at the difference in the way you feel about yourself, and in the results you will get. You will gradually transform your thinking about yourself and what is possible for you. You will become a money magnet and begin to enjoy success out of all proportion to your efforts. There are no limits.

Action Exercises

1. Create a clear mental picture of yourself as completely successful in every area of your life; combine this picture with the feelings of happiness and pride that will accompany your success. Repeat this image, combined with this emotion, frequently during the day.

2. Begin today to build your own success library, with books on success, achievement, and the accomplishments of people you admire. Read them 30 to 60 minutes each day.

3. Get around winners—positive, optimistic people who have goals and who are going somewhere with their lives. Ask them for advice and recommendations, and share your best ideas with them.

4. Talk to yourself positively all the time; become your own cheerleader. Cancel fears of failure by repeating, "I can do it; I can do anything I put my mind to!" Keep this up until you are no longer afraid of anything.

5. Start each day off positively by reading something uplifting, and then by rewriting your goals in the present tense, as if they were already accomplished. Practice the 21-Day Positive Mental Attitude Diet until it becomes a habit.

6. Set a goal today to achieve a net worth of $1 million. Analyze your starting point, make a long-term plan, and set milestones for earnings, savings, and investments. Take action today to begin moving toward it. A journey of a thousand miles begins with a single step.

7. Give yourself a raise. Decide today to increase your current annual income by 50 percent. Write it down as a goal and then make a plan to accomplish it. Take action immediately and never stop until you are successful.

> *"You can have anything you want—if you want it badly enough. You can be anything you want to be, have anything you desire, accomplish anything you set out to accomplish—if you will hold to that desire with singleness of purpose."*
>
> **—Robert Collier**

3

Invest for Success

*"There will come a time when big opportunities
will be presented to you; when they do you must
be in a position to take advantage of them."*

—Sam Walton

If you are really serious about getting rich your own way, the time to start doing something about it is *now*. Financial planning is the tool that you use to get from where you are to the financial independence that you desire. In this chapter you will learn about various investment strategies and concepts that you must know if you are going to build an estate and retire wealthy.

The Financial Planning Stool

The three legs of the financial planning stool are *savings*, *insurance*, and *investments*. Let us begin with savings and insurance. How much do you need? The basic rule with regard to savings is that you should have enough money to cover three to six months of expenses stored away in some form of liquid investment. A liquid investment is one that you can turn into cash quickly, such as savings accounts, certificates of deposit, or even some mutual funds.

Insure Properly

You need sufficient life insurance to protect your loved ones should something happen to you. In addition, you need fire insurance, liability insurance, health insurance, and insurance for any possible financial emergency that you could not write a check to cover.

Life insurance comes first. You should calculate how much your family would require to maintain their standard of living if you died unexpectedly. You then purchase enough life insurance so that the interest from the life insurance proceeds would be sufficient for your family to live on.

For example, if your family requires $50,000 per year and the invested proceeds can earn a return of 10 percent per annum, then you would purchase a $500,000 life insurance policy, owned by an irrevocable trust, with your spouse and family as your beneficiaries.

In your 20s and 30s, the best value in life insurance is term insurance. Term insurance is issued on an annual basis, and because it has no cash-buildup value, it is relatively inexpensive if you are in good health.

As you move into your 40s and 50s, you need permanent insurance. Permanent insurance is more expensive, but it has a cash value that builds up, and the policy can never be canceled once issued, as long as you keep up the payments. With permanent insurance, your estate will receive the face value of the policy in full if ever something were to happen to you.

You should speak to an insurance agent to become fully aware of what you need and the various options that are available to you. But you must be fully insured as a basic part of your financial life.

The Variables of Investing

The third leg of the financial planning stool is investments. The three variable factors in any investment are safety, liquidity, and growth. There is always a trade-off among these three factors.

If the investment has a high degree of safety, such as a government bond, it usually has a low potential for growth. If the investment is highly liquid, such as a savings account, it usually pays a low rate of interest.

If the investment has high growth potential, such as an investment in a start-up business, it is usually far riskier than a savings account or money market fund, and it is not liquid at all. It is very hard to get your money back quickly.

The investments with the greatest potential for safe, long-term, upside increase in value are usually highly nonliquid investments, such as income-producing real estate. This type of investment usually takes a longer time to buy and often a long time to sell.

Each person must choose a combination of investments that he or she feels comfortable with, considering the amount of risk involved. This is something you have to decide for yourself. Financial experts often call this your "risk quotient." The amount of risk you can and should take changes as you get older and as your financial situation changes.

Invest the Way the Wealthy Invest

Affluent Americans, including self-made millionaires, have most of their money in the following five places:

1. Their own businesses.
2. Income-producing real estate.
3. Land held for development.
4. Liquid investments.
5. Stocks and bonds.

Your Own Business

Most wealthy people and self-made millionaires achieve their financial success as a result of starting and building their own businesses. For this reason, most of the affluent have their money tied up in their own companies. In addition, most senior executives of the largest corporations have most of their net worth tied up in the stock of the companies that they manage.

In a survey conducted in New York recently, a cross section of businesspeople, professors, journalists, philosophers, and executives were asked what they thought would be the very best place to invest $100,000 that a person had accumulated from his or her business or work. Surprisingly enough, the most frequently chosen answer was, "The very best place to invest $100,000 would be back into yourself, or your business, getting even better at what you had done to earn that money in the first place."

In every consideration of how you deploy your financial resources, your key concerns should be the level of risk and the certainty of return. If you have less than $100,000 to invest, in many cases the very best place for you to invest your money is back into developing your skills, into getting better at what you are already doing. If you have earned the money in your business, the best place to invest it is probably back into the business or industry where you already have high levels of familiarity and expertise.

Income-Producing Real Estate

Another major investment vehicle for affluent Americans is real estate. This includes single-family homes for rental, income-producing office buildings, apartment buildings, industrial parks, shopping centers, and other properties that can be rented out to produce a steady income stream.

Thousands of Americans have made their fortunes by starting and building their own successful businesses, and then kept their fortunes by careful and systematic investments in commercial real estate. When you take the time to select commercial real estate carefully, and you purchase it on the right terms, it can be the very best long-term investment.

Make Your Fortune in Real Estate

There is probably no area where more myths prevail about wealth and success than in the field of real estate. You will hear people say that 90 percent of all fortunes in the United States come from real estate. You will hear them say, "They aren't making any more of it." Many people say that real estate investing is the surest route to financial independence for the average person, that you can buy it with no money out of your own pocket and have your tenants pay it off for you. Each of these assertions is partially true and partially false.

The field of real estate is one of the most dynamic and competitive in the country, and the real estate industry includes some of the smartest, sharpest, and most experienced and determined business professionals anywhere. And yet, every year, even in boom markets, these people—the experts—lose millions of dollars as a result of decisions and investments that turn out wrong.

No Free Lunch

One of the great truths of business and of life is that there is no such thing as a free lunch. There is no such thing as "easy money." Nowhere in this book will you read that it is *easy* to achieve financial success. This is equally, if not doubly, true in real estate. Yet it is possible to do well in real estate if you approach it as you would any other business.

Real estate investing is not something that you dabble in, if you want to be successful. You must resolve to get into the field of real estate for the long term, a minimum of 10 years, if you want to build a solid portfolio. Real estate is a form of long-term investing and requires long-term thinking.

Real Estate Defined

Let us begin with the definition of real estate in its simplest terms. Here it is: "Real estate is its future earning power." This is an extremely important principle to understand.

The value of any piece of property is determined by the income that can be generated by that property when it is developed to its highest and best use from this moment in time, onward into the future.

There are millions of acres of land throughout the United States that will never have any real value, such as desert land that cannot be developed to satisfy specific human needs and produce income.

When Real Estate Values Decline

There are vast areas of many large cities where property values are declining because growth and development have come and gone, and will probably not return. Every day, men and women are selling homes and property at less than they paid for them, or are losing them to foreclosure, because these properties have declined in earning power and therefore in value.

Starting in Real Estate: Buy 'Em, Fix 'Em

If you sincerely desire to enter the real estate field, to purchase property as an owner and investor, there are many ways that you can do it.

Perhaps the simplest way of all, and the starting point of many real estate fortunes, is called the "buy 'em, fix 'em method." This refers to the strategy of buying properties needing work and fixing them up to increase their value.

There are several steps for you to follow in the buy 'em fix 'em method.

1. Do your research.
2. Keep the down payment low.
3. Move in and renovate.
4. Sell, rent, or refinance the renovated property.
5. Repeat the process.
6. Move up to larger properties.

Do Your Research

Do your research in advance. Select an area in which you want to purchase a home and then look at houses in that area until you find one that is underpriced relative to the neighborhood because it is run-down and needs a lot of work. Real estate agents call this type of house a "handyman's special," and sometimes they advertise it like that in the newspaper. Often they will advertise an older house as a home that needs "TLC" (tender loving care). For you, this type of a house is a "sleeper." This means that it is more valuable than it appears to the average person.

Pay the Lowest Down Payment Possible

Once you have found a home that is underpriced relative to the neighborhood and has the potential to be fixed up, you purchase the house with the lowest possible cash down payment. Very often, the seller will allow you to buy the house with no money down, especially if he or she is eager to move somewhere else and get out from under the mortgage payments. If this is not possible, you can often get the seller to carry back a second mortgage or trust deed on the property for an amount that represents most of his or her equity in the house. (See "No-Money-Down Investing" subsection.)

Move In and Get Busy

You take possession of the house, move in, and begin working evenings and weekends to renovate and refurbish the house, doing most of the work yourself. If necessary, you can take courses in carpentry and home construction, buy your own tools, get advice from other people who have experience in home renovations, and gradually learn how to do it yourself.

Take Action to Maximize Your Investment
When you have renovated and transformed both the house and the yard so that the property looks good, you can then do one of three things.

You can *sell the house* for more than you paid. You can then take the profit from the sale of the house and buy another house to refurbish and renovate.

Another possibility is to *rent out the house* for a monthly payment that more than covers your mortgage payments and gives you extra cash flow in addition.

Finally, you can *refinance the house*, often for as much as you paid for it, based on the new earning power of the property when rented out to a tenant. With a tenant paying you a specific amount each month, you can get a higher appraisal of the property's value. The bank will lend you money, or you can take out a new mortgage on the property, based on this appraisal.

Repeat the Process
You can then repeat this process with another, perhaps larger house, investing your "sweat equity" or human capital in the renovations until you've fixed it up and are ready to either sell, rent, or refinance once again.

Move Up to Larger Properties
As you increase your assets, your cash flow, and your experience, you can repeat this process on a larger scale as you move up to duplexes, triplexes, quadriplexes, and eventually apartment buildings. The rules are largely the same; only the size and number of rental units are greater.

Many of the great real estate fortunes started off with an individual purchasing a single house and then going to work to fix it up personally. He then sold the house, bought another, and invested his time to renovate that house, and so on. Eventually he built a real estate empire that included dozens and often hundreds or thousands of residential units.

Advantages of Buy 'Em, Fix 'Em

There are two main advantages of this buy 'em, fix 'em method. First of all, you can do it while you keep your full-time job, continuing to generate cash flow from your job for repairs and renovations. Second, you can start small, with little or no money, little or no risk, and grow as you gain knowledge and experience.

It is important that you remember that buying and fixing up homes is just another way of starting a business. If you start small and bootstrap, or grow out of your own efforts, you are much more likely to be successful, and you have a very short distance to fall if you make a mistake. It is virtually impossible that you will go broke buying and fixing houses.

No-Money-Down Investing

You have surely heard about the process of "buying real estate with no money down." There is no question that it is possible to buy real estate, especially older homes, with no money down. This is a true statement. What it requires is that you find someone who is a "motivated seller." This is a person who is eager to sell his or her house and who is there-fore willing to carry back a second mortgage or trust deed on the prop-erty, without requiring that you pay out any cash.

Divorce Motivates People to Sell

A motivated seller may be created as the result of several factors. Often, when a couple is divorcing and they are eager to end the marriage and go their separate ways, they will be highly motivated to get out of the house and out from under the mortgage payments. They will be angry and impatient and have no desire or interest in waiting a long time to sell the home. They will therefore be willing to sell you the house on terms that are very favorable to you.

A Death in the Family

When a homeowner has died, the family may be eager to sell off the house and get themselves free of the responsibility of regular payments and maintenance. In this situation, if you come along and offer to take over the home, paying them a regular monthly amount in the form of payments on a second mortgage while making payments on the first mortgage, they will often sign the home over to you.

Financial Problems or Bankruptcy

Sometimes people go bankrupt and are eager to sell their homes and get out from under the monthly payments. Sometimes people are transferred from one part of the country to the other and are eager to put the home behind them. In any case, a motivated seller is one who is willing to accept "no money down" if he or she can be free of the responsibility of making payments on the first mortgage and maintaining the home.

The 100 to 1 Rule

The professionals who teach people how to buy homes with no money down use a rule of thumb called the "100–10–3–1 rule." What this means is that you, as an inexperienced real estate investor, will have to look at 100 houses before you find 10 houses that can be acquired with little or no down payment. Out of these 10 houses, you will make offers to purchase on three of them. Out of the three offers, you will receive one acceptance and buy one home.

In other words, when you start buying homes with no money down, you will have to look at 100 homes before you find a single home that it makes sense to purchase. But if you have lots of time and little money, this is a wonderful way to get started in the real estate business.

How You Buy with No Money Down

This is the way it works. Let us say that a house is for sale for $100,000 and that you can get an 80 percent mortgage on the property. If the seller of the property will carry back a $20,000 second mortgage or a trust deed, you could end up owning the house with no money out of your own pocket.

In other words, the bank would provide $80,000 for a first mortgage, the seller would take back $20,000, and you would have a $100,000 house that you owe $100,000 on, but you would not have spent any money out of your own pocket. You would, of course, be required to make the payments on the first and second mortgages, plus the taxes and any other expenses that go along with the ownership of the house.

Making It Work

If you could then turn around and rent the house for an amount high enough to cover both mortgage payments, the taxes, and the other expenses, the renter of the house would eventually pay off the cost of the house and you would own it with *no money down*.

Alternatively, as discussed earlier, you could move into the house, make the payments while fixing up the house, and then either resell the house at a profit or rent it out at a high enough rent to cover all the payments and give you a positive cash flow. You might even be able to refinance the house based on the new, higher cash flow from your tenant and make a profit in that way.

A Possible Obstacle

You may encounter one obstacle in this system of buying houses with no money down: If the houses are priced reasonably in a normal housing market, the sellers will not have to accept "no money down." There will be a sufficient supply of willing purchasers who will pay them cash for their equity in their homes. This is the way 90 percent or more of all real estate transactions are done.

The Payments Must Be Made

Keep in mind that you will have to have sufficient income to make the payments on both mortgages or the seller will have the right to foreclose and take the house back.

Also, if you rent the house out to a tenant you must be absolutely sure that the tenant will pay the rent in a timely fashion, or you will have to come up with the payments on both mortgages or risk losing the house.

There are many pitfalls and dangers in buying homes or property with no money down, and many people have lost their shirts as the result of the mistakes they made. They have been able to get into a house with no money down, but they have not been able to carry the subsequent payments. Even worse, they have rented the house and the renter has damaged the property. The value of the property then declines and the purchaser ends up owing more than the house is worth.

Tenants Are the Key to Your Success

For the rest of your career in real estate, it is important for you to realize that your choice of renters or tenants is the key to your success or failure as an owner of rental real estate, residential or commercial. Renters unfortunately do damage to rental property. Sometimes they destroy rental property. When you decide to embark on the voyage of real estate investment, you must be extremely careful in your choice of tenants. You must check their backgrounds carefully, especially their history in previous rental properties. *Casualness leads to casualties.*

Land Held for Development

Many affluent Americans store their money in raw land held for development. They buy land on the outskirts of growing cities that have many of the positive economic dynamics that I mentioned earlier. As the city grows and expands, this land increases in value until finally it is purchased for development. At that point, the land value often jumps several times.

Water Is Essential

There are several factors to consider in purchasing raw land. The first, and most important consideration, is to ask, "Where will the water come from?" Land can be developed only if it has an adequate water supply. Check this out carefully.

How Will People Get There?

Another consideration in purchasing raw land is *transportation*. How easy is it to get to the land? Many areas grow rapidly in value after freeways and highways are built that open them up and make them accessible to larger populations. Many people have made fortunes by buying land several years in advance of its development. Then the land can increase in value by 10 and 20 times when the need for homes, schools, and shopping centers reaches that area.

Nearby Population Centers

Anyone thinking of buying raw land should also consider the nearby population centers. For the land to be valuable, it must be capable of providing a service to people of some kind. Where are these people going to come from?

Raw land appreciates in value only as the population of the area increases. Some land will never increase in value because it is lacking in either water, access to major roadways, or population pressures.

Liquid Investments

Affluent Americans also keep their money in certificates of deposit, money market accounts, and other interest-paying liquid investments. Serious money in general is not speculative money. It is careful, conservative money. It is money that has been earned slowly over time and is invested with the aim of wealth preservation.

Stocks and Bonds

The affluent purchase good quality stocks and bonds, usually for the long term. Serious investors in the stock market are what are called "value investors." They carefully research a stock and then purchase that stock based on the underlying fundamental values. They hold the stock for the long term, ignoring the day-to-day fluctuations of the stock market. Warren Buffett is a prime example of this type of investor.

Investment Alternatives Available to You

Let us assume that you are sufficiently insured and that you have enough savings put aside to cover your expenses for three to six months. With your foundation solidly in place, you can now look at some of the places where you can invest your money as you accumulate it.

Where to Put Your Money Conservatively

There are three places (besides savings accounts) where you can park your savings that will give you high degrees of safety and liquidity: money market accounts, certificates of deposit (CDs), and government savings bonds.

Money Market Accounts

Money market accounts are available at your bank and pay a higher rate of interest than savings accounts. Money market accounts require a minimum balance. They are also quite competitive, so you should shop around and look at what different banks offer. As soon as your savings account balance exceeds $1,000, move that money into a money market account at a higher rate of interest.

Certificates of Deposit

Another savings instrument that you may consider is a *certificate of deposit* (CD). These are issued by banks, savings and loans, and other financial institutions for periods of time ranging from 30 days up to 10 years. The longer you lock up your money in a CD, the higher the interest rate you will receive.

The weakness with CDs is that if you need your money back before the date of maturity there are often severe penalties. You should find out what they are before you purchase a CD in the first place.

CDs pay higher interest rates than money market accounts, and are safe places to put your savings. Nonetheless, they are not as flexible as the third option, which is government savings bonds.

Government Savings Bonds

Government savings bonds are the most conservative of investments. There are safe and secure, and they pay reasonable rates of interest. They are easily negotiable into cash if you need the money back at any time. They're backed by the full credit of the issuing government. In other words, you cannot lose money on a government savings bond unless the entire country goes broke.

These three types of investments are perfect places for you to invest your three to six months of savings. You will get the highest return possible with absolute security and safety of principal.

Investing in the Stock Market

When you begin to earn and save amounts of money in excess of your needs for short-term expenses and insurance, the next place you will want to explore is the stock market. There are three major stock markets in the United States: the New York Stock Exchange, the American

Stock Exchange, and the Nasdaq. These stock markets are run by executives and boards of directors who come primarily from the investment firms and brokerages that trade on these markets.

Stock brokerage firms are companies that come together in their respective exchanges to make a market for publicly traded stocks and bonds. You can buy and sell more then 14,000 different stocks, plus hundreds of mutual funds, through a stock brokerage firm, either live with offices like Merrill Lynch or online like Ameritrade and Charles Schwab.

Common Stock

Most of the trading that you hear or read about in the stock market is in what is called "common stock." A share of common stock in a company represents a percentage of ownership of that company. Ownership of the stock entitles you to share in the risks and the rewards of that company, both the upside and the downside.

Your ownership of a company is proportional to the number of shares that you own relative to the number of shares that the company has issued. For example, if the company has one million shares issued and you own one share, then you are entitled to one one-millionth of the profits or losses of the company. When you purchase a share of stock, you actually become an owner of that company for as long as you own the stock.

Betting against the Experts

There are several important factors for you to consider if you are thinking about trading in the stock market. First of all, for you to buy a share of stock, someone else has to be willing to sell that share of stock. Every time a trade takes place, the seller of the stock is betting that the stock price will *decline*, or at least will not go up. The purchaser is betting against the seller, believing that the stock price will *increase*. In this sense, stock market trading is a zero-sum game. Each purchaser or seller is betting his or her knowledge against the other's.

Unless your knowledge of the stock in particular, and the stock market in general, is superior to that of the people whose whole lives are spent working in the market, it is dangerous for you to believe that you can outguess them. The experts simply have too much time and experience for you to make better decisions than they do. You will probably be better off in a mutual fund of some kind.

Index Funds

Some of the most popular and largest mutual funds today (see "Mutual Fund Investing" section later in this chapter) are called "index funds." These funds purchase a cross section of stocks in the Standard & Poor's 500, the Wilshire 5000, or a particular industry. These index funds almost invariably match the overall market in growth or decline. In 80 percent of cases, an index fund will outperform the smartest and most experienced investment managers of stock brokerages or mutual fund companies.

Expectations Move the Market

Stock prices are largely determined by the *expectations* that the purchasers in the market have for the future profitability of the company issuing the stock. Since expectations are volatile and constantly fluctuating with every new piece of information, stock prices can change dramatically, up or down, in a matter of days or even hours.

It is important for you to know that the very best financial minds in the world spend 40 to 60 hours each week studying the stock market and making investment recommendations. In spite of this single-minded focus on stock market values, more than 50 percent of the recommendations of the stock market experts turn out to be *wrong*. The very best you can say is that advice from financial experts is merely a series of educated guesses.

Stock Market Investing Takes Time

Just to avoid making mistakes, much less to pick stocks correctly, you must spend an enormous amount of time and energy studying the market. You must study the individual industry within the market and study the individual company in that industry that you are considering investing in. Fortunately, with the Internet, there is much more information available to you faster today than ever before. But you must still do your homework before you buy a stock.

Contrarian Theory

There are two well-known concepts in the stock market that you will hear about, contrarian theory and the "greater fool" theory. Contrarian theory says that the best time to buy a stock is when nobody else wants the stock, or when everyone else is selling. This approach is partially true and partially false. Sometimes when everyone else is selling the stock there is a very good reason for it, and you should be selling, too.

Nonetheless, contrarian theory is a valuable tool to have at hand when thinking about where and when you invest in the stock market. Sometimes investors pick up real bargains in out-of-favor stocks, but again, you must do your homework.

Buy Stocks at a Discount

Warren Buffett, one of the richest men in the world and probably the most successful stock market investor in history, says that people look for *discounts* in every area except in stock market investing. He has made his fortune by continually looking for discounts, in that the stock is trading well below its intrinsic value. His ability to find these stocks and then move into them and take large stakes has made him and many thousands of other people extremely rich.

The Greater Fool Theory

The other concept that you will hear about, the "greater fool" theory, takes hold in a stock market boom. This theory says that no matter how much you pay for the stock, you don't have to worry because a *greater* fool will come along and pay you even more. The problem with the greater fool theory is that eventually the market runs out of fools. At that point people begin to sell, and the market turns around and goes in the other direction. As more and more people rush to sell, a semipanic can set in and the entire market can drop dramatically.

In the high-tech and dot-com boom of the 1990s, the greater fool theory took over with a vengeance and people began buying stocks at prices that in retrospect were completely ridiculous. Brand-new companies that had never produced or sold anything would make an initial public offering (IPO), and people following the greater fool theory would run the stock up several hundred percent in a single day. Even highly intelligent, sophisticated, conservative, and experienced businesspeople and investors got swept up in the greater fool theory and lost enormous amounts of money. Don't let this happen to you.

The greater fool theory is also applicable to real estate. If you hear someone say that the only direction that something can go is *up*, either don't buy it, or sell it as fast as you can. There is no such thing as a perfectly secure investment that has high potential returns but no downside risk.

Financial Representatives

Here is an important point. Salespeople who work for stock brokerage firms are paid on the basis of straight commission. They sell exactly what they are told to sell by their superiors. The person you speak to on the phone usually knows little or nothing about the stock he or she is recommending. Their jobs are to make up to 200 calls per day, and to sell whatever their management has told them to sell on that particular day.

Most registered representatives are not a source of investment advice. If you take their advice, you must know that you are throwing dice with your eyes closed. You are gambling with your money.

Check the Experience of Others

A good friend of mine is a multimillionaire who earned his money over the years through hard work, savings, and investments. He is often contacted by investment advisers recommending that he invest money into something that they are selling. In some cases, he invites the investment adviser to come and visit him personally.

During this personal visit, he asks the investment adviser about the adviser's own net worth. He says that he does not believe in taking advice from people who are worth less than he is. In addition, he wants to know how familiar they are with what they are recommending.

His experience with investment advisers has been consistent over the years. He finds that they know very little about what they are selling, and that they have not bought any of their investment product themselves. He has never found an investment adviser who is as successful financially as he is.

At the end of the conversation, most of these investment advisers concede that he would be unwise to invest with them. They go away and seldom contact him again.

Who Makes the Money?

There is a moral to this story that is important to you. Almost all the money that is made in the stock market, with few exceptions, is made by the people buying and selling stocks on commission. Very little is made by the actual investors.

In one 22-year study tracking the careers of 1,500 men and women, 83 of whom became millionaires, the researcher found that not a single person in the study became wealthy investing in the stock market. In fact, most of the people in the study were still struggling financially after 22 years of work, and one of the main reasons was because they had lost so much money investing their savings in stocks recommended by financial advisers.

Another point to remember is when the stock market turns down, or the financial market declines, the same people who are giving investment advice are often thrown out of work by the thousands. They often find themselves unemployed and unemployable, or going to work in other fields.

This is not to say that there are not many fine, honorable men and women in the field of financial planning and investment counseling. It is just to say that there are also enormous numbers of people in those fields from whom it would be dangerous to accept advice.

Remember, the only thing easy about money is losing it. However, if you are interested in investing in the stock market successfully, there is a lot of good advice available.

Investment Strategies of a Multimillionaire

Bernard Baruch was one of the most successful stock market speculators in history. As mentioned in Chapter 2, he started his career as a runner on Wall Street and ended up as one of the richest and most respected Americans, and an adviser to six presidents.

In his book, *Baruch: My Own Story* (Henry Holt, 1957), he gives some timeless advice for evaluating a company's stock before investing in it. He singles out three factors:

1. *Examine the real assets.* Examine the assets of the company, the cash in excess of its indebtedness, and the value of its physical properties. Learn how to read a financial statement so that you can clearly understand the assets and liabilities of the company. Remember that you are thinking about paying a certain amount of money for a share in that company. You need to know exactly what it is that you are buying.

2. *What does the company do?* Be sure to ask, "Does this company make something or perform a service that people want or must have?" The most important time period in considering an investment in a company is the *future*. The future of any company is determined by how good its products or services are today, and how much in demand they will be in the future. McDonald's, for example, has been a good stock over the years because what it is selling has been in continual and usually increasing demand.

3. *Study the management.* Another way of evaluating a company's stock is to assess the quality of its management. This is especially important in evaluating whether the company is going to grow in the future. Today, venture capitalists, those specialists who invest in new companies, look to the quality of management as the most important single factor in determining investment success. If the right people are in charge, they will find a way to make the company successful in most cases.

Ten Rules for Investment Success

Here are Bernard Baruch's 10 lessons learned (in quotation marks). Failure to follow these rules has been the reason for losing money for every person who ever violated them in the stock market.

Rule 1. "Don't speculate unless you can make it a full-time job." Remember, every decision you make is a bet against the decision of someone else who is studying the stock market 40, 50, and 60 hours a week.

Rule 2. "Beware of . . . anyone bringing gifts of 'inside' information or 'tips.' " The number one way to lose money in the stock market is to act on tips from people who really don't know what they are talking about, like taxi drivers, bartenders, barbers, and even your close friends at work.

Rule 3. "Before you buy a security, find out everything you can about the company, its management and competitors, its earnings and possibilities for growth." Be patient, disciplined, objective, and unemotional. Take the time to investigate before you invest.

Rule 4. "Don't try to buy at the bottom and sell at the top. This can't be done—except by liars." When you buy a stock, decided at what price you will sell it, and when it hits that price, don't be greedy. With program and computer trading today, you can set a "sell" price on a stock that will be triggered automatically when it hits that price. The fact is that you will never go broke taking a profit.

Rule 5. "Learn how to take your losses quickly and cleanly. Don't expect to be right all the time. If you have made a mistake, [and you see that the stock is going down, sell the stock and] cut your losses as quickly as possible."

The very best technique for cutting your losses in the stock market is called a *stop loss*. With the stop loss technique, you put in an order to sell your stock at 8 percent to 10 percent below the highest price at which you have owned that stock. For example, if you buy a stock at $25 per share, you would put a stop loss for $23 on that stock (approximately 8 percent below your purchase price). If the stock goes up to $30, you would move the stop loss up to $27.50, slightly over 8 percent below the highest price at which you have owned the stock. If the stock declines to this point, it is sold automatically. The use of the stop loss technique can minimize your losses if you have the discipline to stay with it.

Rule 6. "Don't buy too many different securities. Better have only a few investments which can be watched" carefully than to have too many. Diversification spreads your risks, but it also eliminates any chance you might have for major gains if one of your stocks were to increase rapidly in value.

Rule 7. "Make a periodic reappraisal of all your investments to see whether changing developments have altered their prospects." Use *zero-based thinking*. Always ask, when you have new information, "If I had not purchased this stock, knowing what I now know would I purchase it again today?" If the answer is "no," that is your cue to sell.

Rule 8. "Study your tax position to know when you can sell to greatest advantage." Be aware of the capital gains taxes that are applicable to your transactions. Remember that the only thing that counts is the amount that you have left *after* taxes. The timing of stock market purchases and sales to create capital gains and capital losses is an area with which you should be thoroughly familiar.

Rule 9. "Always keep a good part of your capital in a cash reserve. Never invest all your funds." If you keep a cash cushion at all times, you will also be in a position to take advantage of unexpected opportunities that come along. You will also have an emergency reserve to act as a buffer no matter what happens in the marketplace.

Rule 10. "Don't try to be a jack of all investments. Stick to the field you know best." Usually the most successful investors are those who pick one particular industry and concentrate on becoming knowledgeable about the companies in that industry. Pick an industry that interests you so you will enjoy keeping current with it.

Lessons from Successful Investors

Many thousands of successful investors have been interviewed over the years in an attempt to discover their so-called secrets of success. Here are some of their recommendations:

First, if you are not a bit worried about your speculations or your investments, then you are not *risking* enough. You should have enough money invested so that it is a real concern to you. You are far more likely to make the right decision when you are emotionally involved because of the size of your investment. You are also more likely to watch that investment more carefully.

Second, always take your profit too soon. "Conquer greed," as Bernard Baruch says. There is a saying in the stock market: "Bulls make money and bears make money, but pigs never do."

Third, distrust anyone who claims to predict the future, since all financial outcomes are loaded with uncertainty. This means that every investment is a *gamble* of some kind. No one can tell you with accuracy what is going to happen in the future with regard to any stock or investment. Everyone is guessing the very best way they know how.

Fourth, when the ship starts to sink, don't pray; jump. In other words, accept the small losses cheerfully as a fact of investing life. At the very best, about 50 percent of investments will go wrong. They will actually decline in value. They will fail to realize your hopes and expectations for them. But you can still succeed in investing if you minimize your losses on the downside so that you can maximize your profits on the upside.

Fifth, luck is the most powerful single factor in investment success. Because there are no predictable patterns in investing in the stock market, for you to be successful you need a lot of luck. A good question for you to ask is, "How much of my financial future am I willing to entrust to luck?"

Sixth, never fall in love with an investment. Never become emotionally involved with anything that you purchase with the intention of making a profit. This rule also includes real estate, especially your home. Many people fall in love with their investments and are reluctant to admit they have made a mistake. As a result, they ride them all the way down into the cellar, and often end up setting themselves back by several years.

Seventh, never confuse a hunch with a hope. Many people hope that a particular stock or investment is a good one. They then say that they have a very good hunch that it's going to go up. Consciously separate your hunches from your hopes, and don't confuse the two.

Eighth, optimism means expecting the best, but confidence comes from knowing how you will handle the worst. To put it another way, confidence springs from the constructive use of pessimism.

The method that I recommend is for you always to ask, "What is the worst possible thing that can happen in this situation?" Always be willing to face the worst possible outcome. J. Paul Getty, at one time the richest man in the world, said that his secret for success in investing was to objectively assess the worst possible outcome of any business deal before going into it, and then to do everything possible to protect himself should it occur. This you do by putting a stop-loss order on every investment.

Ninth, disregard the majority opinion. Think through every decision for yourself. Don't allow your investment decisions to be influenced by anyone else. Take the time to think them through personally, and then take full responsibility for each choice that you make.

Tenth, if it doesn't pay the first time, forget it. If, based on the information you have, you decide to invest in a stock and it doesn't work out, sell the stock and go on to something else. Keep your ego completely out of the equation. A very wealthy man once told me, "Investment opportunities are like buses; there will always be another one along."

The preceding advice is practiced by many of the most successful people who have ever invested in stocks. Remember, the stock market is highly speculative. It is dominated and controlled by people who are making their livings by buying and selling stock for others. And these people make mistakes every single day.

There are no foolproof ways for making money in the stock market. If you are going to invest in stocks, be careful. Do your homework and watch your investments all the time.

Mutual Fund Investing

There is one way to invest in the stock market with minimal risk, and that is through a mutual fund. A mutual fund is a pool of money made up of the investments of thousands of individuals like yourself. This money is used to purchase a diversified portfolio of stocks. A mutual fund is run by professional money managers, people who make informed investment decisions. These are people who spend their full time in the stock market.

Mutual funds are sold directly by the mutual fund companies themselves, and also through stock brokerage firms, investment advisers, banks, savings and loans, and other outlets. There are thousands of mutual funds available, and they have records of performance that are all over the map. Some of them actually lose money when the stock market is booming, and others make money when the stock market is declining. Once again, this is an area where you must investigate before you invest.

Load versus No-Load Funds

There are two types of mutual funds with regard to cost. The first is called a commission or a *load* fund. In a load fund you pay up to $8^{1}/_{2}$ percent commission, which comes out of your investment when you invest your money in that mutual fund. Most of this commission goes to the person who sold you the mutual fund in the first place. This is how the fund companies compensate their salespeople.

With a commission-based fund, the balance of your investment is put into the portfolio of stocks. The explanation for charging an $8^1/_2$ percent commission is that if the fund is well managed you will make it all back and more in a reasonable amount of time. Sometimes you do, and sometimes you don't.

There are also *no-load* mutual funds. These are mutual funds you can purchase through various intermediaries without paying a commission. One hundred percent of your money will be invested for you.

Countless comparisons have been made over the years between commission funds and no-load funds. The conclusion seems to be that there is very little difference in investment return between the load and no-load funds. Both types seem to be well managed and perform very much the same. There is therefore no need for you to pay a commission when you buy a mutual fund. Your results will likely be no different in the long run, but you will lose a substantial part of your investment at the beginning if you pay a commission. It can take you a year or more just to get back to your original investment.

Key Considerations for Investing in Mutual Funds

There are several factors you should consider when you think about investing in mutual funds. Bear these considerations in mind when you make your choices and decisions.

First, past performance is seldom any indicator of future performance, except in select cases. If your mutual fund is successful, it will usually attract enormous inflows of new money. Soon it can become so large that its money cannot be invested to achieve the same rate of growth that made it famous in the first place. By the time you hear of a successful mutual fund, it is usually too late to get into it and enjoy substantial increases in your investment.

Second, there are certain mutual fund management companies that have long-term above-average records of success and growth. It is not unusual for the shares in a specific mutual fund to increase 10, 20, 30, 40, even 50 percent in a good year in the stock market. Often a large mutual fund can achieve above-market returns for several years.

Third, irrespective of the pros and cons of mutual fund investing, the very best place for the average person to invest in the stock market is through a well-selected mutual fund. Because it holds a diversified portfolio of stocks, your downside is limited. Unfortunately, in most cases, your upside is also limited. Most mutual funds move in tandem with the stock market as a whole. When the stock market goes up, the fund's value goes up, and when the stock market declines, they decline at about the same percent.

Fourth, one of the advantages of a mutual fund, like a stock, is that they are highly liquid. If you need your money back, you can sell your shares, as you can with any stock, and get your cash quickly if you need it, usually within 72 hours.

Fifth, and perhaps most important, mutual fund investing enables you to turn your attention to your career and your business. Once you have invested the money in a mutual fund, you can get on with the rest of your life and work activities and not think about your money again, at least in the short term.

Different Ways to Invest

Other investments that people make have different track records and histories.

Precious Metals

You can invest in gold, silver, and precious metals. These are volatile and dangerous instruments, often sold by questionable people as inflation hedges, based on questionable projections regarding their potential increases in value.

As a rule, be very careful when considering gold, silver, and precious metals. Some of the smartest people in the world are trading in these metals every year. My advice to you would be to *avoid* gold, silver, and precious metals completely.

Antiques and Collectibles

Another type of investment consists of antiques, Persian carpets, coins, stamps, and other collectibles, such as baseball cards. While it is true that this type of investment occasionally goes up in value, it is even truer that investments in these collectibles go down as well, and much more often.

The people who make the most money trading in these areas are the ones who *sell* the antiques, Persian carpets, coins, stamps, and baseball cards to others. Unless you are an expert, this is not a place to invest.

Penny Stocks of All Kinds

Many people invest in oil and gas stocks, mining stocks, and penny stocks. While there are very solid operators in oil, gas, and mining, there are also many questionable stock market hustlers in this type of investment.

With regard to penny stocks, 80 percent to 90 percent of penny stocks never recover to the price at which they are initially sold. They are the greatest waste of investment capital in the country. If someone calls you with a wonderful success story about penny stocks, hang up the phone.

Commodities

Another type of investment that you read about is commodities. Trading in the commodities market is one of the biggest of all gambles. Reputable stock brokerage firms require that you demonstrate to them that you have at least $25,000 to lose before they will accept your investment account. And you can be sure of one thing: You *are* going to lose your $25,000!

Even the most sophisticated commodity traders in the world lose money every single day. Stay away from commodities unless you are willing to make it a full-time life commitment and you have a lot of money with which to learn the field.

Guard Your Money Carefully

Your primary rule for investments of all kinds must be, "Don't lose money." It is better to keep your hard-earned money in an interest-bearing account than to lose it on foolish investments.

Study after study shows that if you simply leave your money growing in a well-chosen mutual fund and let it compound over the course of your working lifetime, you will be further ahead than with almost any other investment except your own business.

The rich are almost always conservative in their dealings with money. They maintain low levels of debt. They handle their money with care, and they continue to look for ways to increase it while minimizing risk.

Learn from the wealthy and do what they do. Follow the leaders, not the followers; remember that the first step to becoming wealthy is to earn the money. The second step is to hold on to it. It is not how much you earn, but how much you keep that counts. Be determined and be careful.

Action Exercises

1. Open a special savings account and begin building it up until you have three to six months of expenses in reserve. This single action will change your personality in a very positive way.

2. Sit down with an insurance agent and ask his/her advice on the type and amount of insurance you need to protect you from any unexpected hazard. When you are properly insured, you feel much better about yourself and your life.

3. Open an account with an online broker and carefully invest your money, starting with a money market account, and then venturing into well-chosen mutual funds. The act of investing in the shares of large corporations changes the way you look at money and business.

4. Do your homework before you purchase an individual stock. Investigate before you invest, and then buy 100 shares (a round lot) in a company and industry in which you have confidence. This will give you invaluable experience.

5. Subscribe to and read magazines and newspapers aimed at people who are serious about their financial futures, such as *Forbes*, *Fortune*, *BusinessWeek*, the *Wall Street Journal*, *Investor's Business Daily*, and *Money*. Keep current.

6. Begin building a cash reserve to use for investment in real estate. Choose a property that is within driving distance of your home, never one that is far away.

7. Think continually about starting and building a business of your own, if you are not already doing it. By building a financial estate, you are laying the groundwork for getting rich your own way.

"The future has several names.
For the weak, it is the impossible.
For the fainthearted, it is the unknown.
For the thoughtful and valiant, it is the ideal."
—**Victor Hugo**

4

Start with Nothing

"The grass is not in fact always greener on the other side of the fence. Not at all. Fences have nothing to do with it. The grass is greenest where it is watered."

—W. Somerset Maugham

When I was starting off in life, I felt sorry for myself because I had no money. I had read the popular editorials that said that life was unfair in the United States because some people had money and some people didn't. They implied that if you had no money to start off with, you had little chance of success later in life.

Then something profound happened to change my thinking. I discovered that the typical American starts off with nothing. Going back to the earliest debates of the Founding Fathers, it was generally assumed that people arrived in this country with little or no money and had to start from scratch. For this reason, the American constitutional system was designed, within a framework of commercial law, to make it possible for anyone, starting from anywhere, to become successful if they worked hard, saved their money, and invested intelligently over the course of their working lifetimes.

The Golden Chains

When I was growing up, and right into my early 30s, despite my short-term successes, I never had any extra money with which I could begin working toward financial independence. There always seemed to be enough bills and expenses to absorb every penny I earned. I was always in debt. The idea of breaking out financially never occurred to me.

Even if a great business opportunity did come along, I would not have been able to do anything about it. Because I had no money, I had no freedom. I was held in the "golden chains" of employment and I couldn't get free.

As I began studying financial success and self-made millionaires, I observed that almost everyone around me was in very much the same condition that I was. No one seemed to have any money. Everyone was in debt. Everyone seemed to worry about money most of the time. The idea of becoming truly wealthy was a distant dream with very little possibility of coming true. You may be in the same situation right now, with more bills and debts than money or assets.

The Statistics Are Dreadful

As I mentioned earlier in this book, the statistics on financial success are a little scary. Of one hundred people who reach retirement age today, according to insurance industry statistics, only one will be wealthy. Four out of the hundred will be financially independent. Fifteen will have some savings put aside. But the other 80 percent will be dependent on pensions, still working, or broke. And this will be after a lifetime of well-paid work in the most affluent society in history. How could this happen?

There are two primary reasons why people retire poor, no matter how much they make in the course of their working lifetimes. First, they never decide to retire rich. They wish and hope and pray, but they never make a firm, unequivocal decision that they are going to become wealthy.

Second, even if they do decide to retire rich, they procrastinate until it is too late. They always have some good reason for putting it off.

Four Steps to Financial Success

If you sincerely want to beat the odds, achieve financial independence, and retire wealthy, there are four keys, all starting with the letter "D."

You Must Really Want It

The first step is *desire*. You must want financial success badly enough to make an unshakable commitment to achieving it. You must be willing to make sacrifices in the short term in order to enjoy financial success in the long term. To break out of the pack financially, you must be willing to delay and defer gratification and expenditures on new cars, clothes, and gadgets, and instead save and invest the money. In the final analysis, the only real determinant of what you can accomplish is the intensity of your desire. If you want it badly enough, you will definitely achieve it.

You Must Make a Decision

The second step is *decision*. You must make a decision, right now, to do whatever is necessary to become financially independent. You must be willing to pay any price and go any distance to achieve your financial goals.

You Must Be Determined

The third "D" stands for *determination*. You must resolve to persist until you succeed in spite of all the problems and obstacles you will experience. No matter how many times you get knocked down, you must be prepared to pick yourself up and continue onward. Determination and persistence are perhaps the most important qualities necessary for financial and personal success.

You Must Make Yourself Do It

The fourth "D" stands for *discipline*. You must develop the discipline, action by action, to master yourself and to develop the habits necessary for achieving financial independence. You must discipline yourself to get up a little earlier, work a little harder, and stay at work a little later. You must discipline yourself to learn everything you need to know to achieve your financial goal. You must discipline yourself to persist resolutely, no matter how many times you experience setbacks, disappointment, and temporary failure.

Give yourself a grade on the four "Ds"—desire, decision, determination, and discipline. You can determine how successful you are going to be in the future by measuring how well you are doing in each of these four qualities on a scale of 1 to 10. Whatever your score, resolve to improve in each area by practicing that quality whenever it is called for.

Five Ways to Become Wealthy

Based on more than 25 years of research into American millionaires, there are basically five ways that you can become wealthy, starting with nothing. We have touched on some of these already.

Inherit the Money

You may be fortunate to inherit the money. Fewer than 10 percent of wealthy Americans inherit all or a part of their money, and the number is declining every year. More and more American fortunes are first-generation; that is, they were earned completely by the person who possesses them.

Become a Professional

You can become wealthy by achieving your wealth professionally. You can become a doctor, a lawyer, an architect, an engineer, or an accountant or take up any other profession that requires long, formalized courses of university study followed by many years of hard work and practice. As a professional, you can become extremely good at what you do, be paid very well as a result, and then carefully save and invest the money you earn.

In the sale of professional services, a person can usually only earn money as long as he or she is working. It is hard to build up equity or residual income in a professional services practice such as medicine, accounting, or law. Sometimes you can sell your practice, but once you stop working, your income slows down and stops as well.

For this reason, professionals who become millionaires almost invariably channel their high earnings into other investments, such as real estate, stocks, bonds, and business ventures that can eventually generate cash flow and dividends for them when they stop working personally.

Become an Executive

Becoming a senior executive of a large corporation may enable you to achieve financial independence. You can get a good education, go to work with a large company, work your way up through the ranks into a senior executive position, be paid very well at your job, and then become wealthy as the result of stock options and investments.

Lightning Strikes

People sometimes become wealthy in America through remarkable, chance events. They win the lottery, write a hit song or best-selling book, invent a timely product or service, or become successful actors or entertainers. The stories of these people fill the newspapers, magazines, and television and radio shows, but they represent less than 1 percent of the wealthy population in the United States.

Your chances of winning the lottery are the equivalent of lightning striking twice in the same place within two years. The odds are millions to one. Fully 95 percent of actors are unemployed at any given time. Only a few of them earn millions of dollars per picture. Most entertainers are underpaid or underemployed, and even if they break into the big time, most of them retire poor as well. They go through the money as fast as they earn it and then end up with nothing at the end of their careers. That's why they say, "easy come, easy go."

The High Road to Riches in America

Perhaps you can become wealthy by starting your own business and earning your wealth all by yourself. Starting your own business has always been the high road to becoming wealthy for most self-made millionaires. Fully 74 percent of wealthy Americans are successful entrepreneurs.

In 2003, the Organization for Economic Cooperation and Development in Paris ranked the United States as "the most entrepreneurial country in the world." Entrepreneurship offers more opportunities and opens more doors than all other possibilities for wealth creation put together. This is why it has been said that if you have the ability to start your own business and you don't do it, you are a fool.

Throughout the rest of this book, I am going to share with you a series of ideas, methods, techniques, and success systems that you can use in a variety of areas to achieve financial independence. Every idea or recommendation in this book has made hundreds and thousands of people into self-made millionaires. What you can accomplish with the ideas you learn in the pages ahead is completely up to you. It will depend solely on your own personal levels of desire, decisiveness, determination, and discipline.

The Starting Point of Riches

Theodore Roosevelt once said, "Do what you can, with what you have, right where you are." If you, like most Americans, are starting off broke or with very little money, where do you start? The answer is that you start by getting your finances under control.

Remember, "It takes money to make money." It is not the money as much as it is the *character* and *discipline* you must have to accumulate money that is essential for financial success. It is only when you can get your finances under control at a low level that you demonstrate that you have the ability to manage and grow your money at a higher level. You have to walk before you run.

Pay Yourself First

One of the great success classics, *The Richest Man in Babylon* by George S. Clason, was written many years ago. His central idea is still valid today. The book is a primer on financial success because its principles are simple, direct, and effective.

Throughout his book Clason says that the starting point of financial success is for you to "pay yourself first." Take 10 percent off the top of your income every time you earn or receive money, and put it aside in your financial independence account. Once you have put it aside, never touch it or spend it for any reason other than to invest it and grow it.

After you have paid yourself first by putting 10 percent of your income away, you then learn to live on 90 percent or less of your income. Fortunately, human beings are creatures of habit. In no time at all, you will develop the habit of living on 90 percent or less of your income. From that point forward, your financial success is largely assured.

Work Hard and Save Your Money

Throughout the history of American enterprise, people have heard the recommendation "work hard and save your money." This is the oldest rule for success.

Why is it that saving money is so important? It is because saving money is a *discipline*, and any discipline affects all other disciplines in your life. Each time you exercise a discipline, your other disciplines become stronger. Each time you fail to discipline yourself in one area, your other disciplines become weaker. You make or break yourself by either developing or failing to develop self-discipline.

If you do not have the discipline to refrain from spending all the money that you earn, then you are simply not qualified to become wealthy. And if by some miracle you do become wealthy, then because you lack discipline and self-control you will not be capable of holding on to your fortune. This is why most lottery winners are bankrupt and back at their old jobs in two to three years. This is why most "overnight successes" are broke and back living in one-bedroom apartments. Because they did not develop the disciplines necessary to hold on to their money, it went through their fingers like water.

Attract the Money You Want

In Chapter 2, you learned about becoming a money magnet. When you save your money, you activate the law of attraction in your life. Each dollar you save will attract another dollar. When you save $5, $10, or $100, you attract more and more money into your life, often in the most remarkable ways.

If you are really serious about your financial future, discipline yourself to go down to your local bank immediately and open a savings account. Put as much money as you can into that account, even if it is only $10. From that day forward, put every bit of money you possibly can into that account to help it to grow.

You will find that the more money you put into that account, the more money you will attract from sources that you cannot now predict. You will get bonuses at work. You will receive unexpected income tax refunds. People will repay old debts. You will find yourself selling used clothes or furniture from around your home or apartment. You may even receive unexpected financial presents. If you can discipline yourself to put each of these "gifts" into your financial independence account, you will *intensify* the magnetic power of that account and begin attracting more and more money into your life.

Starting with Nothing

How do you begin becoming rich if the idea of saving 10 percent of your income is impossible for you at this time? Join the crowd! Most people cannot start off saving 10 percent of their income. Their rent, utilities, car payments, food, and other bills consume everything they earn, and a little bit more besides, usually financed by loans and credit cards. If you are so far behind that you think you are first, how do you begin?

The answer is simple. You begin by saving 1 percent of your income and learning to live on the other 99 percent. If you earn $3,000 per month, this works out to $30 per month, $1 per day. Could you save this amount if your life depended on it? What if your entire financial future depended on it? The fact is that you could find a way to live on 99 percent of your income if your desire for financial independence was intense enough.

Because you are a creature of habit, you will quickly become comfortable living on 99 percent of your income. Then you begin saving 2 percent of your income, and living on the other 98 percent. By increasing your savings rate by 1 percent per month, within one year, you will be living comfortably on 90 percent or less of your income, and you will be on your way to financial independence. But you must get started. You must take action by opening your financial freedom account and beginning to save 1 percent of your income, today.

Pleasure and Pain

One of the main mental blocks that holds people back from saving their money, even when they know they should be doing it, originates in early childhood conditioning. When you were young, your parents encouraged you to save money from your allowance and discouraged you from spending it. But you associated spending money with candy and toys, with pleasure and enjoyment. The idea of saving your money was seen as a deprivation or even a punishment. You therefore developed negative feelings toward the entire concept of saving rather than spending.

In the work of Sigmund Freud, he explains the "pleasure principle." He said that all human action is an attempt to move away from discomfort or pain toward pleasure and enjoyment. Each person, as a child, associates *spending* their money with pleasure and enjoyment, and associates *saving* their money with pain and discomfort. As an adult, this mental conditioning prevails and is a primary reason for financial failure and poverty later in life.

Your goal is to reverse the subconscious programming that you have with regard to spending versus saving. You must begin to think in terms of the pleasure, security and enjoyment that having money in the bank means to you. You must associate saving with happiness and success rather than with deprivation and discomfort. You must begin to look forward to saving money as a source of happiness and satisfaction. This just happens to be the mind-set of all people who become wealthy.

The Wedge Strategy for Financial Success

It is often hard for people to think of curtailing their standard of living, of cutting back in their lifestyle in order to save money. When we suggest that you should be living on 90 percent or less of your income, there is almost always an automatic negative reaction to the idea. You may agree with it *logically*, but you disagree *emotionally* with the cutbacks and sacrifices that this entails.

However, there is a way to counter this natural negative reaction toward savings and accumulation. I call it the "wedge strategy." It may be hard for you to give up spending the money you are earning today. But you should have no problem giving up spending money that you don't have at all.

Here is how the wedge strategy works. From this day forward, resolve that you are going to save 50 percent of every raise, bonus, or increase in pay that you earn for the rest of your career. Almost anyone can agree to save 50 percent of money that they have not yet received. If

I were to offer you one dollar if you would give me 50 cents of it back, you would accept immediately. You must perform this same mental operation on yourself.

Decide in Advance

From now on, if you receive a $100 raise or an increase in pay of any kind, you must decide in advance that you are going to save 50 percent of that amount and put it away into your financial independence savings account. By making this decision in advance, before you even receive the money, you will find it much easier to follow through on your resolution when the inevitable pay increases come to you.

The average pay and cost-of-living increase in the United States is 3 percent to 4 percent per year. By following some of the strategies in this book, you will learn how to increase your annual income by 10, 20, and even 30 percent each year. In every case, you must resolve to save half of your increase and to then invest it carefully for the future. By doing this, if you start early enough and persist long enough, you will become financially independent, if not a millionaire, in the years ahead.

Don't Lose Money

Once you begin to accumulate money, here is an important rule. Invest the money conservatively. Marvin Davis, an American self-made billionaire, was once asked by *Forbes* magazine how he accounted for his financial success. He said that he has two rules for investing money. Rule number one was, "Don't lose money."

He said, "Whenever I see an opportunity to invest where there is a possibility that I could lose money, I just simply refrain from investing in the first place."

Regarding rule number two, Davis said, "Whenever I am tempted, I refer back to rule number one, 'Don't lose money.' "

Warren Buffett, one of the richest men in America, who started with nothing many years ago, practices the same rules with regard to investing. "Don't lose money." You should do the same. The key to riches is to accumulate your funds carefully and then invest them conservatively.

One of the characteristics of self-made millionaires and of old money in the United States is that it is cautiously, conservatively, and prudently invested. Don't try to get rich quickly or make a killing in some area. Instead, concentrate on getting rich slowly. If all you do is save 10 percent or more of your income, invest it carefully, and make it grow at 8 percent to 10 percent per year, that alone will make you wealthy. Even $100 per month, invested at 10.5 percent interest over 40 years, would be worth $1,117,000 at the end of that time.

Strategies of the Wealthy

Some years ago, my accountant was a man who also handled the accounting for many wealthy men and women. He found that they all seemed to have two things in common. First, they had very low debt. Any money that they did owe was solidly backed by income-producing assets. No matter how strong the economy or how low the interest rates, they refused to go into debt unless the return on the money was substantially higher than the cost of the money.

The second quality he found was that none of them got rich quickly, or invested in speculative ventures. Over the years, they concentrated on increasing their net worth by 8 percent to 10 percent each year, year after year, with very little fluctuation. They were not greedy. They accumulated their money slowly and they held on to it, no matter what was happening in the economy around them.

Advice from a Banker

Once I attended the retirement dinner of a banker who had worked with many millionaires over the course of his career. In his address to the group, he talked about the predominant characteristics of the self-made millionaires that he had encountered. He said that he had worked with sailors, farmers, clergymen, laborers, teachers, and crane operators, as well as others from every walk of life, who had become millionaires.

He said that the one characteristic that they all had in common was that they saved their money and then invested it carefully, cautiously, and prudently. From an early age, they each had a long-term perspective, and were prepared to spend many years achieving financial independence.

Change Your Personality

The wonderful result of saving your money is that it develops character, discipline, and self-confidence. When you begin to save money, you will feel like the master of your own destiny. Saving money gives you a sense of being in control of your own life. It gives you a sense of personal power and self-confidence. Having money in the bank actually changes your attitude toward yourself and your world. It even affects your body language.

One of the major reasons why people are unhappy, anxious, and frustrated today is because they don't have any money in the bank. As a result, they worry about money all the time. They can't order from a menu without looking at the right-hand column to see how hungry they are.

But when you begin to save your money and accumulate your funds, you become a different person. Your self-esteem, self-respect, and personal pride increase. Your handshake becomes firmer and you look people directly in the eye. The knowledge that you have money in your pocket and in your bank account translates into a more erect posture, a more confident voice, and a more positive attitude toward yourself and your life.

The Truth about Entrepreneurship

President Calvin Coolidge once said, "The business of America is business." Everything you do in your financial life has something to do with business, in some way. Even if you are a real estate investor or a stock market trader, you are in a form of business. You have sales and revenues. You have profits and losses. You have assets and liabilities. You have choices and decisions to make, and you face continually changing competition and economic forces. Everything that has to do with money involves business principles in some way.

Some statistics suggest that 80 percent of new businesses fail within two years. Another 10 percent to 15 percent of new businesses fail within four years. In many cases, the people starting these businesses invest everything they have, plus everything their families will lend to them, plus two to four years of their lives, only to emerge penniless at the other end.

The primary reason that people do not start businesses is because they are afraid that they are going to fail and lose all their money. And in many cases, they are right.

Lack of Experience

However, if you study the numbers more closely, a different picture emerges. The fact is that most businesses started by *in*experienced businesspeople fail within a few months or a couple of years. This is simply because inexperienced businesspeople do not know how to make sales, generate revenues, deliver products and services satisfactorily, hire people, and manage or administer a fast-moving entrepreneurial enterprise in a highly competitive marketplace. Probably 99 percent of businesses started by people lacking business experience fail within the first two or three years.

Why is the rate of new business failures so high? It is because the entrepreneurs have hopes and dreams, but they don't know exactly what they have to do to make a business successful. They may have an idea for a product or service, but they don't know all the things they need to know to sell and deliver that product or service at a price that enables their business to survive and grow. We'll talk about some of these key success factors in the course of this book.

The Value of Experience

Here's the good news. Fully 90 percent of businesses started by *experienced* businesspeople succeed. Why is this? The reason is because experienced businesspeople know what they have to do to make a business successful. They know how to purchase or produce their products and services. They know how to sell and to market. They know how to generate revenues. They know how to negotiate with their suppliers. They know how to rent premises and negotiate leases. They know how to manage their finances. In other words, they have the experience that is indispensable to business success. For you to start your own business and succeed, these are the things that you must learn as well.

According to Dun & Bradstreet, 96 percent of U.S. businesses that go broke fail because of "managerial incompetence." Managerial incompetence means that the people running the businesses don't know what they are doing. Anyone who has ever built or run a business is continually amazed at how many incompetent people there are out there in the business world, at every level.

Reasons for Business Failure

There are two major areas of managerial incompetence that lead to business failure: poor sales results and poor cost controls.

Poor Sales Results

The first area of incompetence is lack of skill or ability in sales and marketing. Approximately 48 percent of businesses that fail nationwide do so because the business cannot sell enough of its products or services to survive. With declining sales, cash flow—which is like blood to the brain of the business—soon declines to the point where the business collapses.

In a broader sense, this is why people fail personally as well. They fail to generate enough income to cover all of their expenses, both necessary and unnecessary. Eventually they run out of cash and credit. Some 1.5 million Americans declare bankruptcy every year because they do not earn enough money to pay for their living expenses, which are usually out of control.

Poor Cost Controls

According to Dun & Bradstreet, 46 percent of businesses fail because of poor cost controls. The business may be selling and generating sufficient revenues on the front end, but it is losing so much on the back end that it goes broke anyway. Again, this is a major reason for *personal* financial failure, as well. No matter how much people earn, if they cannot get their spending under control the relationship between income and expenses gets so far out of balance that their financial lives collapse.

Both sales and revenue generation in business on the one hand, plus cost controls and cash flow analysis on the other hand, require experience. If you are serious about becoming financially independent, you have to become skilled in both areas.

Business Success Is Predictable

The law of correspondence in business says that your outer world of results will always correspond to your inner world of knowledge, skill, and preparation. To be successful in business, you must learn the skills you need to succeed. Business success is not a matter of luck. Business success is a matter of knowledge, skill, and application. It is a matter of ability. Business success is a matter of experience and intelligence. It consists of skills that you can learn through practice and repetition.

Wonderfully enough, you can learn what you need to learn to be successful in any business. Every single person who is successful in business today, of any kind, at one time had no knowledge or experience of that business at all. Every skill necessary for business success is acquired through learning and practice. And anything that anyone else has done, you can do as well.

Get On-the-Job Experience

One of the best ways to become a business success is to get on-the-job training. About 80 percent of successful businesspeople attribute their success to the training and experience that they acquired working for someone else. As a result, they were able to learn "on the cheap." They may have learned by trial and error, but their employer absorbed the costs of their errors. By paying close attention to what they did right and what they did wrong, they were able to get the experience they needed, and be paid for it at the same time.

Let me repeat. Fully 90 percent of businesses started by *experienced* businesspeople eventually succeed. Companies started by people with more than five years of business experience are far more likely to be successful than any other type of company. They have a 90 percent success rate!

If you are starting off with little or nothing, don't despair. Self-made American millionaires have been broke or nearly broke an average of 3.2 times before they finally developed the skills and experience that they needed to break through financially. Be prepared to have many ups and downs on the way to becoming wealthy. This is simply part of the price that you have to pay to break out of the pack.

Learn While You Earn

Experience is the key. If you sincerely desire to start and build your own successful business, start by going to work for another business in the industry that attracts you. Be prepared to put in five years of hard work to get the training and experience you require. Be prepared to invest as much as 10,000 hours to master the fine points of the business. Be patient. Don't look for shortcuts or get-rich-quick schemes. Settle in for the long haul.

Once you start working for a company, look upon your job as a springboard to future success. Take all the training you can get. Take every course that comes along. Take seminar brochures to your boss and ask if your boss will pay for you to attend these seminars and courses. If your boss won't pay for it, take the courses and pay for them yourself. No matter who signs your paycheck, always view yourself as *self-employed*—because you are. Treat the company you work for as though it belonged to you, because in a way it does.

See Yourself As Self-Employed

The biggest mistake that you can ever make in life is to ever think that you work for anyone else but *yourself*. You are always self-employed. You are the president of your own personal services corporation. The more you act as if you are self-employed and treat your company as though it belonged to you, the faster you will grow and the more you will learn.

The more you treat the company you work for as if you owned 100 percent of the stock, the faster you will come to the attention of people who can help you. By taking personal responsibility for results and for the success of your company, you will attract greater opportunities and responsibilities. You will be paid more and promoted faster. You will be considered to be a far more valuable person than those who just come to work from 9:00 to 5:00 and do only what they are expected to do.

Five Keys to Business Success

There are five essential abilities that you must develop to succeed in business of any kind. These are the keys to starting and building your own successful business, and they are also essential to your making the most valuable contribution you possibly can to the company that you are currently working for.

You can learn each of these skills on the job. You can learn them by transferring from one position to another, or from one company to another, as your career evolves.

Plan, Organize, and Get Results

The first ability you require is the ability to *plan, organize, and get results*. It is the most valuable and highest-paid ability in the country. Your ability to get results, and to take responsibility for results in your company, is the hallmark of the high achiever.

Continually ask yourself, "What results are expected of me?" Look around you at your company. What are the results that are most responsible for the success of the business? Who are the most respected people, and what are they doing? Keep asking yourself, "How can I increase my ability to get the most important results that my company requires to succeed?"

Go the Extra Mile

The key to success in business, either your own or that of someone else, is to do more than you are paid for. Always be prepared to go the extra mile. Remember, there are never any traffic jams on the extra mile. When you dedicate yourself to always doing more than you are paid for, more than your boss expects, you put yourself on the side of the angels. You bring yourself to the attention of people who can help you. You open doors for yourself that remain closed to the average performer.

Since the average employee does only what they are told to do, and no more, when you begin to go the extra mile, you will immediately stand out. Take advantage of your employer. Treat your job as a laboratory in which you can learn a wide variety of skills at someone else's expense. Volunteer for everything. Offer to take on additional responsibilities. Work longer, harder hours than the average. Every single skill and experience you acquire at your work accumulates to make you more valuable and successful in the future.

Market and Sell

You need the ability to communicate, to persuade others, and to sell your products and services. The most important reason for success in any business is high sales. The major reason for failure in any business is low sales. The greater impact you can have on sales revenues and cash flow, the more valuable and important you become to your company.

Whatever position you are in, decide today that you are going to learn how to sell effectively. Read books on the subject. Take courses and seminars from professional sales trainers. Join a Toastmasters International chapter and learn how to speak effectively in public. Look for opportunities to sell, or to become involved in sales activities in your company.

Over the years, I have conducted sales seminars for more than 500,000 sales professionals. Many of these people start off as accountants, engineers, plumbers, truck drivers, and military personnel. They often tell me that initially the whole idea of selling was quite frightening for them, but they could not find any other job at the time.

You Can Learn to Sell

However, as soon as they realized that selling is a skill, like riding a bicycle or typing at a keyboard, their whole attitude toward themselves and their possibilities changed. In a few months or a couple of years, by practicing basic sales skills, many of them became extraordinarily successful and earned far more money than they ever had before. Some of them went on to start their own businesses, and many of them became millionaires as a result.

Be a Good Listener

Probably 85 percent of your success in life, both personal and business, will be determined by your ability to get along well with other people. The better you become at asking good questions and listening intently to the answers, at making presentations and persuading people to cooperate with you, the more impact you will have on your world, and the more valuable you will become. And these are all learnable skills.

Select the Right People

To succeed in business you need the ability to select the right people and to build effective teams. The ability to get people to cooperate and to work together in the achievement of common goals is considered to be the most important of all skills for gaining a promotion.

Every CEO of a Fortune 500 corporation started as a junior employee with no staff at all. By learning how to interact well with one person at a time, they were soon given assistants or the responsibility of organizing other people into a team to achieve a particular business result. The better they became at working with their teams, the more responsibility they were given, along with higher pay.

As you demonstrate your ability to work well with one person, you will soon become a supervisor, and then a manager. At each stage of your career, as you demonstrate your ability to get results through other people, you will be promoted and given even more people to manage and greater results to accomplish. Eventually, you will become an executive and then a leader within your organization.

Master Your Job

When I was 24 years old, I took a job in straight commission sales, going from office to office in the daytime, and from door to door in the evenings. I read everything I could find on sales, listened to sales audiotapes throughout the day and evening, and sought advice from everyone who was ahead of me in my field. In less than a year, I learned how to sell effectively. I increased my income, doubled it, and then doubled it again. I was soon being asked to recruit and train new people, which I did by telling them what I had learned. Soon they were selling successfully as well.

This experience transformed my life. Within two years, I had built a 95-person sales force that was operating successfully in six countries. I had taken myself from rags to riches in professional selling. I had gone from living in a small rooming house to living in a beautiful furnished apartment overlooking the city. I had gone from worrying about money every day to never carrying less than $1,000 in $20 bills. In retrospect, I saw that my success was simply a matter of learning and applying first, the skills of selling, and second, the skills of team building. You can learn these skills as well.

Become a Good Negotiator

You need to be able to negotiate well on your own behalf. All successful businesspeople are good negotiators. They know how to *ask for more* when they are selling, and *offer less* when they are buying. They have developed the ability to negotiate and resolve conflict among the people that they work with. They have learned how to negotiate loans, terms, and conditions with bankers and financial suppliers. They have learned how to negotiate payment terms with suppliers and vendors. They have learned how to negotiate sales with customers. They can negotiate work assignments, responsibilities, and pay with their staff. To be successful in business, you must become an excellent negotiator. The alternative is that you will always be *outnegotiated* by others.

Fortunately, negotiating is a skill you acquire through learning and practice. You can read books, listen to audio programs, and take negotiating seminars. You can learn from the best in the business and then practice on every occasion.

Perhaps the most important word in negotiating is the word *ask*. Develop the habit of asking for what you want, and if you do not like the first answer, ask again, for something different. Ask for better prices and terms. Ask for better conditions. Ask for better seats on airlines and for better rooms in hotels. Ask for better tables in restaurants and better cars when you rent. By developing the habit of continually asking for what you want, you will eventually become an excellent negotiator in every area of your life.

Master the Numbers

An understanding of accounting, business financing, and cost controls will help you to succeed in business. It is amazing how many people have built successful businesses on the front end by selling substantial quantities of their products and services, but then lost all their money on the back end because they did not understand the numbers of their business.

As it happens, most entrepreneurs are more conceptual than detailed. They are more focused on people, products, and sales than they are on financial statements. Nonetheless, financial management is a basic skill that you can learn with a little instruction and practice. After that, you can hire competent bookkeepers and accountants to stay on top of the numbers. But you must be able to read them and interpret them for yourself.

You do not have to become an expert in accounting. But you must understand how to read a financial statement. You must understand the difference between gross and net profit. You must understand the difference between fixed, variable, and semivariable costs. You must learn how to monitor receivables and payables. Above all, you must keep your hand on the pulse of the cash flow in your business. This is the determinant of success or failure.

Dealing with Banks

To start and grow your business, you will usually have to borrow money and arrange lines of credit from your bank. Banks are in the business of making good loans. The completeness and accuracy of your financial projections and your loan requests will largely determine whether you get the money in the first place. Many businesses have actually been forced to close down because the entrepreneur was not capable of putting together an acceptable loan application.

Succeed in Business by Really Trying

These, then, are the five requirements for succeeding in business:

First, you must develop the ability to plan, organize, and get results.

Second, you must develop the ability to sell, communicate, and interact effectively with others.

Third, you must develop the ability to pick the right people and to form them together into effective work teams.

Fourth, you must develop the ability to negotiate on your own behalf, and for your business.

And *fifth*, you must learn how to read financial statements, and develop the ability to understand bookkeeping, accounting, and finances.

The good news is that you can learn each of these through on-the-job training. You can learn them all while you are working for another business.

Use Your Job as a Springboard

What you can't learn on the job you can learn off the job. Your job can serve as an ongoing entrepreneurial training program, a university where you learn the skills you need to become wealthy later on in life.

While you are working, you have *four* advantages. First, you have a paycheck. Second, you have time. Third, you have contacts. And most important, you have increasing experience. Take every advantage you possibly can of the fact that you are employed to learn what you need to learn in preparation for when you eventually go out on your own.

Do Your Research

As you gather knowledge and experience at your job, begin gathering information on various businesses until you find the business that interests you the most. Subscribe to magazines such as *Forbes*, *Fortune*, *BusinessWeek*, *Entrepreneur*, and the *Wall Street Journal*. Read the local business section of your daily newspaper from cover to cover every day. Immerse yourself in the world of business. Sometimes, one single idea, one insight, one article that you read somewhere will open your eyes to an opportunity that will change the direction of your life.

Once you have selected a business that you like, the first thing that you do is to learn every detail of that business. Investigate before you invest. Before you put any of your time or money into a business, learn everything you possibly can about it.

Alex McKenzie, the time management specialist, once said, "Errant assumptions lie at the root of every failure." Peter Drucker said, "Action without thinking is the cause of every failure." In both cases, untested assumptions and incomplete information can lead to mistakes that are fatal to the business.

Practice the 10/90 Rule

Often, the first 10 percent of time that you spend investigating every detail of the business will save you 90 percent of the time and money you might invest or lose later on. Take the time to understand exactly what the product or service does for the customer. Understand how it is developed, produced, sold, delivered, and paid for. Understand the economics and the profit and loss of the business. Especially, take time to fully understand the particular customers for a product or service. Why do they buy? What value do they seek? How specifically does this product or service improve their life or work?

Find out who and what the competitors are for that product or service. What are customers buying today? Why would they switch from their current suppliers to you and buy something different?

Study Successful Companies

When you think of going into a business, take the time to study the companies already in that business. Why are they successful? Why are they unsuccessful? What are they doing right? What are they doing wrong? In every industry, 20 percent of the companies are earning 80 percent of the profits. Identify these top companies and determine exactly why it is they are successful.

Once you have determined why some companies are succeeding and some are failing, take the time to conduct a complete analysis. Analyze the reasons for success. Analyze the reasons for failure. How could you improve the product, service or business in some way? How could you make your product or service so attractive to your customers that they would prefer to buy from you rather than to buy from someone else?

There is a saying that all you have to do is to improve an existing product or service by 10 percent and you can start a new business. All you need to be is 10 percent new, different, or superior to start yourself off on the road to success and financial freedom.

Five Rules for Entrepreneurship

Entrepreneurship is the art of finding profitable solutions to problems. Every successful entrepreneur, every successful businessperson, has been a person who has been able to identify a problem and come up with a solution to it before someone else did. Here are the five rules for success.

Find a Need and Fill It

You can find a need and fill it. Human needs and wants are unlimited. Therefore, the opportunities for entrepreneurship and financial success are unlimited as well. The only constraint on the business opportunities available to you are the limits you place on your own imagination.

Ross Perot was a top salesman for IBM. Many of his customers complained that they needed help processing the massive amounts of data stored in their IBM computers. Ross Perot went to his superiors at IBM and suggested that they move downstream into the data processing business, as an addition to the business of selling mainframe computers. They rejected his idea and turned him down flat. His superiors at IBM told him that they had no interest in diversifying out of the computer business.

He resigned and went out on his own. With a $1,000 loan from his mother, Ross Perot visited several of his IBM customers and proposed to handle all of their data processing needs. He offered to provide these services for less than the companies were already paying, and to split any additional savings on a 50–50 basis. Finally, one of his clients agreed to take him up on his offer, and to advance him the money necessary to set up his first data processing system. And the system worked.

Ross Perot went on to build up Electronic Data Processing, later EDP Industries, processing data for companies all over the country. He eventually sold EDP to General Motors for $2.8 billion, becoming one of the richest men in the world. He found a need and he filled it.

Find a Problem and Solve It

You can find a problem and solve it. Wherever there is a widespread and unsolved customer problem, there is an opportunity for you to start and build a successful business. Once upon a time, before photocopiers, the only way to type multiple copies of a letter was with carbon paper placed between sheets of stationery. But a single mistake would require the typist to go through and erase the mistake on every single copy. This was enormously clumsy and time-consuming.

Then, a secretary working for a small company in Minneapolis began mixing flour with nail varnish in order to *white out* the mistakes she was making in her typing. Her friends in the same office soon asked if she could make some of this liquid for them. To satisfy this demand, she began mixing little bottles of flour and nail varnish on her kitchen table. Soon, people in other offices began asking for it. The demand became so great that she eventually quit her job and began working full-time manufacturing what she called "Liquid Paper." A few years later, the Gillette Corporation came along and bought her out for $47 million cash.

Unlimited Opportunities
There are problems everywhere. Your job is to find one of these problems and solve it better than it has been solved in the past. Find a problem that everyone has and see if you can't come up with a solution for it.

Find a way to supply a product or service better, cheaper, faster, or easier. Use your imagination.

Some years ago, a man named Clemons Wilson took his family on a cross-country vacation. He was frustrated when he could find no hotels that could accommodate traveling families. He pooled all of his savings, and the savings of his friends and family, and started the first Holiday Inn. It was an immediate success. Today, Holiday Inn is one of the most successful hotel chains in the world, and Clemons Wilson retired as a very wealthy man.

Focus on the Customer

The key to success in business is to focus on the customer. Become obsessed with your customer. Become fixated on your customer's wants, needs, and desires. Think of your customer all the time. Think of what your customer is willing to pay for. Think about your customer's problems. See yourself as if you were working for your customer.

This obsession with customer service is the key to entrepreneurial success in every industry. Even Sam Walton, founder of Wal-Mart Stores and one of the richest men in the world, said, "We all have one boss, and that's the customer. And the customer can fire us anytime he likes by simply taking his business somewhere else."

Bootstrap Your Way to Success

Once you have come up with a problem or idea, resolve to invest your time, talent, and energy instead of your money to get started. Most great personal fortunes in the United States were started with an idea and with the sale of personal services. Most great fortunes were started by people with no money, resources, or backing. They were started by individuals who came up with an idea and who then put their whole heart into producing a product or service that someone else would buy.

This is called "sweat equity." Instead of investing cash to start your business, invest your sweat equity. Invest the sweat of your brow to get started. If you have little or no money, look for ways to buy something at a lower price and sell it at a higher price. In this way, you generate positive cash flow and create a foundation for business success. Many of the richest men and women in the country started this way.

Walk Before You Run

To be a big business success, you must first be a *small* business success. To sell many items at high prices, you must first sell a few items at low prices. My first business venture was selling soap at 50 cents a box, door-to-door. My second business venture was selling newspaper subscriptions at $1.75 per week. My third business venture was selling two-dollar discount coupons on Christmas trees for sale at a nearby lot. I moved into the big time when I started mowing lawns around the neighborhood at $2.50 each. Large trees grow from small seeds.

You can begin your drive toward business success with a second income opportunity. Since all your success will ultimately be rooted in your ability to sell products and services, the sooner you learn how to do it, the better it will be for you and the faster you will be successful.

Some people start their business careers by buying items during the week and selling them on the weekends at flea markets and swap meets. Others go to garage sales first thing in the morning with a pickup truck, scoop up all the best items at the lowest prices, and then hold their own garage sales once a month where they sell off everything they have gathered at higher prices than they paid. As a result, they learn how to buy and sell. They learn how to negotiate, buying for less and selling for more. They learn how to communicate and compromise. They learn how to pick products that will sell quickly at higher prices.

Be Prepared to Pay the Price

The only way to triumph is to try. The only way to succeed is to fail, and to learn as a result of your failures. The only way to learn to be successful in business is to practice, practice, practice. If you are not willing to practice and pay the price, you will never gain sufficient experience to succeed. If you are not willing to put in the time necessary to learn basic business skills, you won't stand a chance against someone who is willing to pay that price.

Probably 95 percent of American workers have the ability to start and build their own businesses if they would simply learn how and then give it a try. Business success is based on a series of formulas, combinations, and recipes, all of which are learnable. There are more than 23 million U.S. businesses, with an additional one million new businesses started each year. You can start a new business faster, more easily, and at lower cost in the United States than perhaps any other country on earth. Anyone can do it.

Network Marketing Opportunities

Multilevel, or network marketing is an excellent second income opportunity. Millions of people throughout the world are taking advantage of the opportunity multilevel marketing offers to start and build a successful business quickly and inexpensively. They use the foundation of a network marketing business to learn vital business skills at low cost.

Network marketing has been both maligned and misunderstood. Just as in any business, there are both good and bad network marketing opportunities. But the business model itself has been tried and proven successfully worldwide for more than 50 years. It works for anyone who is willing to invest the necessary sweat equity required by any business.

An Alternate Form of Distribution

In its simplest terms, network marketing is a form of distribution, just like retail, wholesale, catalogs, direct selling, telemarketing, and Internet sales. Network marketing is a way of getting the product or service from the manufacturer or originator to the end customer. The markup in price from manufacturer to retail seller is divided among the various people in the network marketing channel.

For example, if a product has a retail sales price of $10 and it costs $2.50 to manufacture, there is a difference of $7.50 to be used for marketing, sales, advertising, distribution, promotion, packaging, and delivery. In network marketing, this difference between the manufacturing cost and retail price is divided among the various distributors in the sales chain.

When you begin in network marketing, you earn 25 percent to 35 percent of the retail price as your commission for selling the product to the end customer. As you increase your sales volume or recruit additional distributors who achieve certain levels of sales volume, the percentage commission that you receive increases to 40 percent, 45 percent, 50 percent, and so on. You earn an override on the sales of the people under you whose volume is not yet high enough for them to qualify for the higher commissions that you are earning. Everyone benefits; no one loses.

Start Small, Grow Slowly

In network marketing, you get the opportunity to start small, often by investing a few dollars for a sample kit and taking orders from your friends and neighbors, which you then fulfill by buying the product from the distributor and delivering it. In this process, you learn the business skills of selling, organizing, making presentations, accounting, team building, negotiating, persuading, and communicating. Probably 85 percent of what you need to know to be successful in business you can learn from running a successful multilevel marketing business.

Many people have the idea that they are too good to buy and sell small products to the people around them. These people are always amazed when they find that doctors, lawyers, engineers, architects, and other professionals are busy building successful multilevel marketing businesses in order to create second income streams for themselves and their families.

Whatever It Takes

One of the hallmarks of self-made millionaires is that they are always willing to do whatever is necessary on the way up. They are always willing to do what is called "dog work." They are willing to render humble services to their customers, especially at the beginning. They are willing to roll up their sleeves and plunge in. They are willing to make sales calls, pack boxes, deliver products personally, and take care of the bookkeeping and accounting involved in every business, large or small.

People who ultimately become financially successful never think of themselves as being too good for any particular job. They recognize that there is a price to be paid for every success, and the sooner they pay that price, the sooner they can get on to achieving the financial independence they desire.

Meanwhile, the people who think they are too good to start at the bottom are the ones who never succeed and who eventually retire poor. They remain at the bottom.

Eight Qualities of a Good Business

If you are considering a multilevel or network marketing opportunity, there are eight key factors that you should look for before you make a choice. Some of my best friends today are multilevel marketing millionaires. When they began, they spent many months traveling all over the country investigating multilevel marketing business opportunities. They met the key people, tested the products carefully, checked their references with others, and solicited input from their friends and advisers.

When they each finally found the right company and the right opportunity for them, they then made a total commitment to the success of the business. In a few years, they built national and international distribution networks that generated many millions of dollars in sales every month. Here is what to look for.

Quality Products With A Good Reputation

Look for a multilevel business that has quality products that have a good reputation. Never waste your time trying to sell anything that is not of excellent quality. No successful business can ever be built on an average or mediocre product.

Choose a product or service that it is equal to, or better than, any other similar product available in the marketplace at the same price. Every product, to succeed, must have what is called a unique selling proposition (USP). It must possess some special characteristic that makes it decidedly superior to anything else available in the same category. If the product or service you are looking at is not clearly superior in some important way, it will never be successful in the long term.

Fair and Competitive Prices

Second, look for a company that has fair prices that compare favorably with the competition. No one is going to pay more for your product or service if they can get the same or equivalent somewhere else at a lower price. It is essential that you make careful price comparisons.

Unfortunately, there are hundreds of companies that are attempting to sell low-quality products at unreasonably high prices. There are some people who feel that product quality is unimportant. They are convinced that the "business opportunity" is all that people care about. But in the final analysis, it is the customer in the marketplace who will determine the success or failure of any business. And that customer is very sensitive to the amount you charge in comparison with others.

Money-Back Guarantee

Third, every good network marketing company offers a 100 percent unconditional money-back guarantee. This means that the company feels so strongly about the quality of the product and the level of customer satisfaction that it will generate that it is willing to buy it back with no questions. The company is willing to give a 100 percent refund guarantee on anything it sells. This is one of the most important of all principles for business success in multilevel marketing, or in any other area.

The best network marketing companies offer what is called an "empty container" guarantee. This means that you, as a customer, can purchase the product and use its contents completely. If you are not satisfied for any reason, the company will give you a 100 percent refund on the empty container for up to one year from the date of purchase. In today's hotly competitive multilevel market, it is hard to sell anything unless it includes this type of guarantee.

Small Inventory Requirement

Fourth, the best network marketing companies today have a small or zero inventory requirement. This means that you should be able to start a network marketing business with very little money, often not more than $100.

For many years, there were multi-level marketing companies that engaged in an industry practice called "garage loading." They would offer massive discounts, and therefore high potential profit margins, to new distributors who would purchase large quantities of their products even before they had ever made a retail sale. These purchases were not guaranteed and were nonrefundable. Many ambitious young entrepreneurs ended up with a garage full of products that they were unable to sell at any price.

A good network marketing company is focused single-mindedly on *retail* sales to the ultimate consumer of the product. Good companies do not encourage and often they do not allow people to purchase more products than they have already sold at retail. They do not allow people to qualify for higher discounts by simply buying large amounts of product in advance of the actual sale. You should look for this kind of policy in any network marketing opportunity you explore.

Prompt Delivery

Fifth, a good network marketing company provides prompt delivery of your product orders and efficient internal bookkeeping. You can take orders for your product from samples and the company will deliver your products to you, or direct to your customers, within 48 hours. In addition, the company will track sales, commissions, and overrides, and give you accurate financial statements each month.

More and more multilevel marketing companies provide for "auto ship," meaning that you or your customer automatically get a certain quantity each month, usually billed to a credit card. This is always optional, and greatly cuts down on paperwork and administrative activity.

Strong Support Organization

Sixth, look for a strong support organization. It is extremely important to select a network marketing company with a support organization that will offer you training in every aspect of the business. Seek a company that will give you regular seminars on sales effectiveness and product knowledge. Look for sponsors and up lines who will give you motivation and opportunities for personal and business development.

Many people who have started their careers with network marketing companies have gone on to be very successful in their own businesses because of the training they received from their network marketing organization.

The best network marketing companies have the best training systems. The primary reason for success in network marketing is possession of the knowledge and the skills necessary to conduct the business. Failure is always the result of not having the essential skills. If the company you are looking at doesn't have an organized training system, try to find a company that does.

Honesty and Integrity At All Levels

Seventh, look for honesty and integrity at all levels of the company. Make sure that the parent company has an impeccable reputation in the marketplace. Be sure that it is a company that you can be proud to represent and tell your friends about. You should never have to make excuses for the company you are working with.

Check the references of the company just as you would check the references of a new employee you were thinking of hiring for your business. Go onto the Internet and contact people who have worked for the company in the past. Investigate *before* you invest your time and money.

There are individuals who start one network marketing company after another, recruiting inexperienced people with false promises, loading up their garages, and then moving on to the next idea. These companies all have one thing in common: They promise a quick, easy way to make a lot of money in a short period of time. Don't believe them.

Sell Consumable Products

The eighth requirement is very important. The products that you sell in your network marketing business should be consumable, leading to reorders and repeat business. You should sell a product that people use on a regular basis, like vitamins, home maintenance supplies, or beauty products, so that if customers are happy with your product they will continue to reorder month after month. Once you get a satisfied repeat customer, you will often be able to keep that customer for years.

Over the years, I have worked with and used the products of many network marketing companies. Some of them were absolutely excellent. Almost invariably, the best companies score high on the eight factors just discussed. They are a pleasure to work with and can offer an opportunity for you to start from nothing, develop business skills, create positive cash flow, and begin moving toward financial independence.

Money in Your Mailbox

You can start a business in mail order with little money and experience. You can operate from your home with a limited investment and low risk. There are several books written on the subject. These books show you how to start up your business, acquire products at wholesale that you can market, and how and where to write ads that will bring you sales.

Not long ago, a woman who was having trouble earning money to feed her family began developing different ways to prepare hamburger for lunch and dinner. Someone told her that these recipes were unique and different, and that she should assemble them into a booklet. This resulted in a booklet entitled *101 Ways to Serve Hamburger*. She subsequently sold tens of thousands of this booklet by placing small ads in newspapers around the country.

More and more Americans today are buying things through mail order; through articles and ads in magazines, newspapers, and other publications; or via catalogs mailed directly to their homes. Mail order is something that you can get into quite easily and at low cost. But you must still study every detail of the business before you begin, and test every idea carefully in a limited way before you invest money in it.

Get Wired

In 1999, Andrew Grove, president of Intel, stated, "In five years, there will be no more Internet businesses." This statement was greeted with shock and surprise. At that time Internet companies were going public at billion-dollar valuations and people were predicting "the world has changed forever."

But his point was valid. He went on to say that within five years there would be companies that would have an Internet presence, just as companies have telephone numbers and addresses, but many Internet companies would no longer be in business, as they would no longer be able to compete. And his prediction came true.

Anyone Can Do It

Today, every business of consequence, including sole proprietorships and businesses run by people off their kitchen tables, has an Internet site. The good news is that today, "the Internet has been developed by geniuses so that it can be used successfully by morons." Today, anyone can start an Internet business for a few dollars and begin marketing to the entire world. This means you.

There are numerous courses and kits that you can acquire at low cost to start your Internet business. Large companies like Yahoo! and America Online (AOL) will provide you with everything you need to open an Internet store. You can create connections with other Internet businesses in exchange for leads and customers. You can create newsletters and advertisements that eventually reach hundreds, if not thousands, of people. For a small investment, you can create an Internet business that is limited only by your own imagination.

Just as with any business, you should investigate before you invest. Read books, take courses, and even surf the Internet to learn how to start and build an Internet business. Start with a single product for which you feel there is a widespread demand and concentrate on selling more and more of that product to a greater number of customers. As you become more confident and competent selling a single product, you can expand your product offerings. If you do it right, you can soon have a business that earns you thousands of dollars per month.

Building an Internet Business

When I began my speaking, training, and consulting business in 1981, there was no Internet. We used direct mail, direct selling, and telemarketing to generate business. There was no other way.

In 1995, as the Internet began growing and expanding, we set up our first Internet site. It was a bare-bones site with some brief descriptions of the audio and video learning programs we had available. We had it managed by an outside company that charged us a commission on all sales. We set it up for MasterCard, Visa, American Express, and Discover Card, and put in security provisions to guard against loss or theft. Over the next five years, our sales grew to several thousand dollars per month.

As the amount of business being done on the Internet expanded, we realized that we were missing the full benefits available. We therefore invested another $60,000 to completely redesign and upgrade our site. This led to an immediate increase in sales, up to several hundred dollars per day.

Biting the Bullet

Finally, we decided to bite the bullet and develop a world-class Internet business. After a series of mistakes, we found a competent team of Internet development experts who completely rebuilt our site, expanded our offerings to more than 100 products, and connected us to more than 600 other companies that offered our products on their own sites in exchange for a percentage of sales.

Today, our Internet business generates more than $1 million per year in sales. It has more than paid back everything we have invested, and generates substantial profits every month. We sometimes joke among ourselves that we make more money than Amazon.com because we generate net profits every month, while Amazon.com still loses money.

Here is a key point. If thousands and even millions of other people can start with complete ignorance of the Internet and by study, practice, and application can build a profitable Internet business, this is proof that you can as well.

Most of the businesses that are successful today did not exist a few years ago. Most of the best-selling products and services today did not exist a few years ago. Most of the great fortunes of tomorrow will be made in businesses that don't exist today, selling products and services that don't exist today to customers and markets that do not yet exist. This means that the opportunities are everywhere and unlimited.

Start Small

If your goal is to get rich over the course of your working lifetime, it is important that you *take the long view* in everything you do. This means that you can afford to invest a few weeks or a few months at the beginning of your business life to gain the knowledge and experience that you require. As the Roman emperor Augustus said, "Make haste slowly."

One of the best of all success strategies is for you to go to work part-time in a business that interests you. Many people who became wealthy got their start by actually offering to work for free in a business or field that they felt had great potential for the future. As a result of working for free, they brought themselves to the attention of people within the business. By doing the job extremely well, they made themselves so valuable that eventually they were put on the payroll and promoted into positions of responsibility.

Trade Time for Experience

When you start off in the world of work, you will have lots of time but little money. Later in life, if you are fortunate, you will have lots of money and less time. In between, the smartest thing you can do is to invest your spare time in learning how to make the kind of money you want to earn later on. By working for a company in a field that interests you, you get an invaluable form of on-the-job training. You learn how the business works on the inside. You get valuable insights and experience that tell you whether this is the right field for you to dedicate your future to.

Even if you are working full-time at another job, you can work part-time evenings or weekends in another field to learn about it. You can volunteer to work on your annual vacations from work. You can work on holidays. But there is no alternative to putting in the hours and getting the experience you require if you are determined to be financially successful.

Remember, the primary reason that businesses fail is because of *managerial incompetence*. This means that the people in charge make the wrong decisions. They make the wrong investments. They make mistakes that cost money that often cannot be recouped. Don't let this happen to you. Take the time to learn what you need to know to succeed. Be patient. The time you invest before you start will pay off over and over again in the months and years ahead.

Seven Steps to Business Success

There are seven steps that you can take throughout your business career to assure that you achieve the very most in sales and profitability with the very least in effort and loss. Any attempt to short-circuit or sidestep these seven steps can end up costing you far more than you could ever imagine.

Step 1. Set Specific Financial Goals

Set a specific financial goal for yourself and then begin to visualize it as a reality. Play and replay the picture of your goal on the screen of your mind as if it were already a reality, over and over again. The greater the clarity, frequency, intensity, and duration with which you visualize your goal, the faster you will attract into your life the people, circumstances, ideas, and resources necessary to achieve it.

Step 2. Offer a Superior Product

Look for a need that you can fill, or a problem that you can solve, with a product or service that is both of high quality and a good value. All successful businesses are based on products or services that are excellent in some way. Refuse to spend a minute of your time producing or promoting a product or service that is not superior in some way to whatever else is available in the marketplace.

Step 3. Start Small and Grow Slowly

Start small and learn your business thoroughly. Be patient. Invest your time rather than your money, especially at the beginning.

One of the best ways to build a business is to bootstrap. This approach requires that you start off with a little money and you grow your business with the profits that you earn from the sale of your products or services, rather than from outside financing.

Many people who think of starting a business immediately begin looking around to find someone who will lend them money. The fact is that most new businesses are started with what is called "love money." This is money that people such as your family or friends give to you or lend to you because they love you. This money is hard to get and easy to lose. It is much better that you finance your business out of your profits.

Step 4. Test Before You Invest

Take the time to test every major move before you invest money in it. The three rules for success in marketing and selling are: "Test, test, test."

One of the reasons that entrepreneurs fail is because they are too *impatient*. The get a good idea and then they plunge into business without doing their homework. It is much better that you move ahead carefully, one step at a time. Take feedback from your mistakes and make corrections to your course.

The fact is that 99 percent of new ideas in business do not work, at least in their initial form. Nine out of 10 things that you try in business will not produce the results that you expected. It is much better for you to make small bets and learn from each one rather than to gamble your whole bankroll on one great idea that turns out to be a failure.

Step 5. Grow from Your Profits

Only expand your business on the basis of your successes, out of your profits from your business activities. Only expand your business with money that you have earned in the business, not on borrowed capital.

In study after study, business analysts have found that starting off with a limited amount of money is often the best of all possible strategies. When you have very little money at the beginning, you are forced to use your imagination, creativity, and energy to generate sales and profits. You do not have the luxury of a big bank account that enables you to make expensive decisions or engage in costly advertising activities.

During the Internet boom, thousands of companies were able to arrange millions of dollars of venture capital on the basis of an idea. Inexperienced businesspeople who had not yet created a product or service that had sold and made a profit were suddenly flooded with enormous amounts of capital. In almost every case, they went a little crazy with so much money. They built expensive offices and bought corporate jets, limousines, and huge houses with expensive furnishings. They threw money around like drunken sailors. In no time at all they ran out of money, and there was no more capital available. Some 95 percent of those Internet companies subsequently went bankrupt, with everybody losing everything they had invested.

But when you start off slowly, one step at a time, you learn to appreciate how hard it is to sell a product or service and make a profit. As a result, you appreciate every dollar you earn. You delay or defer every expense possible. You become fixated on the top line and on cash flow. You check the bank account every day. You become tightfisted in business from an early age and develop the attitude toward money that will assure that you become rich over the course of your career.

Step 6. Select People Carefully

Fully 95 percent of business success is in the *selection* process. Be extremely careful in selecting the people to help you expand and grow your business. The biggest mistakes that you will ever make will be in picking the wrong people to work with, so take your time.

All productivity comes from people. All sales and marketing success is the result of having good people in key places. All business success comes from having competent people in the key jobs in your company. One incompetent person in a key job can be enough to doom an enterprise. Don't let this happen to you.

The rule is to hire slowly and carefully, and fire quickly. If you realize that you have made a mistake, that a person is not working out, deal with the situation quickly and efficiently. Do not keep incompetent people in important positions. This demotivates everyone and can actually cause the failure of the business.

My friend Harvey Mackay tells about how he spent six months trying to find a new salesperson. He interviewed 35 different candidates for the job, and finally ended up hiring no one at all. He said later that it was better to leave the job vacant than to hire the wrong person and have to fire him later. This is good advice.

Step 7. Use Financial Leverage

Use financial leverage whenever you possibly can. Financial leverage comes in the form of business borrowing and lines of credit from the bank, which are based on the cash flow from your successful business.

The key to the success of any business is cash flow. If you have positive cash flow—if you are generating profits from your daily, weekly, and monthly business activities—you can accomplish almost anything in the business world. When you have a history of positive cash flow, banks will be open to lending you the money that you need to take advantage of additional opportunities.

Your business goal is to develop a continuous stream of positive cash flow and then to build cash reserves against any fluctuations in sales. Banks will then lend you all the money you need because they will be confident that you will be able to service the debt and pay it back.

Be Action-Oriented

Many businesspeople achieve their greatest successes in unexpected areas. They begin a business and then find that it isn't as profitable as they had anticipated. But because they remain flexible, they change direction, using their experience and momentum to try something else. They often strike pay dirt in a completely different field.

The most important thing is to begin, to take action. The key to success is to get started and then to move forward one step at a time, learning and growing as you go. There is enough information available in virtually every field for you to become knowledgeable enough to achieve success. But continuous action is essential.

Take a Chance

Success author Orison Swett Marden once wrote, "The first part of success is *get-to-it-iveness*. The second part of success is *stick-to-it-iveness*." Every business begins with an act of faith and courage, a bold leap into the unknown. As Peter Drucker wrote, "Whenever you see a successful business, someone once took a big chance."

Only 1 in 10 people who want to start their own businesses ever develops enough courage to begin and has sufficient persistence to continue. The keys to success are always *get-to-it-iveness* and *stick-to-it-iveness*. The fear of failure holds people back more than any other factor. The fear of failure puts a brake on your potential and paralyzes your actions. And the fear of failure makes failure inevitable. Don't let it hold you back.

Seven Steps to Financial Independence

Fortunately, even if you know nothing about business, you can begin with a dream, a castle in the air, and then build a foundation under it. The starting point of many great fortunes has been these seven simple steps:

First, set a goal and back it with a burning desire.

Second, begin accumulating capital with a regular savings program. If you cannot save money, nothing else is possible for you. You cannot move forward until you have some money set aside.

Third, use your current job as a springboard to later success. Learn while you earn. Take the long view, and always do more than you are paid for. Put yourself on the side of the angels.

Fourth, experiment in business on a limited scale so that you can learn the key skills necessary for success. Don't look for shortcuts or get-rich-quick schemes. Be prepared to pay the price for success by learning what you need to learn before you launch your business venture.

Fifth, search for problems unsolved, needs unmet, and products or services you can supply of high quality and at reasonable prices. All you need to start building a fortune is a single excellent product for which there is a profitable market opportunity.

Sixth, read everything you can find in your chosen field. Learn everything you can about the subject. Be open to new information and be willing to change your mind if what you learn is not consistent with what you initially thought. Remain flexible.

The *seventh* and final, step is to launch your goals and plans with courage and persistence. Develop complete faith in your ability to succeed, and never, never give up.

Action Exercises

1. Get your feet wet. Start your own business today, even if it is just a sole proprietorship that you can start at home without registering anywhere. Open a bank account in the name of your new business and use your Social Security number as your tax ID number.

2. Imagine that you already have lots of money; what kind of business would you want to get into if you had no limits? Begin doing research in that area.

3. Take the long view. Determine what subjects you need to learn and what skills you have to acquire to start and build a successful business. Make a plan and get started today.

4. Determine the kind of products or services that you like and enjoy consuming, and that you feel you could offer and sell to others. Look for something of good quality that you would be proud to represent.

5. Look at your current job and decide what additional skills you could learn and acquire on the job or by taking extra courses. Use your job as a springboard to future success.

6. Experience is the key to success. Identify the areas where you need more experience in order to get better results where you work, and in your own business. Make plans to get into at least one of those areas immediately.

7. Look for business opportunities everywhere; develop an entrepreneurial mind-set, and continually be open and curious about needs not satisfied and problems not solved. One idea is all you need to make your first million.

"Men who are resolved to find a way for themselves will always find opportunities enough; and if they do not lie ready to their hand, they will make them."

—**Samuel Smiles**

5

Build Your Own Business

*"Don't wait for extraordinary opportunities. Seize
common occasions and make them great. Weak
men wait for opportunities; great men make them."*

—Orison Swett Marden

Ambitious men and women are starting more than one million new businesses every year. There are currently more than 23,000,000 businesses nationwide, ranging from single individuals working off their kitchen tables all the way up to companies like Microsoft, Motorola, and General Motors.

Each of these businesses offers products or services that are in some way distinct and different from those of any other company. The opportunities for finding and developing a new business idea are all around you, and with proper preparation, the possibilities for your success in business are virtually unlimited.

As many as 80 percent of all the products and services in common use today, at home, in business, and in organizations large and small, will be obsolete in five years. They will be replaced by newer, better, cheaper, and more efficient products and services. The rapid development of new technology and the desire of people for new, better, or cheaper products and services mean that you can start your fortune more easily today than at any other time in history.

The Failure Rate Is High

However, we know that 80 percent to 90 percent of new businesses fail in the first two to four years due to a variety of factors. As we discussed, the primary reason for business failure is incompetence of some kind on the part of the person or persons starting the business. This incompetence is usually manifested in an inability to sell the product or service in sufficient quantities or to control the costs of producing and selling the product.

Another major reason for business failure is offering the wrong product at the wrong price to the wrong market at the wrong time, or a combination of these. If your product or service is wrong for today's market, even the best marketing efforts and cost controls will not help you to be successful.

The Wrong Product at the Wrong Time

Ford Motor Company's introduction of the Edsel in the 1950s is a perfect example of the wrong product at the wrong time and price. After spending $250 million in development and research, Ford brought the car to the market only to discover that there was no market for a car of that kind at that price.

Many of the dot-com companies, like Webvan.com, offering groceries, and Pets.com, offering pet food and supplies, went broke and took down hundreds of millions of dollars of investors' capital with them. It turned out that there was not a sufficient market for groceries and pet supplies ordered over the Internet and delivered by mail or personal courier.

Many small businesspeople often make the same mistake, but on a smaller scale. They invest an enormous amount of time and money bringing a product to market without ever determining, in advance, if there is sufficient demand at that price.

Seven Principles
for Business Success

In this chapter, you will learn a series of ideas on how to find a product or service, how to test-market it before you invest a lot of money in it, how to promote it properly, and how to expand your business once you get started. Here are some key principles for business success.

Start at the Beginning

The first principle with regard to selecting any new product or service is to determine if it fills a genuine, existing need that customers have right now. A new product or service must solve a problem of some kind for the customer, or make the life or work of the customer better in a cost-effective way. You must be very clear, from the beginning, about exactly what your product or service does to improve the quality of life of your customer.

Offer Good Quality at a Fair Price

To be successful, a new product or service must be of good quality at a fair price. If it is in competition with other similar products or services, it must have what is called a unique selling proposition (USP). It must have some beneficial feature or attraction that makes it unique, different, and superior to any competitive alternative.

This area of uniqueness is central to success in business. No product or service can succeed unless it is somehow different and superior to any other product or service that competes with it. There is seldom any opportunity to build a business around a me-too product or service— one that is just the same as all the others, the only difference being that it is you who happens to be selling it.

The very safest business strategy is to start off with an accepted product for which there is already a widespread market, and then find a way to improve it in some way. Deliver it faster, make it better or of higher quality, or lower the price of the product or service in some way. Instead of trying to invent a new business or industry, start off with a product or service that people are already using and find some way to make it more desirable.

Practice Frugality at all Times

Tight financial controls and good budgeting are necessary for business success. Successful companies are those that use accurate bookkeeping and accounting systems. They put these systems in place at the very beginning and carefully account for every penny they spend.

Even the largest multinational companies, doing billions of dollars in sales each year, tend to be very careful with their expenditures. They are constantly looking for ways to cut costs while maintaining the same level of quality. They focus on frugality at all times.

Cash Flow Is Like Blood to the Brain

Especially with a small business, you must hold on to your cash as a drowning man would hold on to a life preserver. Cash is the lifeblood of the business. Cash flow is the critical measure and determinant of business success. All successful entrepreneurs install careful financial controls and monitor them every day. They carefully consider every expenditure. They take the time to analyze the use of every dollar. They work from detailed budgets and they review them every week and every month.

The basic rule for entrepreneurial success is to spend money only to earn money. This is because in business there are only two basic categories, revenue and expense. The basic rule for running your business is that "if it's not revenue, it's expense!"

Guard Your Cash Carefully

The key to business success, with regard to your operations, is "frugality, frugality, frugality." Once I worked for a man who had started with nothing and built an $800-million business empire by the time he was 55. I was amazed to see that he ate lunch at a small diner across the street from the office and drove a used car. He delighted in saving money.

When Sam Walton was worth more than $25 billion, he still drove his own pickup truck to and from work. This attitude of frugality from the top permeated every aspect of the business, all the way down and throughout every department. The practice of frugality assured that the business was profitable, year after year.

Maximize Your Marketing

Perhaps the most important principle for business success is strong momentum in the sales department. This requires an emphasis on marketing that permeates the entire organization.

What is the purpose of a business? Some people say that it is to "make a profit." But this is not correct. The true purpose of a business is to "create and keep a customer." Profits are the result of creating and keeping a sufficient number of customers in a cost-effective way. All emphasis has to be on creating and keeping customers.

Selling Is the Core Skill of Business Success

The keys to business success are simple. With regard to the product, the keys are to "Sell! Sell! Sell!" The most important single skill you must develop for succeeding in your own business is the ability to sell yourself and your product to your customers.

In fact, the ability to sell is one of the key skills for a successful life. With very few exceptions, all successful businesses begin with a single person who is excited about the product and who is very good at selling it to others. This entrepreneur likes the product so much that he or she can hardly wait to talk to other people about it. This individual is eager to make new customer contacts. But where there is no sales expertise, the finest product or service will fail.

Love Your Customers

In successful businesses, concern for the customer at all times is a top priority. In a successful business, everyone in the business thinks about creating, serving, and satisfying customers all day long. Ten years after the book *In Search of Excellence* by Peters and Waterman came out and became a best seller, a journalist asked Tom Peters which of the seven principles in the book he felt was still the most important. He replied, without hesitating, that it was "an obsession with customer service."

In the best businesses, large and small, the key people *love* their customers. They think about their customers day and night. They see themselves as personal representatives or agents of their customers, working on the customers' behalf. This attitude of devotion to customer wants and needs permeates the entire organization, and causes people to want to do business with the company and continue doing business with it in the future.

You can always tell a good business by the way it treats customers. You can tell a good business by the way people answer the phone and deal with customer requests and inquiries. You can tell a good business by the way they deal with customer needs and complaints. Concern for the customer at all times is a top priority in all successful businesses.

Develop a Complete Business Plan Before Starting

A major reason for business success is that the founders developed a complete business plan before starting operations. Successful businesses are those who have carefully thought through every part of the business, completed very careful budgets, and conducted a breakeven analysis on their activities before they open their doors. They have organized and laid out a business plan, like a blueprint, before they begin spending money and engaging in business activities.

Here is an interesting discovery. Once the business plan is developed, it is seldom referred to. Very often, companies will spend many months developing a business plan and spend several weeks each year updating the business plan; but once it is complete, it is put into a drawer and seldom referred to until it is time to update it again.

Why is this? The reason is that what usually happens in a business, once operations begin, is quite different from what was expected or predicted. What use, then, is a business plan? The answer is that the very exercise of working out a business plan in advance forces the entrepreneur to think through all the critical issues that are involved, or will be involved, in the operation of the business.

Think Through the Critical Issues

Writing out a business plan forces the business owner to think about the products and services to be offered, the prices at which they will be sold, and the likely volume of sales that will be achieved. It forces the business owner to carefully think through all of the expenses that will be incurred in bringing that product to the market. It forces the business owner to project the people who will be required; the offices and facilities that will be necessary; the money that will be needed for rent, utilities, and payroll; and all the little factors that go into making a business successful. By writing out a business plan in advance, the entrepreneur is forced to think through and carefully analyze every one of these numbers, and combine them into a total blueprint before starting.

Can You Get There from Here?

Over the years, I have worked with entrepreneurs who were eager to start a new business. However, once they were forced to think through and gather all the information necessary to complete a business plan, they realized that the business would not work. Either they could not charge enough for the product or service relative to the costs of bringing it to the market, or the market was not large enough. Sometimes the length of time to break even was too long, or some other factor that they hadn't considered came up. You've heard the saying, "You can't get there from here." By writing up a business plan, it often becomes clear that *this* business is not a good idea in the first place.

Interestingly enough, when you go to a bank to borrow money or to a venture capitalist, or even undertake to hire a senior executive, the very first thing they will ask you for is a business plan. If you do not have a business plan, you immediately reveal yourself as an incompetent manager, the number one reason for business failure. With no business plan, you have no credibility and you will find it almost impossible to get the support that you need to build your business.

Never Give Up

An important key to business success is a high degree of determination, persistence, and patience on the part of the business owner. Venture capitalists are people who look at hundreds of business plans and seldom fund more than 1 percent of them. They will tell you that they look for character and ability more than anything else in deciding whether to invest in a business. They look at not only the product or service to be offered, but the people whose talents, abilities and experience will be essential to making the business successful.

Determination, persistence, and patience go hand in hand with business success. Nothing ever works out the way you think it will. You will continually have to chop and change and go in different directions. Your best-laid plans will meet with disappointment and frustration. But your ability to persist and to continue seeking faster, better, more innovative ways of achieving your business goals is the key to your future.

It Takes Time to Succeed

Based on studies of many thousands of businesses, there are some simple rules of thumb in terms of the time you can expect to invest. First, it takes two years to *break* even in an average business. For the first two years of the business, you will be learning about that business at a rapid rate. During this time, you will almost invariably be scrambling financially, trying to keep your head above water. You will borrow from friends and relatives, and often go deeply in debt. This is a part of the normal price that an entrepreneur has to pay to learn the skill of starting and running a successful business.

Profitability Takes Four Years

It takes four years for a new business to *show a profit*. As Peter Drucker said, "No business makes a real profit within four years." Every attempt to break this rule ends up in financial disaster for the entrepreneur. Look at what happened to all the dot-com companies that spent millions of dollars on Super Bowl advertising in an attempt to jump-start their businesses into immediate sales and profitability rather than building slowly over time.

In the third and fourth year of your business, you will be making a profit, and bringing in more money than it is costing you to stay in business. During this time, you will be paying back all the loans and bills that you accumulated in the first two years.

The third rule of thumb is that you will break into serious profitability at about the seventh year of your business. It takes this long for you to master the skills of entrepreneurship. And there are no shortcuts. You have to be patient. Henry Ford once wrote, "The two most important requirements for success in business are foresight and patience. And the man who lacks patience lacks the critical quality for success in any business venture."

The Factor of Three

There is a basic rule that any new product or service, to enter into the marketplace and succeed, must be superior to its competitors in at least *three* ways. Your job is to find three different ways in which you can improve the desirability of your product for a customer who already uses a similar product supplied by a different company.

The entire convenience store industry was built around the three concepts of moving the stores closer to the customer, offering a narrow range of the most popular products, and remaining open longer hours to make it more convenient for the customer to buy. By focusing on these three differentiators, the convenience store industry now achieves many billions of dollars in annual sales.

Most fortunes are made by providing established products and services in established markets to established customers, but finding a way to improve the process of production, selling, delivery, and service in some respect.

The success rate for brand-new products or services in the United States is only 10 percent. The success rate for *improved* products or services is about 80 percent. By following the market and bringing out an improved product or service in an established market, you can increase your odds of success from 10 percent to 80 percent. This can make all the difference between success and failure.

Questions You Must Ask and Answer to Succeed in Business

There are several questions that you must be able to answer to succeed in a competitive market. Look at what you are doing right now and apply these questions and their answers to your business.

Is Your Product Suitable?

First, the product or service must be well suited to the needs of the current market. This means that customers want it, need it, can use it, and can afford it, plus they are willing to buy it, right now. If there is no immediate and pressing need or desire for the product or service, it will probably fail in a competitive market.

Have You Analyzed the Market?

A major reason for business success is that you do careful market analysis before you start business operations. In other words, you invest considerable thought into whether there is a market before you even create the product or service.

When I do marketing and sales consulting for corporations, I always ask three basic questions about a product or service that they are thinking about bringing to the market, or have already released but which is not selling particularly well.

Marketing Question One. Is there actually a market for this product? Remember, "Errant assumptions lie at the root of every failure." Many entrepreneurs become excited about bringing a product or service to the market without ever standing back and objectively assessing whether there are customers who will buy this product or service in competition with whatever they are currently using or whatever else is available. Is there a market for what you want to sell?

Marketing Question Two. Is the market *large* enough? The costs of developing a new product or service and bringing it to the market can be extremely high. There must therefore be a large enough market for the product or service to justify all of the time and expense necessary to produce it in the first place.

Gillette just released its new Four-blade razor, the Quadra, but only after having invested 10 years and more than $500 million in its development. The market for that razor will have to be enormous and extend for several years to pay back the costs of producing the razor in the first place.

Marketing Question Three. Is the market *concentrated* enough? Are there large numbers of customers in specific geographic locations or accessible by advertising and promotional efforts without bankrupting your company?

Today, with the Internet or pinpointed direct mail, it is possible to reach potential customers all over the world quickly and inexpensively. But the question of how you are going to make your product or service availability known to enough customers in a cost-efficient way can determine the success or failure of your business.

There may be a market for 100,000 units of a particular product in the United States. But if the demand is only one or two per community throughout the country, it may be impossible to reach those people with any kind of advertising or sales effort. Even if there is a large demand for a new product, if it is not concentrated enough to be reached in a cost-effective way, a company can go broke bringing it to the market.

Who Is Your Customer?

Identify the customer for this product or service. This is the central question of marketing research. Who is your *ideal* customer, in terms of age, occupation, position, income level, gender, tastes, hobbies, and interests? The greater accuracy with which you can identify your ideal customer, the easier it becomes for you to design the product or service appropriately and to market it effectively.

The biggest mistake you can make is to sell aggressively and professionally to the wrong customer, the person who cannot or will not buy from you, no matter how good your product or service is.

Why Would They Buy from You?

Determine why your ideal customer will buy from you. What value does he or she seek? What is it that your product or service will do for your customer that will cause him or her to buy from you, rather than from someone else? Why would your ideal customer switch from his or her existing supplier for your product or service, rather than continue buying it from the current supplier? Many small companies go broke because they do not have a good enough reason for customers to switch from their current suppliers to the new product or service.

What Are the Alternatives?

Determine what else is available. What other products or services are available to the same customer to satisfy the same need or solve the same problem? How is your product or service superior in a meaningful way to your competitors' products and services?

Especially, how do you *position* yourself against your competitors in such a way that your prospective customer sees your product or service as superior and more desirable than anything else available?

What Does Each Customer Cost?

One of the most important concepts in business is called "cost of acquisition." This is the amount of money that you will have to pay in advertising, promotion, marketing, direct mail, telemarketing, and commissions to gain a single customer. This amount has to be calculated in advance and built into your financial projections. The failure to accurately determine your cost of acquisition per customer can quickly undermine the finances of your entire business.

You have heard it said jokingly, "We lose money on every sale, but we make it up on the volume." It is no joke, though. There are many companies that sell high volumes of products, but because their costs of acquisition are so high, they actually lose money on every sale. Don't let this happen to you.

The Great Marketing Questions

Here is a summary question that I write out and then break down, line by line, when I work with small and large companies. Your ability to ask and answer every part of this question will largely determine your success or failure in business. An incomplete or inaccurate answer to any part of this question can lead to insurmountable problems that will bring down the enterprise. Here it is:

"**What** exactly is going to be sold to **whom**, and at **what** price, and **how** is it going to be sold, and by **whom**, and **how** is it going to be paid for, produced, delivered, and serviced?"

1. **What** exactly is the product or service, in terms of what it *does* to change or improve the life or work of the customer?
2. To **whom** is it going to be sold, exactly?
3. At **what** price is it going to be sold to this customer?
4. **How** is it going to be sold to this customer at this price?
5. **Who** is going to sell it in this way to this customer at this price?
6. **How** is it going to be paid for, and when?
7. **How** is it going to be produced, delivered, and serviced?

Failure to ask and answer these sevens questions can be fatal to the business. Changing any one of these answers can change your results completely.

In the final analysis, your ability to sell your product in a cost-effective way, including marketing, advertising, selling, commissions, travel, and all promotional costs, is the key to business success. Becoming or finding the right salesperson, developing an effective sales presentation, and talking to a large enough number of prospective customers is central to the entire business process. As the rule says, "Nothing happens until a sale takes place."

Since cash flow is the life energy of the business, spend money only to generate additional cash flow. Delay, defer, and cancel any expenditure that does not increase sales and revenues. A primary reason for business *success* is tight financial controls, especially at the beginning. A primary reason for business *failure* is spending too much money on non-cash-generating expenditures, especially at the beginning of the business.

Getting into the Game

Let us say that you have now decided to start your own business. How do you find a new product or service, recognizing that 80 percent or more of products or services will be new or different in five years? Here are 16 approaches that have been used by successful entrepreneurs over the years.

Start with Yourself

Look into yourself. Begin with your own talents, your own abilities, your experience, knowledge, interest, background, education, and so on.

Look carefully at your current work, your current business, your current position, or your current product or service. Look within your own life and work, under your own feet, for your own "Acres of Diamonds."

Here is a question. What qualities do you have that account for your greatest successes in life so far? What personal skills and abilities have gotten you to where you are today? How could you apply those same skills and abilities to starting and building a new business?

If you already have a company, what are the special talents, abilities, experiences, knowledge, interests, and backgrounds of your business today? What qualities, talents, and skills have enabled your company to succeed up until now? What are the things you do best? What are the greatest opportunities within your business right now?

Many fortunes begin when individuals see customer needs that are not being satisfied and that their current companies have no interest in satisfying. Often the impetus comes as the result of customer inquiries or complaints. Finally, the individual decides that he or she will start a new business, sometimes on the side, to give these customers what they are asking for. It could be Tom Fatjo handing garbage in his community after hours, or Ross Perot taking over the data processing activities of large organizations. Sometimes there is a great business opportunity staring you in the face, right where you are today.

What Can You Get Excited About?

Look for a product or service about which you can really become *enthusiastic*. Sometimes people become wealthy by translating or transforming their hobbies into a business. Pierre Omydar collected PEZ dispensers as a hobby. In an attempt to find a market for his collection of PEZ dispensers, he started a little Internet business, which has grown into eBay, with 95 million customers worldwide.

You will always be most successful doing something or marketing something that you really love and care about. Every product or service, and every business, must have a *champion*. This is someone who believes intensely in the goodness and value of the product or service for the customer. Every product or service must have someone in the business who really loves the product or service and is eager to get out and tell other people about it.

What Can You Improve Upon?

Look for something that is an improvement on an existing product or service rather than something brand-new. Look for something that is cheaper or of better quality. Look for something that has additional features or functions that current products don't offer. Look for something that is an improvement in some way on something that people are already buying and using.

Improving an existing successful product or service is the fastest and surest way to build a successful business. An idea only needs to be 10 percent newer and better to capture substantial market share. Common, popular types of products are safe ways to start into business. Brand-new products, for which there is no demonstrated market, are very risky.

For almost 100 years, companies have been manufacturing and selling doughnuts. There are many thousands of doughnut shops doing successful business all over the country. Then, a few years ago a new company, Krispy Kreme, entered the market offering a type of doughnut that was only slightly different from and superior to products of other doughnut companies that had been in business for decades.

Within a few years, Krispy Kreme swept the country. The average sales per square foot of a Krispy Kreme doughnut franchise are 500 percent greater than that of almost any other doughnut shop or fast-food franchise in the country. A small difference in quality and presentation has translated into an enormous difference in financial results. Where might this be possible for you?

Find Ways to Offer Value

Another key to finding a new product or service is to look for something that represents genuine value. Seek a product or service that makes an important contribution to the quality of life or work of the customer. Don't look for easy money. Don't look for gimmicks or useless knick-knacks. Don't look for get-rich-quick schemes or rewards without working. There aren't any.

Keep Your Eyes Open

An excellent way to find a new product or service is to read newspaper stories, articles, advertisements, and classified ads. Very often when companies have new products or services to sell, they advertise in magazines and newspapers under "Business Opportunities."

You will find these "Business Opportunities" sections in the back of business magazines, the *Wall Street Journal*, *USA Today*, and your local newspapers. At the very least, if you see a product or service that interests you, pick up the telephone and ask the company to send you some information. Many people have become rich this way.

Read Trade Magazines in Your Field

Reading trade magazines, especially in your field of knowledge or expertise, can help you to find new products and services. A large city library usually has a wide selection of trade magazines. Even better, you should subscribe to all the magazines in your field and read them through, page by page, each month.

Once you get an idea for a new product or service, go onto the Internet, put the name of the product or service into Google, and then begin Web surfing. You can get more information in a few minutes surfing the Web than you used to be able to get in several days or even weeks of conventional research.

Whenever there is a new breakthrough business idea or product, it is written about in the publications read by the people who would be most interested in using or selling that product or service in their business. For example, in one of my businesses, we saw a story about a new process that had been developed in the eastern United States that would go perfectly with our existing operations. We immediately phoned the developer, flew down, examined the product thoroughly, and tied up the exclusive rights for it in the state of California. If this new process turns out to be successful, it will be extraordinarily profitable. You can often do the same.

Attend Trade Shows and Exhibitions

A wonderful way to find new products or services is to go to trade shows. There are trade shows specializing in particular products or services being held all over the country and all over the world, all the time. All you need to get into a trade show is a business card and the payment of a small fee.

Whenever a company wants to introduce a new product to as wide an audience as possible, it immediately takes space in a trade show that will be attended by buyers from all over the country. The primary goal of companies at trade shows is to find retail and wholesale distributors for their products in markets where they don't yet have representation.

Position Yourself as a Retail Buyer

When you go to a trade show, present yourself as a retail buyer. Sign up at the registration desk, pay the entrance fee, and introduce yourself as a buyer looking to buy the products offered in the trade show. Walk around the trade show and talk to the people manning the booths. Find out what it is that they are offering and selling. Find out about the size of the market and the direction the market is going. Ask them about industry trends. Ask them what is successful and what is unsuccessful.

You can learn more about a national industry in a few hours at a trade show than you could in many days or even weeks of research on your own. The people who man the booths at the trade shows are usually extremely knowledgeable about the entire industry. They can give you ideas and insights that can be invaluable to you in starting and building a successful business.

In addition, many of them will be competing with each other. By asking different people how their products or services compare with other companies offering the same general product, you will get priceless information that will enable you to make better business decisions.

Ask Your Friends

Tell your friends that you are thinking of starting a new business and that you are looking for new product ideas. Say that you are looking for something to sell or distribute. Have them keep an eye out for you. Sometimes your friends will meet people you won't meet and see things you won't see. Often they will come across ideas for new products or services when they are traveling and pass them onto you.

Keep Current with Business Magazines

An excellent way to find new products or services is to read magazines such as *Entrepreneur, Inc., Money, Fortune, Forbes,* and *BusinessWeek*. Read magazines where people advertise new products, services, or business opportunities. Especially, read magazines written for people in the field in which you are interested. Read everything that you possibly can.

Look for Products Worldwide

An excellent source of new product ideas is contained in foreign publications. Every country in Asia with a large export market has a catalog that is available through its consulate that lists all the products for which its companies are seeking distributors worldwide. You can phone or visit the consulate or go onto the Internet and get a wide range of information on the type of products that you can import into the United States on an exclusive basis and build a business around.

There are catalogs available for products that are made in Europe, country by country, and often for Europe as a whole. These catalogs contain hundreds of products that are made by European corporations seeking U.S. distributors. Sometimes the distribution rights for these products are available for the asking, because no one else has thought of asking for them.

Seek Out Hidden Opportunities

Some 95 percent of all products are never sold outside of their country of origin. Most small and medium-sized manufacturers of products, in any country, are so busy selling as much of their product as they can locally that they never give any thought to a national or international market. Herein lies a great potential opportunity for you.

Your objective, when you find a new product or service anywhere, is to acquire the rights to sell that product *exclusively* in your market area. Sometimes these rights are available for the asking. The manufacturer of the product is so busy with its current business that it has not given much thought to more widespread distribution. This can be the starting point of your own successful business.

Introduce Something New and Different

Some years ago, a young entrepreneur got a catalog of products manufactured in Holland that were available for worldwide distribution. He had a background in gardening, and as a result he was fascinated to read about a special type of plastic wheelbarrow that appeared to be stronger and cheaper than anything available in the U.S. market.

He wrote to the company and asked for the exclusive rights to sell the product in the U.S. and Canadian markets. The Dutch company sent him a sample of the wheelbarrow for his inspection. He took this sample wheelbarrow to a national gardening trade show and demonstrated it to buyers for national chains of department and gardening stores.

These professional buyers immediately saw the potential in this new style of wheelbarrow and placed orders with him for 50,000 wheelbarrows at the first show. Because it was innovative, light, corrosion-free, and inexpensive, it was an immediate hit. His profit was more than $10 per wheelbarrow. He made more than $500,000 profit from his first venture, with no investment. It pays to keep your eyes open.

Look under Your Own Feet

A great place to find a new product or service is within your own field or skill. You may have a million-dollar idea in your own mind. Many people have had the experience of an idea for a product or service nagging at them over and over again, while they kept pushing it away or ignoring it. Then someone else comes up with the same idea, introduces it to the marketplace, and makes a million dollars.

It is estimated that people on average have *four* ideas each day driving to and from work, any one of which would make them a million dollars if they would just follow it up. There is a natural tendency for people to sell themselves short and to think that, if it is their idea, it can't be worth very much. Don't let this happen to you. Look into your own field and skills. Look into your own mind, and trust your own ideas.

Keep Your Eyes Open When You Travel

Another way to find a new product or service is to travel. Keep your eyes open for opportunities. Sometimes just finding a new product or service that is doing well somewhere else, but hasn't yet come to your market, can make you wealthy.

A friend of mine was flying back East to look into a business opportunity he had read about in a magazine. On the plane, he sat next to a business development specialist for a national franchise chain. This representative was returning from California after an unsuccessful trip looking for a franchisee for his business. My friend asked him a series of questions and immediately recognized that this was the kind of franchise he was looking for. He signed the papers for the franchise on the plane, turned around at the airport in New York, and flew back to California to start the business.

Don't Be Afraid to Ask

He immediately went to a new shopping center that was almost complete and applied for a prime location. As it happened, that space had been leased to another company that had backed out of the deal at the last moment. The shopping center owner was reluctant to rent to an inexperienced businessperson, but he wanted the shopping center to be full when it opened in a few weeks. He took a chance on my friend and leased him the space.

The location turned out to be perfect. The business boomed. It began throwing off hundreds of dollars a day in net profits, which my friend used to open additional franchises and buy real estate. Seven years later he was a millionaire and one of the most successful young businesspeople in the city. Similar opportunities are all around you.

Move Quickly on Opportunities

An aggressive entrepreneur, Peter Thomas, who lived at that time in Vancouver, British Columbia, followed this strategy of quick action exactly. He was sitting on the beach in Hawaii during his Christmas vacation when he read a story about a new real estate franchise in California called Century 21. He immediately got up from the beach, checked out of his hotel, and flew to Irvine, California, where he walked into the offices of Century 21 to ask for the franchise rights for Canada.

After a short discussion, he brought the rights to set up the Century 21 real estate franchise in Canada. It was a runaway success, from coast to coast. It made Peter Thomas a millionaire many times over.

Very often, all you have to do to get the rights to sell a product in your market area is to ask for it. But there is one reservation. Before you bring a new product or service back to your market, be absolutely sure that it is selling well somewhere else. Many manufacturers and distributors attempt to promote products outside of their market areas because they are not selling well at home. Be sure that the product is already successful before you invest time and money selling it in a different area.

Continually Scan the Radar of Opportunity

Keep your eyes open and alert to new business opportunities occurring around you. Develop a moneymaking attitude. Constantly think in terms of creating and keeping customers. Look for products that customers want, or places that customers go where new products and services can be offered.

A friend of mine became a millionaire with a simple strategy. When a new shopping center was announced anywhere in the city, he would immediately approach to the landowners of the properties across the street from the shopping center and offer to buy their land. Over time, he was able to buy and develop commercial properties at low cost that benefited from the large amount of traffic generated by the shopping center when it was complete. He repeated this strategy several times, leveraging off of each piece of property, until he was financially independent.

Find Something You Like and Believe In

The final rule for business success is that you will only be successful marketing and selling something that you believe in, use yourself, and would recommend to your best friend. I quite often see people making the critical mistake of trying to sell a product or a service that they themselves do not use. Sometimes they try to sell a product that they personally cannot afford or do not find attractive. They would not recommend it to their friends or family, but they think that somehow other people will buy it, even though they wouldn't.

There seems to be a direct relationship between how strongly you believe in the goodness and value of your product or service and how capable you are of selling it to others. You must be excited about it. You must absolutely believe that this product or service can enhance the life or work of someone else, and be eager to tell them about it.

These are just 16 ways that you can find a new product or service idea. There are many more. The fact is that you are surrounded by more moneymaking ideas for products and services than you could pursue in many lifetimes. If you are serious about finding a new business idea, there are no limits.

Test Your Idea Before You Invest

There is a process of scientific investigation called the "negative hypothesis." Because entrepreneurs sometimes become extremely excited about a business opportunity, it is essential that you use a "negative hypothesis" approach to any product or service that you are thinking of investing time, money, and emotion in bringing to the market.

With a negative hypothesis, the scientist will take a proposition that he or she wants to prove and create a negative version of the proposition. For example, the scientist could say, "Taking an aspirin each day thins the blood and lowers the possibility of a heart attack in older men and women."

The scientist will then create the negative hypothesis: "Taking an aspirin a day does *not* lower the likelihood of a heart attack in older men and women." The scientist will then try to prove that the negative hypothesis is true by conducting every type of double blind and placebo test on individuals in an effort to prove that aspirin has no positive effect on reducing heart attacks.

If, at the end of the experimentation, in spite of the scientist's best efforts he or she has been *unable* to prove this negative statement, then the positive form of the proposition may still be proven: "Taking an aspirin each day reduces the risk of heart attack for older men and women."

Be Your Own Devil's Advocate

Before you introduce a new product or service to the market, you should perform a negative hypothesis on it as well. As an exercise, attempt to disprove the idea that there exists a profitable demand for the product or service. If you cannot disprove this proposition, then by default you have reason to be confident that it is a marketable product or service.

Fast, Cheap Market Research

How can you conduct fast, cheap market research? How can you find out whether the product will sell before you invest too much time or money in it? These are critical questions that often determine your success or failure in business.

Before embarking on any new business venture, you must invest considerable time and money in research. The payoff will be in excess of 10-to-1 in time and money saved or earned. For every dollar, for every hour that you put into market testing, you will save $10, $20, or $30 or hours in lost time or money later on. Here are some of the ways that you can be sure, in advance, that there exists a large enough and profitable enough market for your new product or service.

Do Your Homework

Find out every detail of the product or business. Study it carefully. Do your research. Visit other companies in the same industry. Ask questions of people who sell the product and people who use the product. Accept nothing on faith.

At the beginning of the automotive age, there were more than 300 automobile manufacturers in the United States. Walter Chrysler, the founder of Chrysler Corporation, was convinced that it was possible to build a car that was superior to any competitor. His strategy was simple. He went out and bought several of the most popular and best-selling automobiles. He took them home to his garage and disassembled them completely, down to the very last nut and bolt. He then put them back together again.

By the time he had disassembled and reassembled every automobile, he had developed some excellent ideas on how to create a car that was superior to any other individual automobile. Armed with this information, he attracted financial backers, formed Chrysler Motor Corporation, and created one of the largest fortunes in the country.

Find Out What Others Are Saying and Writing

Before you embark on a new business venture, read the trade magazines, articles, and stories on the business, industry, or occupation. Here is a technique you can use. At every major city library, there is a publication called the *Readers' Guide to Periodical Literature*. The *Readers' Guide* lists every article that has been written on every subject in most American publications each month. The librarian can guide you to the periodicals index and show you how to use it. The monthly indexes are cumulated into annual volumes.

Once you have determined the articles that you want to read, you can go to microfiche in the library files, or even the Internet, to get all the information that has been written on a particular product or service in the last week, month, year, or five years. You can make yourself an expert on a particular subject area by using the *Readers' Guide to Periodical Literature.*

Many consultants will tell you that when their clients ask them for information and advice on a particular subject, they go down to the library and go through the periodicals index on that subject. They often invest several hours becoming extremely well informed on everything that is going on in that subject area at the present time. They often sell that advice, in the form of consulting services, for several hundred dollars per hour to their clients. You can do the same thing. Check the *Readers' Guide.* Become intimately familiar with the business before you begin.

Ask the Opinions of Others

Pick out people who are already in the same business and ask their opinions of the product or service. Many people have saved themselves an enormous amount of time or money by finding that people who are already in the business wish they were not in the business in the first place. They wish they had invested more time or more money before they got into the business, and now it is too late. Go and talk to them. Ask them what they think about the business. Ask them if they would recommend that someone else get into that business.

Don't be shy or secretive about asking for information. Very often at my seminars, people come up to me and ask for advice on a business they are thinking about getting into. I will then inquire, "Well, what is your business idea?" And surprisingly enough, they won't tell me their exact business idea. They say that they are afraid that someone will steal their idea. They want to keep it a secret.

Ideas Are a Dime a Dozen
The fact is that business ideas are a dime a dozen. Fully 99 percent of new business ideas don't work in any case. The dumbest thing you can possibly do is to keep an idea for a new business, for the sales and marketing of a new product or service, a secret to yourself. Instead, be perfectly open. Tell people what you are thinking of doing. Get feedback from people who are already in the business. This advice alone has saved

me hundreds of thousands of dollars. It may even have saved my financial life on a couple of occasions.

When you go to people who are already in the business and tell them an idea that you have to change or improve the business in some way, don't worry about them taking your idea away from you. Most people in business have already thought of your idea years ago, or have no interest in it in any case. Usually, they are so busy trying to make their own business successful, they have no time or money to even think about testing an idea that someone else has suggested.

Rely on Your Bank Manager

Ask your bank manager for his or her opinion and advice. A bank manager who deals with commercial accounts often has an extremely accurate sense for what kind of businesses will succeed and what kind will not. A single five-minute interview with my bank manager a few years ago saved me $200,000 in an investment I was considering. He pointed out to me the weaknesses in that particular business. He asked me questions about the products, the customer market, the levels of profitability, and the competition. I was unable to give him intelligent answers. As a result, I didn't go into the business. The people who told me that I didn't know what I was talking about and went ahead and invested their money in the business anyway lost every penny.

Be sure to ask your bank manager for advice. The bank manager works with hundreds of businesses over the years and has a very good sense for what will work and what will not in today's competitive marketplace. Your bank manager can be one of the very best sources of business advice in your world, and at no cost to you.

Ask Your Friends and Family for Input

Ask your friends, your family, and even your acquaintances for information. Family members are not only good sources of information, but they are also excellent targets for market research. Ask your family and friends if they would buy the product or service that you are thinking of offering. How much would they pay for it? Listen to their questions. Listen to their criticisms. Listen to their concerns. If you can't answer their questions and concerns in a logical and believable way, it could be that there is something wrong with your idea.

Get a Customer's Opinion

Visit prospective customers for the product or service and ask if they would buy it. If you are thinking of selling something to a company, go to the type of company that you would sell it to and ask if they would buy it if you produced it and made it available. If you are thinking of selling something at retail, go to the retail outlets and ask them if they would buy it and offer it in their store. Ask the prospective customer for the product if he or she would buy it.

Prospective customers are usually open and candid. Sometimes they will give you insights that will be worth their weight in gold. If you are going to sell to retailers, ask them if they could sell the product if they were selling it at the price you had in mind. Why or why not?

Study Your Competition

Research all the competitors for the product or service that you are thinking of offering and ask this question: "Why would someone switch to buy from me?" If there is already a similar product or service on the market, why would somebody drop a product or service that they are comfortable with in order to buy your product or service that they don't know anything about? Is your product, service, or idea cheaper, better, or of higher quality? How can you convince enough customers of this to stay in business?

Especially, study your most successful competitors carefully and learn what it is that they are doing that enables them to beat their competition. Throughout your career as a business owner, make it a habit to admire those people in your industry who are doing well. Then look for ways to do them one better.

Become a Pessimistic Optimist

An excellent way to do fast, cheap market research is to become suspicious. Be wary. Develop a cynical, pessimistic attitude and accept nothing on faith. Look for the *fatal flaw* in your business proposition.

Whenever I do consulting for a corporation, especially when they ask me to research an investment or a new product or service, I always look for the fatal flaw. I always look for the one thing that is wrong with this investment that could cost my client a lot of money.

And do you know what happens? In 99 out of 100 cases, I find the fatal flaw in the investment. I find something in a contract or mortgage agreement, or something in the way the land is laid out, or the way the distribution agreements are signed. I look for something that, if it were not discovered, would lead to the failure of the business.

No One Sells a Successful Business

Whenever someone is attempting to sell you an existing business, always look for the reasons why. If a successful business is for sale for any reason, there is almost always a fatal flaw somewhere. Whenever someone is trying to sell you a successful moneymaking opportunity, there is almost invariably something wrong with it. If you can't find the fatal flaw and are thoroughly convinced there is none, only then should you go ahead with it.

Usually people who are selling a business are selling it because they are losing money in it. Sometimes they will say, "The reason I am selling this business is because I want to concentrate on something else." But the real reason they are selling the business is because they are losing money. Take the time to find out why a person would be selling a successful business. It is very seldom the reason that you are given.

Look for Hidden Possibilities

A friend of mine was offered a company for sale that was doing about $1 million in sales each year, but which was never profitable; it was only breaking even. My friend studied the financial statements carefully and then offered the owner $100,000 cash for the business. The owner accepted the offer and volunteered to continue running the business if the new owner wanted to keep him on.

But my friend, who was an accountant, noticed that over the years the owner of the business had increased his personal salary to $200,000 per year, and was paying his longtime secretary $75,000 per year. The day after my friend closed the purchase, he fired them both, cutting the operating expenses by $275,000 per year. He then hired a general manager at $50,000 a year and an assistant for the general manager at $25,000 a year, taking the company from breakeven to $200,000 profit per year almost overnight. The fatal flaw was that the salary structure of the key people had gotten completely out of control. Sometimes you can spot an opportunity like this if you learn how to read financial statements.

Think Long-Term about the Business

Look at the business before you go into it as though you are going to be operating it for the next 20 years. The rule is, "Long-term perspective sharpens short-term decision making." If you look at any business venture, any product or service, as though you are going to be doing this 20 years from now, you will find that you are much more astute in making decisions in the short term.

Be Open to Negative Input

Seek out and listen carefully to people who are negative toward your idea. Your aim is to be a "realistic optimist," but you should look for *negative* thinkers to temper your optimism. The viewpoints of negative people can be invaluable and often save you a fortune in time and money.

A friend of mine is a business lawyer. He gives advice to many people on investments. When someone comes to him and wants to make an investment that they are not sure about, he performs a little exercise.

He takes them into his office and says, "I want you to sit behind my desk and imagine that you are me. Then I am going to come in and present this investment to you. I want you to critique this investment as if you were my adviser."

When his clients begin critiquing the investments they are thinking about getting into and are forced to become skeptical about the proposed investment, he says that they are astonished at how bad the investments really are. He has saved his clients millions of dollars by compelling them to be negative thinkers about their own ideas, simply by switching roles and sitting in front of a desk while they sit behind the desk. You should do the same thing.

A Great Entrepreneurial Success Story

You do not need to be overly influenced by negative thinkers even though you do need to take their viewpoints into consideration. There is the famous story of Mary Hudson, who started off with $200 in the middle of the Great Depression. She leased a gas station that two men had gone broke running on two different occasions. Everyone told her that it would be impossible for a woman to run a successful gas station if two men had failed at it in the past.

She ignored their advice. From that gas station, she built a company called Hudson Oil, which became one of the biggest independent distributors of gas and oil in the United States. From the $200 investment, even though everyone told her she would fail, she became one of the richest women in the country. It is helpful to listen to negative thinkers, but you don't necessarily have to accept their advice.

Test-Market Your Product or Service

How do you test-market a product or service? How do you find out if people are actually going to buy it? There are several steps you can take before you invest too much time or money in an idea that might not be successful. Here they are.

Step 1. Get or Make a Sample

Make or obtain a prototype of the product. Create or get a sample. If it is being manufactured somewhere else, get a sample of it that you can show to other people.

If you are going to manufacture a product yourself, create a prototype so that you can show it, demonstrate it, and photograph it. Have a sample so that you can let people see it, touch it, feel it, and give you an opinion on it.

Step 2. Show It Around

Some years ago, I negotiated with the Suzuki Motor Company of Japan to bring their four-wheel-drive vehicles into North America for the first time. My first request was for three samples of the vehicles, which they sent over on the next ship. We then drove the vehicles around to about 30 different dealerships and let people look at them, touch them, smell them, feel them, and test-drive them. In addition, we took the three vehicles to several trade shows, large and small, and spoke to more than 4,000 potential buyers over a series of weeks.

Once people could see them and test-drive them, they immediately wanted to buy and own the Suzuki vehicles. We knew that we had a winner. We signed the importation and distribution agreement, brought in thousands of vehicles, and sold them through 65 dealerships. It was a great success. But the starting point was a prototype that people could actually see and feel.

Step 3. Know What It Costs

Get accurate prices and delivery dates from your suppliers. If you are going to show the prototype or sample, you must be able to tell the prospective buyer how much it will cost and how long it will take to get delivery. Be sure that you have these answers.

Step 4. Ask a Buyer

Get a buyer's personal opinion. Go to people you will expect to buy the product or service and get them to tell you how they think and feel about your offering. Ask them, "Would you buy this?" If it is a retail operation, you ask, "At what price could you sell it?" Always call on the individual who makes the buying decisions. Always call on the person who can sign the check.

Step 5. Be Objective

Compare your product or service with other products on the market. And again, ask yourself this question: "Why would someone buy from me instead of from someone else? What is it about the product that makes it faster, better, cheaper, or superior in some way to what is already available?"

Step 6. Do a One-Store Test

Try a one-store test. See if you cannot find a store that will carry your product on a limited basis and see how customers respond to it. Try a one-customer test. If it is a product or service, find one customer who will buy and use the product or service and give you candid feedback.

Step 7. Show It Off

Take your product or service to a trade show. As I mentioned earlier, there are 15,000 trade shows each year all over the country. Sophisticated buyers go to trade shows. They will tell you immediately whether you have a winner. They will tell you quite quickly whether there is a market demand for your product at the price you will have to charge to make it available.

Sometimes these professional buyers are right, and sometimes they are wrong. The people who developed the game Trivial Pursuit took it to a toy and hobby show in Toronto and sold only 132 sets. Two months later, they took it to another toy and hobby show in Montreal and sold only 144 sets. The trade show strategy was not working for them.

They then changed their strategy and directly approached a major toy and game company in New York, Hasbro Industries. Hasbro buyers saw the potential in the game and agreed to distribute it. The following year they sold $750 million worth of Trivial Pursuit.

Step 8. Ask Your Friends

Ask your friends if they would buy the product, or if they would use the service. Ask your relatives. Even ask your spouse. Sometimes your mother is a good test subject. Sometimes your father is the person to ask. Sometimes your brothers, sisters, or friends will give you accurate feedback on whether you have a winner.

If they say they would buy the product or service, ask for a firm commitment. Take an order and give them a date for delivery. Ask them for a check.

Sometimes people will tell you that you have a great product or service, and encourage you to get into a new line of business that they don't really believe in. When you go back to them later, you will find that they will not be your customers at all. When you ask them for a check, when you ask them to actually part with money, they will come up with a thousand reasons for not buying.

The essence of successful business is really quite simple. It is your ability to offer a product or service that people will pay for at a price sufficiently above your costs, thereby giving you a profit that enables you to buy and offer more products and services. It's not complicated.

How to Build a Profitable Business

There are several ways to build a profitable business.

Look for Ways to Add Value

One way to add value to the product is by bringing the product or service from another place and making it available in your existing market. You can generate profits by creating a product or service and selling it at a price higher than your total costs of production. You can become wealthy either by selling a few products or services at high profits or by selling many products or services at low prices and smaller profits.

Your very best strategy is, of course, to sell a larger volume of products with a smaller profit on each item. Most great fortunes have been made selling large quantities of products over a wide area, thereby broadening the market and reducing your dependency on just a few customers.

For example, look at the difference between selling yachts and selling chewing gum or candy. There are a few fortunes that are based on selling yachts, but there are many fortunes that are based on selling chewing gum and candy. The basic rule is, "If you want to dine with the classes, you must sell to the masses." The very best way to build a large, profitable business is to sell a high volume of products with a small, dependable, consistent profit on each one.

Start in an Established Field

Another key to business success is to start off in an established field and experiment with new products or services only out of your profits from your established business. One reason that many entrepreneurs fail is that they have grandiose ideas of being the first into the market with a brand-new, untried, unproven product. Don't fall into this trap.

Trust Your Inner Voice

Read every publication, and explore every opportunity. Remain open to all ideas. But in the final analysis, trust yourself. Trust your inner voice to tell you the right thing to do. All great businesspeople become great by listening to their inner guides.

This inner voice will never fail to lead you to your highest good. The more knowledge and experience that you acquire, the sharper, better, and more accurate will be this inner voice.

When you begin to magnetize your mind with visual images of wealth and success, and as you begin looking everywhere for profitable ideas, you will begin to attract into your life the people and opportunities you need to achieve your goals. Your success will become inevitable.

Business Opportunities Are Everywhere

There have never been more opportunities for more people to start and build successful businesses than there are today. The possibilities open to you are limited only by your imagination. And since your imagination is unlimited, your opportunities are unlimited as well. In the next chapter, you will learn how to market and sell any product or service on which you decide to build your business.

Action Exercises

1. Look into yourself and determine the kind of product or service you could really get excited about producing and selling. How you feel personally about your business will determine whether you make it a success.

2. Look at the market and identify needs unmet and problems unsolved that you could do something about with a new or existing product or service. Look for opportunities everywhere.

3. Test your ideas for new products or services by getting as many opinions from others as possible. Be open to negative reactions and skepticism. They can contain seeds of truth and ideas for improvement.

4. Subscribe today to several of the most popular magazines and trade journals in your field. Read the "Business Opportunities" sections and call for information. The more ideas you have, the more successful you will be.

5. Go onto the Internet and identify the trade shows being held in your area of interest. Make plans to attend and spend a day or two talking to the exhibitors about the future possibilities in your business.

6. Take the time to develop a business plan before you start spending time and money on a new venture. Determine where your sales will come from, how much they will cost, and how profitable they are likely to be.

7. Make it a habit to use your intelligence and imagination rather than money and frantic activity to succeed in your business. Practice frugality at all times. Preserve cash.

"There will always be a frontier
where there is an open mind and a willing hand."
—Charles F. Kettering

6

Market and Sell Anything

"Marketing is the whole business seen from the point of view of its final result, that is, from the customer's point of view. Concern and responsibility for marketing must therefore permeate all areas of the enterprise."

—Peter Drucker

The major reason for business success is invariably the ability of the individual or the owner to move the product to the customer in an efficient, cost-effective manner. Major reasons for business failure are poor marketing, lack of sales ability, and lack of momentum in the sales department.

In almost every troubled company I have worked with, ineffective marketing, resulting in poor sales, has been the major problem or cause of declining revenues and growing problems.

Marketing and Sales Defined

Marketing can be defined as the "process of studying the market and determining what it is that people want, need, can use, and will pay for, and then providing that product or service in a timely and cost-effective manner."

Marketing analysis enables you or your company to bring the correct product and services to your market, at the right time. Selling, on the other hand, is the process of attracting or finding customers for the product or service and demonstrating to them that your product or service will give them the benefit that they desire. Selling is the process of demonstrating that your product is the solution to their problems or satisfaction of their needs, at a reasonable price.

As Peter Drucker says, "The purpose of marketing is to make selling unnecessary." It is not likely that you will ever make selling completely unnecessary, but your marketing skills will account for 90 percent of your success in business. Fortunately, marketing is a learnable skill. You can improve your marketing dramatically by making small changes and adjustments to what you are doing today.

The Marketing Mix

There are four parts of any marketing plan. When you are thinking of setting up, starting, or expanding your business, or selling any product or service, the four elements that you have to think about continually are product, price, place, and promotion.

The Product

The first element is the *product* or *service*. Exactly what product or service are you going to sell to this market? Define your product or service in terms of what it does for your customer. How does it help your customer to achieve, avoid, or preserve something? You must be clear about the benefit you offer, and how the customer's life or work will be improved if he or she buys what you sell.

The Price

How much are you going to charge for your product or service, and on what basis? How are you going to price it to sell at retail? How are you going to sell it at wholesale? How are you going to charge for volume discounts? Is your price correct based on your costs and the prices of your competitors?

The Place

Where are you going to sell this product at this price? Are you going to sell directly from your own company, or through wholesalers, retailers, direct mail, catalogs, or the Internet? To put it another way, at what location will customers buy your product or service? Where will they be? Where are they today?

The Promotion

Promotion includes every aspect of advertising, brochures, packaging, salespeople, and sales methodology. How are you going to promote, advertise, and sell this product at this price at this location? What will be the process from the first contact with a prospect through to the completed sale?

Creative marketing comes from continually questioning the existing situation and looking for ways to change this *marketing mix*—the product, price, place, and promotion. Creative marketing often involves adding new products or services or modifying existing ones. It may require changes in pricing, place of sale, or promotional methods. Sometimes marketing requires that you delete existing products or services, sell them at different prices, or offer them in different places or promote them differently.

You can change any one of these elements and then test to determine whether this change improves sales or profitability. Sometimes you may have to change two or more factors at once to achieve a quantum leap upward in sales results. In any case, the marketing mix is a dynamic combination of elements that is always changing.

Five Rules for Selling Anything, Anywhere

Once you have decided on your marketing mix, there are five cardinal rules for selling anything, anywhere, at any time. Any violation of any one of these rules can lead to the failure of your sales efforts, and often does.

Rule 1. Your product or service must be ideally suited to the current market. It must be competitively priced and vigorously promoted. Nothing sells itself. Products and services are sold, not bought.

Rule 2. People buy *benefits*, not products. They buy *solutions* to their problems. They buy ways to achieve their goals. It must be clear what problem your product can solve, what benefits it can offer, or what goal it can help a customer to achieve.

Rule 3. The product or service must satisfy an *existing* want or need of the customer or *create* an immediate want or need. The main reason for business failure is that there is no real need for what the company is selling. The more and better you test your product or service before you bring it to the market, the greater assurance you will have that the need actually exists.

Rule 4. Customers must *believe* the salesperson, trust the company, and be convinced that the product or service is the best for them, all things considered at the present time. Credibility is everything. The level of trust that the customer has in you and your company is the critical factor in whether he or she buys from you at all.

Rule 5. The customer must be willing and *able* to pay for the product or service and have a sincere desire to enjoy the benefits that you are offering. It is worse than useless to market to a customer who, in the final analysis, does not have the money to pay for your product or service, or who doesn't really want it in the first place.

Five Questions You Must Answer

There are five questions that you must be prepared to answer before you can make a sale. These questions lurk in the back of the mind of each customer, and are seldom spoken aloud. Nonetheless, failure to answer any of these questions can cost you the sale, even from a qualified prospect. You must design your sales presentation and methodology around answering these questions.

Question 1. "Why should I listen to you?" All advertising, promotion, and sales efforts are designed to break the preoccupation of the customer and answer the question, "Why should I listen to you?" If you don't answer this question right at the start, usually within the first few seconds, you seldom get a chance to sell your product.

The scarcest commodity in the United States today is "attention." The average customer is bombarded by hundreds and even thousands of commercial messages every day. From the time customers get up in the morning, radio, television, newspapers, billboards, and the Internet are all bombarding them with hundreds of messages, all shouting in some way, "Buy me! Buy me!" To even get a chance to sell, you must break through this preoccupation by answering the question, "Why should I listen to you?"

Question 2. "What is it and what does it do?" Once you have the customer's attention, you have to tell the customer, quickly and clearly, exactly what your product or service is. How does it improve the life or work of the customer? What need does it fill, or what problem does it solve?

It is amazing how many advertisements, on radio, television, and in print, fail to answer this question. After you have seen or read the advertisement, you are still not clear what it is that the company is selling, or why you should be interested in proceeding further.

Question 3. "Who says so?" Customers are skeptical and suspicious of any sales advertisement or claim. You need immediate proof that your product does what you say it does. You need testimonials from satisfied customers. You need some kind of independent research. You must overcome the customers' natural skepticism by offering some proof that your product or service will deliver the result or benefit that you promise.

Question 4. "Who else has used it?" No one wants to be the first person to try your product or service. There is safety in numbers. Customers want to know the names or types of customers who have already used your product or service satisfactorily.

Question 5. "What do I get?" Everybody's favorite radio station is WII-FM, "what's in it for me?" You must get to the bottom line quickly. The rule for effective advertising or selling is that a 10-year-old child should be able to read your advertisement and then be able to explain to another 10-year-old child exactly what it is you're selling and why he or she would be interested in buying it. If your advertisement is any more complicated than that, it will probably not succeed.

Evaluate every piece of advertising or promotional material that goes out of your office to make sure that it answers those five questions: *"Why should I listen to you?" "What is it and what does it do?" "Who says so?" "Who else has used it?"* and *"What do I get?"*

Selling Your Product or Service

There are many different ways to sell your product or service. In sales and marketing, the more different options you have and the more different possibilities you can conceive of, the more likely it is that you will take that critical first step to becoming wealthy. The more techniques and strategies you have, the more likely it is that you will take the necessary steps toward achieving your financial goals.

The purpose of this book is to open your mind and expand your horizons to all the possibilities that are open to you in starting and building your own successful business in America. The goal is to take you from wherever you are today, and to introduce you to specific, concrete actions that you can take to where you want to be in the future.

Multiple Ways to Sell

There are dozens of different ways to sell a product or service. The average business uses only one or two of these methods. Fortunately, the more of these methods you are familiar with and with which you experiment on a limited scale, the more likely you are to pinpoint a formula for sales success that will make you wealthy.

Personal Sales

Personal direct selling is the best of all sales methodologies. This is something that you are doing, one way or another, from the first day you start in business. You are selling your product or service. You are selling your ideas. You are selling yourself and your leadership. You are selling your abilities to pay to your suppliers, your backers, and your bankers. You are selling your authority to your staff. You are selling continually.

Retail Sales

Another way to sell a product is through retail sales. You can sell your products through your own store, or you can sell to retailers and have them carry your products. Many tens of thousands of products are designed, developed, manufactured, and sold through wholesalers and retailers. This is perhaps the largest single method of sales in the world.

Distributors

You can recruit distributors for your product in other market areas than the one where you do business. Selling through a distributorship can be as *simple* as giving individuals or companies the exclusive or nonexclusive right to sell your products in their areas or to their existing customers.

Setting up distributorships can be as *complex* as selecting the right people and companies, training them thoroughly in how to sell and deliver your product or service, supplying them with all the products and materials they need to conduct their business, and supporting them 24/7 to assure that they are successful in selling your products.

Distributors are invariably independent businesses with their own names and identities, and their own ideas about how to conduct their businesses. Aside from requiring them to agree to certain performance standards and working as closely with them as they will allow, you have little control over how they carry on their business. Nonetheless, setting up distributors for your products or services can enable you to expand nationally and internationally in a short period of time.

Newspapers

You can sell a product through the newspaper. The purpose of newspaper advertising is to generate direct and immediate responses that translate into sales and profits greatly in excess of the cost of advertising. All newspaper advertising is aimed at getting people to take action *now*. It is aimed at getting them to phone you and buy or to come into your store in person so that you can present your products and sell to them immediately.

Is It Paying for Itself?

A marketing consultant who worked for me many years ago had a simple formula: "Creative advertising sells!" He said that immediate responses and sales results were the only measure of whether the advertising was any good.

Some years ago, I was promoting a product with radio and newspaper advertising that had been written by an agency that was apparently not very good at what it did. One day, in the midst of this advertising campaign, another advertising executive, representing his own advertising agency, phoned me and asked me how sales were going. A bit embarrassed, I told him that sales were going fine. He said, "I have only one question for you: Is your phone ringing?"

As it happened, in spite of many thousands of dollars of advertising, the phone was not ringing at all. I invited him in to make me a new proposal for a different approach to our advertising. His ideas were excellent. We accepted them, and within one week the new ads were causing our phones to ring off the hook. I always apply that same test to the advertising of my clients: "Is your phone ringing?" If it's not, change your advertising immediately.

Direct Mail

Direct mail allows you to pinpoint your market and aim your promotions at exactly those people who would be the most likely to buy your product in the shortest amount of time.

Successful direct mail depends on your ability to acquire a good *mailing list*, and then having a product that is tailored to that specific group of customers. Direct mail allows you to focus on doctors, dentists, lawyers, sports car owners, seminar attendees, or any other demographic group that you can identify.

There are several organizations throughout the country that develop and supply mailing lists for people who want to use direct mail to contact customers. Dun & Bradstreet has been a market leader in this area for many years. USA Direct of Omaha has the names, addresses, and data on more than 100 million customers, in every category, throughout the United States. There are mailing list brokers in the Yellow Pages in virtually every major city. You can also find all the information you need regarding mailing lists on the Internet.

The number, sophistication, and quality of mailing lists available today are absolutely remarkable. The more specific you can be about the very best type of prospect for what you are selling, the more precise your mailing list can be made, and the more effective your direct mailing campaign will be.

Mail Order

To sell through mail order, you can place large or small ads in selected publications that appeal to your particular customer group. The entrepreneur Paul Hawkins built a $45 million business selling garden tools by running small ads in magazines that were read by people who garden as a hobby. Other small business people get started by contracting for products at wholesale and then selling them at retail in the classified sections of magazines and newspapers.

The Internet

You can set up your own Internet site or store, offer specialized products and services to a particular type of customer, and then work in cooperation with other Internet sites and businesses that appeal to that same type of customer.

The era of spam marketing through the Internet is coming to an end through government regulation. For the foreseeable future you will sell on the Internet by offering free information in a specialized area and making your offer widely known. When customers come to your site to take advantage of your free offer, you can then sell them high-quality products and services, backed by an unconditional guarantee. As you develop an expanding network of happy customers, they will tell other people about your site, and your customer list will start to grow.

There are many misunderstandings about the Internet. Some people suggest that it is easy to start an Internet business and make a lot of money. The fact is that it is not easy to start *any* business and make a lot of money. Every business requires a tremendous amount of thoughtful planning and preparation before you begin. It then takes a good deal of time to build your business, one sale at a time.

Almost all products sold on the Internet are clear and specific. Customers know exactly what they are looking for when they go to the Internet in the first place. It is almost impossible to create a demand for a new product on the Internet, because it is impossible to touch, taste, feel, or experiment with it. The most successful Internet businesses are those that sell known products at competitive prices with unconditional guarantees. Think about Amazon.com or Barnes&Noble.com as well as travel sites such as Expedia.com and Priceline.com.

Direct Selling

You can sell your products by direct selling, from office to office or door to door. This form of selling requires an ability to write or telephone to set up appointments, to visit the prospect personally, to identify the prospect's needs, and then to make an effective sales presentation.

Often direct selling requires *cold calling*. This means that you have to phone or visit people you have never seen or met before. In cold calling, the rejection level is high. You need a tremendous amount of toughness and persistence. However, once you learn that *rejection is not personal*, and you get over your fear of cold calling, you can start and build successful sales in virtually any market.

Seminar Selling

You can advertise and bring together prospective customers who are interested in your product or service for a group presentation. During this presentation, you can explain what it is that you offer and why it is an ideal product or service for those in the audience, and encourage the seminar attendees to buy what you are selling or arrange for a private meeting at a later time.

Seminar selling is used primarily to sell business seminars or services, or financial advice and planning. The key to success in this method of selling is to give excellent value and instruction on your subject to demonstrate your expertise and to create a desire to learn more. This way of selling can be very successful if you can attract a large enough group of qualified prospects, usually via newspaper, direct mail, and radio.

Party Plan

Perhaps your products can be sold through what is called a "party plan." Some product lines like Tupperware and beauty products, as well as specialty foods and certain clothing lines, can be sold in homes by having the resident invite friends over for a presentation. The salesperson then demonstrates and sells the products to those in attendance. The host or hostess receives a premium or commission on all sales that the attendees place. Hundreds of millions of dollars are sold on the party plan system every year.

Co-Op Mailings

You can sell your product or service through co-op mailings. Many large mailing firms, or other companies, will include your product flyer or your product brochure with their mailings or invoices in exchange for a share of the gross sales.

If you have an American Express, MasterCard, or Visa card, you will be familiar with the special offers that you receive with each invoice. These companies send out information on dozens of products throughout the year along with their invoices.

One of the great advantages to co-op mailings is that there is no cost to you except the printing of the promotional material until the sales are generated.

The Government

Different governments—city, county, state, and federal—may be interested in your product or service. The government is the biggest single customer in the country, consuming hundreds of billions of dollars' worth of products and services each year. You can make a fortune by just finding a product that government organizations need and want at a particular time.

If you have a product or service that can be used by government agencies, you should approach city, county, state, and federal government offices. Find out everything you can about how to sell to government officials. Find out how to get onto their bidding lists. Find out who does the purchasing, and why they buy in the first place. Sometimes you can even develop a product that is specific for various governments or for a specific government department such as the Defense Department.

Manufacturers' Representatives

You can sell your product through manufacturers' representatives. There are companies throughout the country that represent a variety of different products in specific market areas. Often they will specialize in selling to a particular type of customer, or in carrying a particular type of product line.

You can advertise for manufacturers' representatives to work for you on commission in other market areas. Advertise in the specific magazines and publications that they read. The best part is that you pay them on straight commission. There is no cost to you unless they make a sale.

Chain Stores

Sometimes chain stores have hundreds of outlets nationwide. You only need to sell your product to one person—to one buyer at the head office—and it will go into hundreds of stores.

Many entrepreneurs have made their fortunes by getting a company like Wal-Mart or Kmart to carry their products in all their outlets. Even though these big buyers will squeeze the entrepreneurs down to the last penny, the volume of sales can still make being carried by these large chain stores extremely profitable.

Discount Stores

You can sell your product through discount stores. Discount stores prefer to carry products at below the normal retail price. Sometimes you can repackage or even relabel your product to sell through discount stores so that it won't hurt your sales at full retail price by other methods.

Supermarkets

Supermarket chains often carry a large number of nonfood items. If one chain of supermarkets will carry your product and it is appropriate for their type of customer, you could sell an enormous amount in a short period of time.

Department Stores

You can sell your products through department stores. Their product buyers are very astute, but if they like your product, they can become major customers for you.

One of the most important things to do, before you begin producing or importing a particular product or service, is to visit product buyers at these stores and get their opinions. These people deal with vendors all day long and usually have excellent instincts for what will sell in the current market. They are not always correct, but their input can save you an enormous amount of time and money.

Wholesalers

Wholesalers will often carry your products to sell along with their other lines, direct to their retail customers.

If you use wholesalers, you will have to sell to them at well below retail prices. Their primary concern will be the profit margin they can earn between the prices they pay you for your product and how much they can sell it for to their retail customers. As a result, they will do everything possible to squeeze your prices down as low as possible.

Turnover and Profit per Sale

Here is an important point. Whenever you are selling to wholesalers, retailers, discount stores, department stores, chain stores, or grocery stores, they will all have one measure in common. Their primary concern is *turnover*. How quickly will the product sell, and how much profit will they make per unit? Sometimes this is referred to as "velocity." What will be the speed of turnover multiplied by the amount of money they can make from the sale of these items?

These people have only one thought in their business lives. It is *profit per sale*. They are not interested in prestige, status, attractiveness, or appealing to a narrow market segment. All they care about is the volume of sales multiplied by the amount of profit they can earn from each item. When you talk to them, the *quality* of your product will be of some concern to them but the *profitability* of carrying your product will be all-important. Be sure to appeal to this main interest in everything you do and say.

Premium Sales

Companies may purchase your products to give away as a prize, an award, or a bonus for purchasing something else. If your product is inexpensive enough and has a high enough perceived value, very often companies will buy it and give it away as a low-cost incentive to get people to purchase their main product or service.

Look for companies that use prizes, bonuses, and awards to get new business. Sometimes these companies can buy your product in large quantities. Often, you can private-label your product or service for a company that wants to give away a large number of them.

Advertising Specialty

You can sell your product as an advertising specialty. Companies may purchase your product to imprint with their name and give away as gifts and incentives to their customers. Some advertising specialties you are familiar with are embossed pens, ashtrays, Frisbees, or baseball caps. Often companies will give away pocket calendars, radios, and even small computers as advertising specialties.

Franchising

Your product can be sold in large quantities through franchising. Many businesses have the capacity to be franchised and to be rolled out to other areas. Franchise businesses now count for many billions of dollars in retail sales, not only throughout the United States, but throughout the world.

A franchise is a *proven success system*. It is a business system from which all the bugs and defects have been removed. It is a profit-making system that can work for anybody, virtually anywhere, if the franchisee follows the business system exactly the way it has been designed.

Once you have developed a successful business system, such as McDonald's, Kinko's, or Krispy Kreme doughnut franchises, you have a model that is replicable. Like a recipe, it can be duplicated over and over again, getting the same results for each new franchise.

McDonald's has more than 30,000 franchises worldwide. Because the McDonald's franchise system has been tested and proven so many thousands of times, in every type of market, there have been only one or two failures of a McDonald's franchise in history.

A Proven System
With a good franchise, the sellers of the franchise can predict with some accuracy exactly how much the owner will earn each year as the result of following the system.

But franchising requires that you develop a successful system *first*. Franchising requires that you develop a profitable business that can be multiplied many times over. It is amazing how many people come up with a business idea and begin thinking about franchising it before they have even made it successful the first time. The fact is that the average company that franchises does not do so until it has been in business for 8 to 10 years. Most companies never franchise at all. If you are considering buying a franchise, investigate before you invest, and look for a track record of success.

Trade Shows

You can sell your product through trade shows. Buyers from thousands of companies attend trade shows every year to find new products to offer to their customers. They know that the cutting edge of new product development is represented in trade shows, and that one new product, at the right time, can earn millions of dollars.

As I mentioned earlier, there are more then 15,000 trade shows each year. Many companies develop their entire business around their appearances in trade shows.

Displays and Exhibits

You can move your product to the market through fairs, expositions, or even exhibits at conventions and fund-raising shows. High traffic count can result in big sales. Look for places where you can appear and display your product where a lot of potential buyers will be walking past. You want to be continually seeking ways to put your product in front of as many potential customers as possible.

Fund-Raisers

You can often sell your product through churches, charitable organizations, the chamber of commerce, or schools that will in-turn sell it as a fund-raiser. You can sell candy, nuts, toys, and items for schools, bands, and other fund-raising organizations.

Most of these ideas require energy and imagination more than money and risk. In many cases, you can take orders for the product before you place your orders with the manufacturer, thereby keeping your exposure limited until you develop a steady volume of sales.

Start Small, Grow Slowly

The key to business success is to conserve cash at all times. Poor inventory control, which means purchasing too much stock that ends up not being sold, is one of the major reasons why businesses get into trouble. Whenever possible, arrange to sell the product and get firm orders before you place your orders with the supplier or manufacturer.

Make haste slowly. Take one step at a time. Be patient. Don't try to cream the market or to get rich quickly. Instead, get rich slowly but surely. Test each step as you go, and whatever you do, don't lose money.

Master the Art of Selling

All successful businesspeople are good salespeople. They are good persuaders. As Robert Louis Stevenson once said, "Everybody makes their living by selling something to someone." The only question is, "How good are you at selling?"

Rich or Poor?

Here is an important point. The primary reason that people retire poor in the United States is because they don't know how to sell, or they're afraid to sell, or they think that they are too good to sell. Selling is one of the highest-paid professions in the world. Some 5 percent of all self-made U.S. millionaires have been salespeople all their lives, working for other companies. An additional 74 percent of self-made American millionaires are entrepreneurs who started their businesses as a result of being able to sell something to someone. Selling is the high road to business success.

What do you say to people who feel they are too good to sell? It is inspiring to think of people like Lee Iacocca, who as the president of Chrysler Corporation went on television and radio and traveled around the country as a spokesperson and salesman for Chrysler products. People like Bill Gates, Larry Ellison, Warren Buffett, and Michael Dell—some of the richest people in the world—are continually standing up before critical audiences and selling them on the virtues and values of their products and services. The most successful people are always selling something to someone.

Selling Is a Learnable Skill

The only question you need to ask yourself is whether you are going to become good at selling. Fortunately, selling is a learnable skill, as are all business skills. Even if you have never sold anything to anyone in the past, you can learn to be a confident enough salesperson to start and build a successful business.

If for any reason you are not good at selling and you are not willing to become good at selling, you can grow a business only if you can find someone else to do the selling for you. But the challenge is that people who are good at selling either will not work for you in the first place or will want a large share of your business in exchange for their ability to bring in revenues. Many small businesspeople hire a salesperson and then become completely dependent on that salesperson. If that salesperson leaves and takes the business with them, the company can collapse.

Control the Revenues

There are certain skills in business that you can hire out or hire in. There are other skills that you absolutely, positively, must master yourself if you are going to be both successful and independent. Marketing and selling are the two key skills of the business owner that cannot be delegated successfully to someone else.

The sooner you become excellent at selling, the sooner it will be that you become financially independent and create the kind of life that you desire.

Thomas J. Watson Sr., the founder of IBM, started off at as a young salesman selling cash registers for the National Cash Register Company. Building on his sales skills, he took over a small punch card processing company and changed its name to International Business Machines. By focusing on selling and salespeople, he eventually built IBM into one of the most successful companies in the world.

Richard Sears, who co-founded Sears, Roebuck and Company, started his career by buying watches at wholesale and selling them at retail at stations along the railroad. He liked the process of buying and selling so much, and he did it so well, that he eventually partnered with Alvin Roebuck and went on to build one of the most successful retail sales corporations in the world.

Almost every successful business starts off with someone who can sell the product or service. Personal selling is the starting point for most of the great fortunes in the United States. Make a decision to learn how, and excel at it, today.

Opportunity Gap Analysis

Opportunity gap analysis is a good exercise to expand your mind and your business for your product or service. With opportunity gap analysis, you use your creativity to find different ways to move more of your product or service to more customers.

Here are 10 questions you can ask to find newer or better ways to distribute your product or services:

1. *What other ways could you sell your product?* Remember, there are dozens of different ways that we have identified earlier. Simply taking a product that is being sold one way and selling it in a different way can be all that it takes to start a successful business, or turn around an existing one.

2. *What additional customers are there for this product?* Where are these additional customers? Who are these additional customers? Finding a new customer base for an existing product can be the key to making your business successful.

3. *How could you modify or change your existing products or services to make them more attractive to your customers?* How could you change the packaging? Change the functions? Change the features? Increase the size or reduce the complexity? Decrease the size or simplify the product? Continually look for ways to offer your product or service in such a way that it is more appealing to the same or to a different customer group.

4. *What noncustomers could you develop for this product?* Who can you think of who could use, benefit from, and afford this product, who is not buying from anyone at present? What customer groups are not using this product at all at this time? How could you appeal to these people?

5. *What new products do your customers want?* If you already have an existing customer base, what else do your customers need that you are not yet supplying to them? What else can you produce that your customers can use in conjunction with what you are already selling them?

6. *What additional methods of distribution exist for your product?* How else could you get your product to your customers? Think of the different ways listed earlier. Which of them could work for you?

7. *What additional products could you distribute through your existing marketing channels?* If you already have distribution channels—retail, direct selling, or direct mail—what other products could you offer that you could sell using the same channels to the same customers?

8. *What new products could you develop for your existing distribution channels or existing customers?* What else could you sell through these distribution channels to your current customers?

9. *What new markets exist for your new products and for your current distribution channels?* In other words, where are there people or customers who are not currently using your products or services that you could reach with your existing distribution channels?

10. *What additional products could you produce with your existing facilities?* With your existing staff? With your existing knowledge? With your existing skills and abilities? What else could you produce? What additional products and services could you create for your existing market?

Most companies and people get stuck in a comfort zone. They start off selling in a particular way, and ever after, they continue to sell and deliver their products in the same way. But the only real test is *sales*. Are your sales high enough? Is your business profitable enough? In what ways could you change the way you sell and deliver to get better results? In times of rapid change, you must continually ask and answer these questions, because your competitors are asking them, every single day.

Getting Free Publicity

Over the years, I have personally used various techniques to get tens of thousands of dollars' worth of free publicity in newspapers, magazines, radio, and television. These methods work everywhere and for almost everyone. Often, your ability to get free publicity can be the key to launching and growing your business or your product successfully.

Once you have a product or service that you are ready to take to the market, begin thinking immediately about how you could make it *newsworthy* so that people would write about it and talk about it without your having to spend money advertising it.

Here are the rules for getting free publicity:

Rule 1. Ask for It

If you want publicity, ask for it. People will not seek you out to give you publicity, but very often they will give it to you if you ask them to.

Rule 2. Prepare a Press Release

Compose a publicity notice or press release, and send it to all the relevant media. Look in the Yellow Pages for every newspaper, radio station, television station, magazine, and other publication and write a letter to the editor on your company stationery. Include a 100-word description of your new product or service. Write it like a news story and make it interesting.

Rule 3. Make It Newsworthy

Ask the question, "Is it news?" Give your new product or service an interesting twist. Some years ago, an entrepreneur spent all his money importing a long-life lightbulb that would burn for thousands of hours without replacement. He tried to sell it for three years and almost went bankrupt because no one was willing to pay the higher price he had to charge.

Finally, he did something to make it newsworthy. He announced that his lightbulb would last for "50,000 hours." This got media attention. Soon he was on radio and television shows talking about this remarkable scientific development. People wanted to hear about it. They thought it was interesting. Almost overnight, his sales went up astronomically and he became financially successful.

Rule 4. Pinpoint Your Audience

Answer the question, "Who is my customer or customer segment?" Then seek out the radio stations, television stations, newspapers, and magazines that are listened to, watched, or read by your specific potential customers.

Rule 5. Select Your Media Carefully

Carefully consider what media you should contact. Look in the book *Standard Rates and Data*. This is the bible of the advertising industry. It gives you the names, addresses, phone numbers, and all the critical information about media advertising in your market area and throughout the country. It tells you what types of stories and articles the media are interested in and what markets they appeal to.

Rule 6. Create Good Working Tools

What you need to get free publicity is good letterhead and clear, crisp copy. In other words, write about your product or service so that it is newsworthy. Write it like a news story. Write your description so that the staff could take it from your letter and run it on the air, or print it in the newspaper or magazine, without changing it. Make it interesting and appealing.

Rule 7. Send a Photograph

Send a photograph of your product in use. If you can get a photograph of someone using your product or service, this is more interesting and more likely to be newsworthy.

Rule 8. Use Direct Mail

Use direct mail to select media and particular sections of newspapers and magazines. For example, if you have a product that appeals to lifestyle, gardening, or sports enthusiasts, send a letter to the editor of that particular department of the newspaper or magazine or at the radio or television station. These people are always looking for a newsworthy item to pass along to their audiences.

Rule 9. Go on Radio and Television

Get onto radio and television talk shows, if you possibly can. This gets you exposure to thousands of people quite quickly and can often lead to tremendous sales of your product or services.

The first step in getting onto talk shows, in addition to having a newsworthy product or service, is to prepare a fact sheet for the announcer. Prepare a summary of the benefits or interesting features of your product or service so that the announcer can read it quickly and then begin the interview. Make it as easy as possible for the interviewer to look and sound intelligent.

If you get onto a television show, create a questionnaire to act as a prompter for the host of the show. Give him or her a series of 10 to 12 questions that you know people who would be interested in your product or service might ask. Encourage the host to ask you these questions so that you can answer them.

Once you start to answer the questions on radio or television, don't try to be an entertainer. Instead, sell with good information. Give as much valuable information about your product or service and how helpful it can be to the listener as you can in the shortest possible period of time. Think and talk in terms of benefits for the customer.

Rule 10. Offer Something Free

Whenever possible on a radio or television show, offer something free to the audience. Invite them to phone you for a free list or report. Ask them to send a self-addressed, stamped envelope and offer something of value to prospective customers. Send them to your Internet site to get a free download of something that can help them in their life or work. The people who will contact you to get something free will often turn out to be your best paying customers.

Rule 11. Leave Information Behind

When you have finished your appearance on a radio or television show, leave your brochure, your business card, and any other information about your product or company that you possibly can with the receptionist. You may be amazed at how many people telephone a radio or television station sometime after you have been on the air looking for you or your company. When you leave this information with the receptionist, it can be passed on to anyone who phones in.

Some years ago, I gave a one-hour interview on a popular radio call-in show in the middle of the morning. I offered a free gift to anyone who called. The station got so many phone calls in the next hour that the switchboard actually shorted out and shut down. They had never seen that volume of call-in traffic before.

Some months later, when another guest failed to show up, they decided to rerun my interview again, using different introductions and tag lines. Once again, they received more than 500 calls and burned out the switchboard. But by this time they had lost the information that we had given them and the callers had no way of getting in touch with us. We lost a tremendous amount of potential business.

Always leave information behind you, wherever you go. Be especially friendly to the receptionists and the assistants. Be polite and gracious. Treat them like the important people they are. Introduce yourself and give them the necessary information so when other people phone in they can get in touch with you.

Opportunities Everywhere

There is an old saying, "The successful person makes more opportunities than he finds." The fact is that there are unlimited opportunities for the creative minority. If you are determined to enter a world of entrepreneurship, to start your own business, the only limits on what you can accomplish are the limits that you place on yourself. They are largely self-imposed.

Every day, almost 3,000 men and women make the decision to go out on their own. They are willing to take a chance to realize their dreams of freedom, success, and financial independence. And what they have done you can do as well.

Just Do It!

There are numerous ways for you to begin. Today, there are more ways for you to succeed in business than you could imagine. There are more ways to sell your products and services than you could explore in a lifetime. What is required from you, more than anything else, is *action*. Nothing will take the place of focus, persistence, and continuous action toward your goal.

When you are ready to take the necessary actions, you will learn the lessons you need. You will find the people to help you. You will uncover the opportunities you are seeking. You will achieve the success you desire, if you only act decisively.

Take action today. Do it now. Act without doubt, delay, or procrastination. Don't wait. Just do it!

Action Exercises

1. Make a decision that you are going to be in business within 30 days. Identify a product or service that you like and feel you can sell, and make arrangements to bring it to the market. Get on with it.

2. Decide on a method of sale that seems logical for the product or service you have chosen, and then concentrate single-mindedly on mastering that distribution channel.

3. If you are already in business, select a way of selling and marketing that you are not currently using and focus on learning everything you can to offer your product or service in that new way.

4. Study your distribution channels and determine what you could do differently to offer more or different products in different ways to different customers. Remain open-minded and optimistic.

5. Upgrade your sales skills. Some 95 percent of full-time sales professionals could learn how to sell more, better, and faster than they are doing today. Resolve to invest any amount of time and money necessary to become excellent at sales.

6. Get around the right people. Form a mastermind group with other people in similar businesses, and get together once per week to share ideas and experiences. You will never live long enough to learn it all on your own.

7. Be prepared to fail your way to success. Nothing works the first time. Resolve to try, and try again. Learn from every mistake, and resolve in advance that you will never give up.

"It is an economic fact that in a competitive marketplace, the effectiveness of marketing is the primary determinant of business success."
—Sonia Rappaport

7

Get the Money You Need

*"You have powers you never dreamed of.
You can do things you never thought you could do.
There are no limitations on what you can do
except the limitations of your own mind."*
—**Darwin P. Kingsley**

There are three main reasons why people never follow their dreams to start their own businesses and achieve the financial independence they desire. The first reason is *fear of failure*, the single biggest reason for failure in adult life.

Fear of failure settles in your solar plexus and paralyzes you, stopping you from even taking the first step. In order to be all you can be, including becoming a millionaire, the first thing you have to learn to do is to confront your fears. You must learn to control your fears, to master your fears, and to act in spite of your fears.

Ignorance Holds You Back

The second major reason for financial underachievement and failure is just plain *ignorance*. Most people do not know how to start and build a business, or how to invest in stocks, bonds, real estate, or other financial vehicles, and for some reason they never bother to learn. They live lives

179

of quiet desperation, admiring others who strike out on their own, but doing nothing themselves. They go to their graves with their music still in them.

Lack of Money

The third reason why people don't start and succeed in their own businesses is perceived *lack of money*. They think that they don't have enough money, and they feel that they cannot get the money they need from other sources.

Most aspiring, would-be entrepreneurs go to their local banks to borrow money to fund their entrepreneurial ideas. When they are repeatedly turned down by the banks, they conclude that there is no money available for them. Having come to this conclusion, they just give up and go back to working for wages.

As it happens, the most valuable assets you have are ambition, energy, imagination, and a burning desire for financial success. If you have these qualities, plus a willingness to work and sacrifice, you will eventually earn, attract, or acquire, all the money you need.

Money Is Available Everywhere

There are several sources of money that you can tap to start and build your own business. In my entrepreneurial career, starting and building businesses over the years, I have used every one of them. Here they are.

Dip into Your Own Savings

First, and usually the most important, is your own personal savings account. In earlier chapters I emphasize how important it is for you to save money. If you cannot discipline yourself to save and accumulate money to get started, you probably do not have the character and discipline to succeed once your business gets going.

Sell Some Assets

You can raise money by the sale of assets. You can sell your house, your car, your motor home, or some of your furniture. You can sell everything that you own. You can cash in your life insurance for its cash value. Sometimes you can sell stocks, bonds, or securities or liquidate your retirement account to get the cash you need to start your own business.

Most people who start a business for the first time end up selling everything they have to get enough money for their own business.

Use Your Credit Cards

Another source of money that you can tap into to start or build your business is credit cards. Many of the most successful U.S. businesses were started by people who took out as many credit cards as possible while they were working and possessed a solid credit rating, and then borrowed against and lived off those credit cards for two or three years until their businesses became profitable.

A friend of mine, working for a Fortune 500 company, worked his credit rating up to $50,000 worth of cash value on his credit cards before he resigned. He was then able to start his business and eventually break through to financial independence on credit card cash.

This is not a great strategy, nor is it a recommendation. Credit card cash is very expensive, sometimes charging 18 percent interest per year. But if it makes the difference between going broke and staying in business long enough to turn the corner, it is an increasingly common way for entrepreneurs to launch their businesses.

Take Out Personal Loans

You can get personal loans. These are loans that are made to you on the basis of your job, your past credit rating, and your character. Sometimes you can get a personal line of credit from the bank, based on your assets. You can then use this line of credit to underwrite your business until you achieve sufficient sales and profitability.

It is essential that you build up a good credit rating and that you maintain that rating. If you are thinking of starting a business in the future, it is a wise idea for you to begin borrowing and repaying loans from your bank so that the bankers become familiar with your trustworthiness.

Banks Like to Make Good Loans
The goal of the loan officer or the bank manager is to make good loans that are paid back promptly, with interest. When you can convince bank officers that you are a dependable borrower, they will loan you all the

money that they feel that you can properly service and repay. But you must have a credit rating to start with.

A friend of mine prided himself on paying for everything in cash. He had no loans and no credit cards and never used banks for financing purchases of any kind. When he decided to start his own business, even though he had accumulated substantial assets and was creditworthy in every respect, no bank would lend him any money because he had no borrowing history.

A basic rule for building up bank credit is to "borrow big and pay back early." If necessary, get someone with a high degree of creditworthiness to co-sign a loan with you; then pay it back well in advance of the due date. After you have done this a couple of times, you will have your own credit rating and you will be able to borrow money without a co-signer. You should go through this exercise of building up your creditworthiness while you have a full-time job, and well before you start your own business.

Borrow against Collateral

You can borrow money by taking out what is called a collateral loan. You can borrow against something you own. You can borrow against your car, your furniture, your boat, or your motor home. You can even borrow against your house. Many businesses have been started by the business owner mortgaging, financing, or borrowing against every single thing he or she owns.

Acquire Love Money

The basic source of most new business financing, probably 99 percent, is what is called "love money." Love money is money that people give or lend to you because they love you. This is money from friends, relatives, business associates, your parents, and so on.

New business start-ups are extremely risky, and banks are not in the business of taking risks. They are in the business of *avoiding* risks. For this reason, very few banks will ever lend to a person starting a business, unless they are convinced that that person has sufficient funds and collateral to repay the loan even if the business is a failure.

The only people who will take a risk with a new business are the people who love you. They will advance you the money because they believe in you and are hoping for the best.

Get a Business Loan

Take out a business loan. Business loans require a liquid asset coverage of at least $2 for every $1 that you wish to borrow. Business loans also require a minimum of one to two years of successful business history. To borrow money for your business, you will need up-to-date financial statements, plus *personal* guarantees that cover everything that you own, or ever will own.

Many people will tell you not to give personal guarantees when you take out a loan for your business. This is silly. Before banks will lend you money for your business, they will want personal guarantees not only from you, but also from your spouse, and often from your parents. Banks are not in the business of taking risks.

Five Factors That Banks Look For

There are five factors that banks look for before making a loan to you, or to any businessperson. These are called the "five C's" of lending or borrowing. You must be prepared to demonstrate all five when you approach a bank for a loan.

1. *Collateral.* First, banks look for collateral. What assets are you going to put up to cover the loan? Collateral is something that can be sold for cash fairly quickly to repay the bank in case your business is not successful.
2. *Character.* Banks look for character. What is your previous track record with regard to loans? What kind of character do you have, in terms of honesty and dependability? Who knows you? Who will vouch for you?
3. *Credit Rating.* Banks look at your current credit rating. How much money have you borrowed and repaid in the past? How good is your credit history today?

   Some years ago, as a small business owner, I made a 20 percent deposit on a new home purchase and applied for a mortgage for the balance. This is usually a standard loan, and easily approved. But a few years before, while I was out of town for several weeks, a credit card bill had arrived in the mail and had not been paid until after the 30-day deadline. This black mark went onto my credit rating and caused my mortgage loan application to be rejected several years later.

   My point is that your credit rating is a very precious thing that follows you wherever you go. I have known many people whose entire adult lives have been ruined because they have been sloppy or indifferent with their credit. They have failed to make credit card payments, car payments, utility payments, or rent payments when they were due. In one or more of these cases, they have been reported to a national credit bureau. This negative credit rating has then dogged them for as long as 10 years, wherever they went, anywhere in the country. Don't let this happen to you.

4. *Capital.* Banks want to know the amount of capital you have. How much of your own money are you willing to invest? This is a measure of how deeply committed you are to the success of the enterprise.

5. *Confidence.* The last factor that banks use to determine whether to lend you money is their level of confidence in you. In the final analysis, the individual banker must have confidence that you are the kind of person who is going to succeed in the business that he or she is lending you money to start or build.

Banking Relationships Mature over Time

Borrowing money from banks is a progressive series of financial transactions that develop over time. When you first attempt to borrow money, most banks will want $5 worth of collateral, personal investments, and other assets for every $1 that they will lend you. They will also want personal guarantees that extend beyond bankruptcy, should you declare it. But after a bank has several years of experience with you and comes to know you and trust you, its lending requirements decline, step by step.

After five years of successfully borrowing and repaying money from the bank, its requirements for cash, collateral, assets, and even personal guarantees will drop off. The bank officers will be content for you to pledge the cash flow and the assets of your business to support the loans that you are taking out from them. At a certain point, they will even come to you and offer to lend you more money to expand your business or to make other investments.

Lease or Rent

Another way that you can finance your business is through leasing. Instead of paying cash for cars, furniture, buildings, or office equipment, you can make monthly payments by renting or leasing them month by month and year by year. This is a prudent way to get started, especially since your sales and cash flow are often unpredictable in the early stages of your business.

During the dot-com boom in Silicon Valley and throughout the United States in the late 1990s, many inexperienced businesspeople were able to raise large quantities of venture capital on the basis of sketchy business plans. They then made the mistake of sinking huge amounts of cash into beautiful office buildings, expensive furniture, imported automobiles, airplanes, and Super Bowl ads. Inevitably, they ran out of cash and were unable to borrow more. As a result, their businesses quickly collapsed, and the investors lost everything. Whenever possible, lease or rent rather than buying.

Bootstrap Your Way to Success

An excellent way to finance and build your business, and one of the most popular and effective strategies in business, is called "bootstrapping." Bootstrapping requires that you start small, generate sales and profits, reinvest your profits back into your business, and then make more sales and repeat the process.

Thousands of men and women who are today millionaires and multimillionaires began with little or no money and built their fortunes one dollar at a time through bootstrapping. Even though you start more slowly with bootstrapping, there are certain distinct advantages of this process that make it superior, in many cases, to starting off with a lot of money.

Develop Creativity and Learn Fast

When you are forced to bootstrap and to build your business slowly, you have to replace money and investment with hard work and creativity. You have to work with what you have, right where you are. Because you have so little money, you cannot afford to make mistakes. This makes you sharper and quicker than people who have the luxury of too much money in the bank to fall back on. Remember what happened to the dot-com millionaires, many of whom are at home living with their parents today.

Many businesses that start with too much money get into trouble quickly because they have not learned how to handle the money. When you bootstrap, you remain conscious and aware of every dollar that comes into or out of your business. You get smarter at a faster rate than other people. As you build your business out of your own sales and cash flow, you are much more likely to create a business that lasts for years.

Use Customer Financing

You can finance your business by using what is called "customer financing." With this method, your customers give you the money that you need to produce the goods and services that you sell to them for the money that they've already paid you in advance.

Ross Perot, who is today a multibillionaire, started EDP Industries with $1,000, borrowed from his mother (love money!). After dozens of sales calls, he finally found one customer who would buy into his idea of handling all of the data management services of the customer's corporation. Perot talked his first customer into paying 50 percent of the fees in advance so that Perot could afford to purchase the computer equipment and deliver the services in the first place. The rest is history.

Request a Deposit

Many businesses will request a 50 percent deposit on an order when they make the sale. With this money, they will then buy the raw materials and pay for the labor to produce the product that they have sold. Their profit is contained in the other 50 percent that they collect upon successful delivery of the product or service.

Get Paid First

Many companies use customer financing to get started. They make the sale and ask the customer to pay for all or part of the order when the order is placed. If this is not possible they get the customer to agree to pay upon delivery of the order, rather than waiting 30, 60, or 90 days. They then take this money and pay their suppliers.

This is called "kiting" and is very common in small businesses. You arrange 30- or 60-day credit terms from your suppliers. You sell the product, get paid for it, and then turn around and pay your supplier before the bill becomes due. In this way, you have no capital of your own tied up. By selling a product, receiving payment, and then paying your supplier, you can actually be in business with little or no cash investment or exposure.

Sell a Subscription

Another way of customer financing is the sale of newsletters, seminars, and subscriptions of any kind. The customers pay for the product or service in advance, prior to delivery. With a subscription, customers pay for the entire year of the product prior to receiving the first issue.

Direct Mail Selling
Direct mail marketing is another form of customer financing. Your up-front investment is in the advertising, but then you take the orders before you fill them and deliver the product. You actually receive the money by cash or credit card before you have to purchase and deliver the product or service. Your customers are actually paying for the business as you go along.

License the Rights
You can use customer financing by licensing the right to manufacture or market a product that you own or control in exchange for a royalty or a fee.

Get a Retainer
You can use customer financing in consulting. Many small businesses start with a person who has expert knowledge in a particular area. He or she goes out and offers his or her services as a consultant on what is called a "retainer basis." On this basis, clients pay you a monthly retainer to work with them for a certain number of days or hours each month. In exchange, they give you progress payments, usually on the first of the month.

    If you are working on a consulting basis for several days or weeks, you can bill the customer as you go along, on a weekly or monthly basis. In this way, the customer finances your operations.

Multilevel Marketing
Multilevel marketing is another way of customer financing. In multilevel marketing, all you require is a sample kit to get started. After demonstrating the samples, you can take orders and collect payment. You can then buy the products from the manufacturer, deliver the orders, and keep the profits.

Factor Your Receivables
Many companies use banks to factor their purchase orders from their customers. Especially if you receive an order from a large company with a good reputation, the purchase order is a guarantee to pay if and when you deliver the product or service that you have sold. Because of the

creditworthiness of your customer, banks will lend you 70 percent or 80 percent of the face value of the purchase order. They will then charge you interest on the loan for carrying the balance between the time that they give you the money and the time at which you collect the money from your customer and repay the bank.

Franchise Your Business

Customer financing is a popular way of raising capital that you see being used around you all the time. For example, franchising is a form of customer financing. The franchisor expands the business by selling the right to use his business system and name in another market area. The franchisee pays a franchise fee that provides the money necessary to support the newly franchised business. McDonald's now has 30,000 franchises worldwide based on this concept of customer financing.

Seek Venture Capital

Some companies are financed by venture capital. This is sophisticated money managed by experienced people that is pooled as high-risk capital to invest in potentially fast-growth companies. This type of money is well known but very hard to get hold of.

Many young entrepreneurs try to raise venture capital to start their businesses. They are absolutely amazed at how difficult this is. Fewer than 1 percent of business proposals received by venture capitalists are ever funded because new businesses are so risky. Fully 99 percent of all business plans and proposals submitted to venture capitalists are eventually thrown in the wastebasket. Venture capitalists are not in the business of losing money for their clients.

Three Requirements for Venture Capital

Venture capitalists will invest in a business today only when it has three things going for it. First, it has to have a proven success record. The business has to have been in operation successfully for at least two years. At this stage, the business owner approaches venture capitalists for money to expand the business to take advantage of larger market opportunities.

Second, the entrepreneur or business owner must submit a complete business plan. A complete business plan may take anywhere from two to six months to produce, and may require from 100 to 300 hours. It may cost anywhere from $25,000 to $50,000 to have it done by an outside consultant. The venture capitalist will not even talk to a person without a complete, detailed business plan that the entrepreneur thoroughly understands and can explain, page for page, number for number.

The third ingredient, and often the most important factor that venture capitalists look for before they will invest in your company, is a competent management team in place. Venture capitalists today look more closely at the experience of the managers of the company than at any other factor when making a decision to lend money.

If for any reason you do not have a proven success record of building and operating a profitable business, plus a complete business plan explaining exactly why you want the money and what you intend to do with it, as well as a competent, proven management team in place, it is better to look for other sources of capital than from venture capitalists.

Consult the Small Business Administration

You can often tap into the Small Business Administration (SBA). The SBA will look at business plans as what is called a "lender of last resort. This means that it will consider your business plan and your loan application only when you have been turned down or rejected by at least two other banks or financial institutions.

The good news is that, because the SBA is a government organization, even if it will not approve your loan, the staff will help you to operate your business more successfully. They will provide you with consulting services at low cost, and sometimes for free. The SBA also has publications, books, pamphlets, and so on that can help you in your marketing, financing, selling, and other aspects of your business. Many small and medium-sized companies have been saved or turned around by the Small Business Administration.

Seek Funding from Small Business Investment Companies

You can sometimes raise money through small business investment companies (SBICs). These are risk groups that put together pools of money to invest in small, up-and-coming companies. They are similar to venture capital groups in that they require some kind of a track record before they will invest with you.

Both venture capital suppliers and small business investment companies will require equity in your company. Very often they will require controlling equity, 51 percent or more of the stock in your business, before they will invest. If you do not perform and generate the profits that you promised, they want to be in a position to take over your company, replace you with competent management, and recover their investment.

Issue a Public Stock Offering

You can raise money for your business with a public stock offering. During the dot-com boom, many companies were going to market, selling stock, and raising large amounts of money even before they had built or sold a single product or service. They were called "prerevenue" companies. This type of investing—going public in advance of having a functioning business—had never happened before, and probably never will happen again.

Normally, a public stock offering requires a record of proven profitability, usually for several years. It requires two to three years of audited financial statements. A public offering is done through a stock brokerage firm, which will handle most of the details and then offer the stock to the public and to their clients.

Price-Earnings Ratios

Going public is one of the fastest ways to become wealthy in the United States. By building a business with a track record of growing earnings, you can sell stock to the public based on a multiple of those earnings. For example, the average price-earnings ratio of companies in the S&P 500 has been about 15:1 for the past 50 years, with fluctuations. This means that if your company is earning $1 million in profit each year, the stock market would value the company at $15 million and you could set your share price based on that valuation.

If purchasers in the stock market believe that your company is going to grow and increase its profitability in the years ahead, they will often pay 20 and 30 times the expected earnings for the stock. During the dot-com boom, companies with no earnings were selling for as much as 300 times projected earnings. Intelligent investors were willing to pay outrageous amounts based on extraordinarily optimistic projections. But those days are gone forever.

Full Disclosure Is Required

You can often make a *private* stock offering to individual investors who will invest in your company without your having to go public. In either case, the investors will require a "due diligence" report on your company. This means that they will require that experts carefully evaluate every word and number in your financial statements and projections, including every detail of your history, to assure themselves that everything you say is absolutely true and verifiable.

The wonderful thing about a *public* stock offering is that it provides a market for your shares in the company. When your company begins to grow and you go public, you can sell 30 percent or 40 percent of its stock into the public market. The public market price will then set a value on the shares of your remaining stock. With this value set by the public market, you can borrow against your own stock, use it for equity financing, and even use your stock to buy other companies.

Obtain Supplier Financing

You can raise cash for your business with what is called "supplier financing." Many companies that supply you with goods and services to sell to your customers will offer you delayed billing, if you ask for it. If you have a good track record and credit rating with your suppliers, they will often be willing to wait 60 or 90 days for payment. This gives you an opportunity to purchase products and services, even raw materials, from your suppliers to produce the goods and services that you have sold to your customers, and then to get paid for them, all before payment is due to your suppliers.

With good credit, a person can start a business, make sales, fulfill the sales, and make profits long before having to pay for the products or services that have already been sold. The ability to do this depends very much on your character, your reputation, your credit rating, and the confidence that your supplier has in you and your ability to pay.

Better Sources of Credit

Here is an important note: Smaller or newer companies are more likely to offer you credit terms than larger companies. Smaller or newer companies are often easier to deal with because they are hungry and are eager for the business.

The key to getting generous credit terms from your suppliers is for you to go and visit them *personally*. Sell the sales or the credit manager and on you and your reason for requiring credit. Take along your financial statement. Show your business plan. Explain what you are doing, and very often your suppliers will extend you credit and help you to build your business.

In a famous story, Victor Kiam purchased Remington Products, a $150 million company, with almost 100 percent financing by the owners. The people who wanted to sell the company structured the deal in such a way that they financed almost the entire purchase. They received their money back later out of the cash flow and profits of the company.

Determinants of Credit

There are two other factors that influence whether you can or should get financing for your business. The first is the type of business or industry you are going into. If you are going into a business that is largely a cash business, it is going to be hard for you to raise long-term financing. Suppliers of capital will expect you to collect and repay them immediately as you sell.

The second factor that will influence whether you can or should get financing is the geographic area that you are operating in. Some parts of the city, county, state, or country are easier places to borrow money for expansion than others.

In some fast-growing areas, banks and other financial institutions are very open to lending you money. In other areas, they will be very cautious and will often not lend you money at all, no matter how good your business plan.

Choosing the Ideal Business for You

What kind of business should you think of going into? The very best way to answer this question is for you to do your homework in advance. According to *Inc.* magazine, the fastest-growing businesses in the United States, by sector, are service businesses of all kinds (47 percent). Twenty-three percent of the fastest-growing businesses are in manufacturing, 15 percent are in distribution, 8 percent are in retail, and 7 percent are in construction.

By industry, 29 percent of the fastest-growing businesses are computer-related or high-tech businesses, 17 percent are in business services, 14 percent are in consumer goods, 8 percent are in construction, 7 percent are in industrial equipment, 4 percent are in publishing and media, 3 percent are in telecommunications, and 3 percent are in medical and pharmaceutical goods. These numbers change each year.

Select a Growth Business in a Growth Area

It is important that you know these percentages because banks and lending officers study them carefully when deciding whether to lend to a particular business.

It is also important that you know these statistics when you decide what kind of a business to go into yourself. Service businesses, computer-related businesses, and business services are the most successful and fastest-growing businesses in the United States. Please note that these percentages are continually changing, so check your local statistics and keep your numbers current.

The percentages of the best and fastest-growing businesses will be different from state to state, from city to city, and from one part of the country to another. The fact is that you can make more progress in a shorter period of time in a rapidly growing industry, in a rapidly growing part of the country, than you could working your entire lifetime in a part of the country or an industry that is declining and losing either population or market share.

The Best Places to Locate

The key variable in determining the fastest-growing and the most prosperous areas to locate is the number of new businesses being started each year in a particular area. The rate of new business formation is the best single indicator of how rapidly an area is growing.

According to economists, 8 to 10 percent of jobs in any given area are lost each year through attrition, layoffs, shutdowns, bankruptcies, mergers, and other reasons. For an area to grow economically, not only must it absorb the 8 to 10 percent of jobs that are being lost each year, but also it must create more jobs in addition because of the new people coming into the workforce.

Fortune magazine says that the best bets for economic growth are metropolitan areas with large concentrations of university graduates, plus a range of lifestyle features that attract creative people. On this basis, some of the fastest-growing metropolitan areas in the United States turn out to be Boston, Palo Alto, Los Angeles, San Diego, Austin, Raleigh-Durham, Atlanta, Miami, and Seattle. These areas have large numbers of well-educated people plus attractive lifestyle features that cause people to want to live there and raise their families.

Lifestyle Is Paramount

Two of the most popular cities in the United States today, for example, are San Diego and Atlanta. This is because of the quality of life that is available in those cities. More and more people are deciding *where* they want to live before they decide what they want to do. Here are the top cities for business development—in order.

Los Angeles. The fastest-growing areas in the United States for the foreseeable future will be cities like Los Angeles. It is now the nation's number one job and population center. It has one of the fastest rates of growth and new job and company creation of any city in the country.

New York/New Jersey. The second most powerful hub for new company and job creation is New York, especially on the fringes of the city, up the Hudson River and across into New Jersey.

Dallas. The third area of rapid growth is Dallas. Dallas has a strongly diversified economy no longer dependent on oil, and is going to be one of the best cities to live in the foreseeable future.

San Diego. The fourth most popular area is San Diego and the greater San Diego area. San Diego has become a magnet for people and new business start-ups, along with having perhaps the best climate and one of most attractive lifestyles in the United States.

Houston. Houston is the fifth most popular city for new business development and population growth in the country. It has become a major center for medical, technology and computer software.

Boston. The sixth fastest-growing area in the United States is Boston and its suburbs. High-tech growth around Boston is largely attributed to its having the nation's largest concentration of universities and educational institutions. There are more universities per capita in the Boston area than in any other metropolitan area in North America.

Atlanta. The seventh fastest-growing U.S. city is Atlanta. It has been growing at a rapid rate for the past 10 years, and it continues to expand. The joke in Atlanta is that the city is always "under construction."

Other Fast-Growth Cities

There are two more cities that are slated for rapid growth, Austin in Texas and Raleigh-Durham in North Carolina. Both of these cities are close to universities. They are enjoying steady population growth. The large number of new business start-ups means there is rapid job growth in the area.

Even though they are smaller in population, the two fastest-growing areas in the United States today (2004) are San Bernardino/Riverside, California, and Las Vegas, Nevada. Businesses are starting up in these cities at a rapid rate, thousands of new jobs are being created, and real estate development is exploding. This is likely to continue for many years.

In any one of these cities, if you have the desire and the determination behind an idea to fill a need, you can and will find the money you need to get started. You can start small and grow your business as you accumulate experience and cash flow.

You Can Start Today

You can start by borrowing on your credit cards, your life insurance, and your personal possessions. You can borrow from your friends and relatives. You can even borrow from your current employer or your future customers. You can save your money through hard work and sacrifice to build up a nest egg. You can take the extra time to study and learn more about your business. Thousands of the most successful businesses were started on a shoestring, often in a garage, with the major investment being the time and energy of the founder.

Whatever others have done before, within reason, you can do as well, starting today. The only questions you have to answer are, "How badly do you want it?" and "Are you willing to pay the price?" If you want to start and build your own successful business long enough and hard enough, and you are willing to pay the price in advance to achieve success, nothing will stop you as long as you refuse to make excuses for not moving ahead.

Action Exercises

1. Determine exactly how much money you will need to start and build your own successful business, to launch new products, and to expand your operations. You must be clear and accurate.

2. Decide on one or more methods of financing your business and begin using the magic word for business success, "ask." Remember, before you ask, the answer is "no." You have nothing to lose.

3. Begin today to clean up your credit rating and put your financial affairs in order. This can benefit you all the years of your business life.

4. Begin building up a solid credit rating by borrowing and repaying early. Visit and get to know your bank manager. Build your reputation for character and competence.

5. Bootstrap your way to financial success by starting right where you are and growing out of your sales and profits.

6. Think continually in terms of revenue generation—of making sales, delivering what you have sold, and getting paid for it quickly.

7. Keep accurate financial accounts and records of every cost and transaction. Hire an accountant or bookkeeper, full-time or part-time. Stay on top of the numbers. Never leave them to chance.

"There are ways that lead to everything,
and if we have sufficient will
we shall always have sufficient means."
—François de la Rochefoucauld

Think and Grow Rich

*"Because its purpose is to create a customer, the
business has two—and only these two—basic
functions: marketing and innovation. Marketing
and innovation produce results; all the rest are "costs."*
—Peter Drucker

You have probably heard it said many times that the way to become
wealthy is to "work hard and save your money." This is partially true and
partially false. There are a lot of people who are hardworking and frugal,
but they are just getting by.

Nonetheless, there is some truth to this rule as well. Hard work
is extremely important, as is the necessity to save and nurture your
capital. However, the sad fact is that you cannot become wealthy by
simply working longer, harder hours. You must work *smarter* as well.
You must learn to tap into your creative capacities, into the 90 percent
of your mental abilities that resides in your subconscious and *super-
conscious* minds.

There is a direct relationship between how much of your creativity
you use and how wealthy you become. All you need is one good idea to
start you off on the road to a fortune.

In this chapter, you will learn why creativity is so important to success, some of the blocks to creativity that you need to remove, and several ways to stimulate your creativity on a daily basis. You will learn

some key questions you can ask to test the worth of your new ideas, and how to develop the qualities of genius.

You Are a Potential Genius

My many years of studying intelligence and teaching creativity have convinced me that each person has the seed of genius lying within him or her. You have a creative imagination that you can tap into to bring you everything you could ever really want in life. Your job is to learn how to access this mental storehouse of ideas.

Your goal is to learn how to use your creative mind to *achieve* any goal, *overcome* any obstacle, and *solve* every problem on the path to becoming a self-made millionaire. If you want financial success badly enough and you are willing to work hard enough, nothing can stop you. Your mind will show you the way.

Why Creativity Is So Important

There are three main reasons why creativity is important in building your fortune. First, solving problems and making decisions are the key functions of the entrepreneur. As much as 50 percent to 60 percent of your time in business and in life is spent solving problems of some kind. The better you become at thinking up creative ways to solve the inevitable and unavoidable problems of daily life and work, and making effective decisions, the more successful you will be.

Second, each of us wants to make more money. We all want to be more successful and enjoy greater status, esteem, and recognition. Your problem-solving ability is a key determinant of how much money you earn and how successful you become.

Third, you can earn more only by producing more. You can become wealthy only by doing things faster, better, or cheaper and by becoming more productive. You can move to the top only by performing higher-value tasks, and this requires that you use more of your intelligence and creativity.

Use More of Your Intelligence

Most people function with very little creativity at all. The average person has enormous reserves of intelligence that he or she habitually fails to use.

You have heard that people on average use less than 10 percent of their brainpower, and therefore their mental potential. According to the Stanford Brain Institute, the amount is actually closer to 2 percent. This small quantity is usually spent on day-to-day activities, doing the same things in the same old way, watching television, and generally performing far below one's potential.

The average person therefore has 90 percent or more of their potential in reserve, *unused*. When you learn how to tap into that enormous reserve capacity, you will be able to do anything you really want in life. You will begin to perform at genius levels.

Multiply Your Results

By sharpening your thinking skills and exercising your natural creative powers, you can multiply the value of your efforts and increase the quantity of your rewards. You can make yourself more valuable in everything you do. You can accomplish far more in a shorter period of time.

Fortunately, creativity is a skill that can be *learned* and that can dramatically accelerate your personal and professional development and growth. Like playing a sport or musical instrument, your creative ability can be improved with practice. You can actually make yourself smarter and more mentally agile by doing certain things in a certain way, as you will learn in the pages ahead.

As Within, So Without

Everything you are, or ever will be, is the direct result of the way you think. Your outer world is a reflection of your inner world (the law of correspondence). If you improve the quality of your thinking, you must very quickly improve the quality of your life. There is no other sure way of achieving your goals. And there are no limits except the limits you impose on yourself with your own doubts about how smart you really are.

Stimulate Your Thinking

Physically, there are foods that are better for you than others, in that they give you greater health, vitality, and energy. In the same way, there are *mental* foods as well that stimulate your thinking and enable you to make better decisions, get better results, and achieve your goals of wealth and financial independence faster and easier. Just as with physical exercise, the more of these mental exercises you practice, the sharper and more alert you become. You will release more of your natural creativity and trigger better insights and ideas to achieve your financial goals.

Think Positively

The first stimulant to creativity is a positive mental attitude. It is a decision in advance to look on the bright side of every situation. This is why a positive mental attitude has been well defined as a "constructive response to stress."

The most creative people tend to be *optimists*. Most of the time they think and talk about what they want and the steps they can take to achieve their goals. They look for the good in every situation. They look for the valuable lesson in every setback or difficulty. They confidently expect to gain something from every problem or disappointment.

Thinking positively is very much a choice you make. And the payoff is extraordinary. As you develop the habit of positive thinking, you will experience higher levels of self-confidence and self-assurance. The more positive you become toward yourself and your future, the more willing you will be to try new and different things, and even to sound or appear foolish.

Resolve today to become a *possibility thinker* in your own life. Think in terms of "I can" rather than "I can't." Think continually about all the different ways that your goals can be achieved, rather than thinking about the obstacles and problems that may be holding you back right now.

Set Clear Goals and Objectives

Think on paper. Sit down and write out clear goals and objectives to which you are committed. Nothing stimulates your creativity more rapidly and predictably then your making a clear decision about exactly what you want and then making a plan to achieve it.

Remember, you become what you think about most of the time. Think about your goals continually. Dwell upon them throughout the day. Think about them the last thing before you go to sleep at night and first thing when you wake up in the morning.

The very act of thinking about your goals and how you might achieve them makes you a more positive and creative person. The more often you think about your goals, the more often you activate your subconscious and conscious minds to bring you ideas and insights, and the energy necessary to implement them. Thinking about your goals activates the law of attraction, and begins attracting into your life people and circumstances that can help you achieve them in ways that you cannot even imagine today. By thinking about your goals, you turn your mind into a force field of energy in the universe that draws you toward your goals, and draws your goals toward you.

Stimulate Your Curiosity

Develop a questioning, curious attitude toward your life and work. One of the hallmarks of intelligence is curiosity, and curiosity often leads to innovative approaches to solving problems and achieving goals. Whatever you are doing, don't be afraid to ask questions about what is being done, and *why*. Asking why or why not, and how things work, not only increases your knowledge, but also gives you insights and ideas that you can use to improve the situation. Whenever you see a customer need unmet or a problem unsolved, ask as many questions as you can to find out why this situation is occurring.

Asking questions about what is going on around you can give you information and insights that can lead to ideas for new products and services, new businesses, and maybe even the beginning of your fortune.

Stimulate Your Mind

Feed yourself on a stimulating mental diet. Continually bombard your mind with books, courses, audio programs, different magazines, seminars, people, and alternate forms of information. The more you stimulate your mind with new and different ideas, people, and viewpoints, the more likely you are to come up with ideas that will lead to solving your problems and overcoming your obstacles.

There seems to be a direct relationship between the number of new ideas you expose yourself to and the likelihood that you will come across exactly the right idea at exactly the right time for you.

Most new ideas don't work, at least not in their original form. But sometimes when two or more ideas are combined, a breakthrough occurs that can change your financial life. Keep your mind open at all times.

Practice Creative Visualization

A wonderful way to stimulate your thinking and release the genius within you is to continually imagine and visualize your goal as if it were already achieved. The greater clarity you can create in your mind of the goal that you desire, the more you will come up with ideas to help make your goal a reality. In addition, once you are clear about exactly what it is you want, create clear mental pictures of yourself actually doing those things that you will have to do to achieve the goal.

If you need to make a sales presentation, negotiate a loan, or gain the cooperation or assistance of someone else, practice "mental rehearsal." Just as if you were trying out for a stage play, rehearse the upcoming event in your mind. Go through the entire meeting or presentation mentally, from beginning to end, and imagine every detail in the situation. Visualize and see yourself as calm, confident, and relaxed. See the other person responding to you in a positive, open, and helpful way. Replay this scene over and over until you feel comfortable and confident about your ability to perform at your best. This is an effective way of stimulating your creativity.

Learn to Laugh at Yourself

One of the best ways to remain positive and creative is for you to develop a sense of humor about yourself and your life. The greater your sense of humor, the more ideas you will have. Make it a habit not only to look on the bright side, but also to see the funny side of people, situations, and experiences. Don't take yourself too seriously.

How much you laugh, your sense of humor, and how creative you are are all directly related. Each time you laugh, you release endorphins and dopamines in your brain, which simulate your creativity and give you a greater sense of well-being. People who laugh a lot tend to be far more creative than people who do not.

When we take business groups through brainstorming exercises, we encourage them to come up with the most ridiculous ideas possible. Everyone can laugh or comment, but no one is allowed to criticize or ridicule. Often, the best solutions to complex problems emerge as the result of a group of people laughing together and throwing ridiculous ideas onto the table. The more people laugh together, the better seems to be the quality and quantity of ideas they come up with.

Get Physically Active

A great way to trigger creativity is through vigorous physical exercise. When you engage in aerobic exercises, such as running, cycling, or swimming, or any other activity that increases your heart rate and makes you perspire, you accelerate the flow of highly oxygenated blood to your brain. After 20 to 25 minutes of vigorous exercise, you begin to experience the "exercise effect." Your brain releases endorphins, which give you a heightened feeling of self-awareness, increase your intelligence, and make you feel happier and more relaxed.

In study after study, researchers have found that people who exercise aerobically in the morning are more creative and intelligent all day long than people who do not. They are brighter, sharper, and more alert. They grasp new information faster and have better memories. They even get better grades on standardized tests. Their IQs actually improve.

The fitter and healthier you are as the result of daily exercise, the brighter and sharper you will be in solving problems, making decisions, and coming up with creative, innovative solutions to help you achieve your goals. Vigorous physical fitness can give you the winning edge in business and in life.

Practice Intense Concentration

An excellent way to improve your creativity is by the deliberate practice of intense concentration. Your mind is like a muscle. When you work out *physically* with weights, you pump large amounts of blood into your muscles, which causes them to grow and become stronger. When you work out *mentally*, you drive large amounts of blood into your brain, stimulating the growth and activation of additional neurons, ganglia, and dendrites.

The key to activating more of your mental powers through concentration is for you to focus intently on one thing at a time. You can concentrate on information gathering—for example, on assembling every bit of data available on a particular problem or project. This will often generate insights, ideas, and solutions. You can concentrate on formulating the problem clearly and on defining it in several different ways. This exercise can lead to new approaches and different ways of solving it. You can concentrate on generating multiple solutions to a single problem, rather than settling for the first idea you come up with.

The more you concentrate, the smarter you become. The more you concentrate, the more of your intelligence becomes available to you. The more you concentrate, the more and better creative solutions you discover.

Expect the Best

Another way to stimulate your creativity is to develop an attitude of positive expectancy or confident expectations. The more confidently you expect to be successful and to get the results you desire, the more optimistic and cheerful you will be. When you confidently expect that there is an ideal solution or answer to any problem you face, you will almost always find it.

The most creative people make it a habit to approach any problem with a confident belief that there is a logical, workable solution just waiting to be found. No matter how many difficulties they experience, they proceed as if a successful outcome was preordained. They remain calm, positive, and cheerful. Surprisingly enough, this attitude almost always enables them to find a solution, to find something good in every problem, or to learn a valuable lesson from every difficulty.

Take Charge of Your Life

One of the most important keys to stimulating creativity is the acceptance of 100 percent responsibility for yourself and for the problem, whatever it is. Whenever you have a difficulty of any kind, immediately seize *mental* control of the situation by saying, "I am responsible." When you accept responsibility, you immediately take control over your mind and the situation. With this sense of control, your self-confidence and self-esteem will increase. You will feel more powerful and confident. You will feel more capable of making the right decisions and taking the right actions. Most of all, you will activate your higher mental powers and use more of your creative faculties.

The root cause of almost all negative emotions is the tendency that many people have to *blame others* for their problems, both past and present. Unfortunately, when you blame another person you unwittingly position yourself as a victim. Instead of feeling powerful and capable of dealing with whatever life throws at you, the act of blaming someone else for a problem or difficulty makes you feel angry and powerless. The best parts of your brain shut down, and all your emotions become channeled toward rationalizing and justifying your negative feelings.

But when you accept complete responsibility for achieving a goal or solving a problem, you immediately feel stronger and more confident. You switch from anger and negativity to optimism and positive thinking. The instant that you accept responsibility for your situation, your creative mind goes to work to generate insights and ideas you can use to solve the problem or improve the situation.

Develop a Burning Desire

The final key to stimulating your creativity is the quality of desire. You must have a burning desire to achieve a particular goal as well as an intense desire to realize your full potential as a person. You must really want to become everything that you are capable of becoming.

Ambition is the driving force that causes you to strive continually toward being all you can be. With sufficient ambition and a burning desire, you can break out of your comfort zone, take risks, and move forward. The more ambitious you are, the more likely it is that you will generate the creative breakthrough ideas you need to achieve all your goals.

The Qualities of Genius

Geniuses have been studied throughout the ages, going back to thousands of years. In analyzing the lives and activities of the great thinkers of the ages, researchers have concluded that geniuses seem to have three qualities in common. Each of these qualities is a habitual way of thinking or dealing with the world that you can learn by practice and repetition. As you do, you actually become *smarter*.

Many people are convinced that genius is a matter of IQ, usually demonstrated in the ability to earn good grades in school. However, there are countless stories of people who did poorly in school or who failed to score very high on conventional IQ tests, who nonetheless performed at genius levels later in life. Genius is not a matter of good grades or high test scores. It is instead reflected in your *way of acting*. If you act intelligently, you show you are smart. If you act stupidly, you are stupid, irrespective of your IQ or your academic record.

It turns out that many of the great creative geniuses of history had only average or slightly above-average IQs, but they used them in an outstanding fashion.

As mentioned, there are three ways of acting that all geniuses seem to have in common. Each of these ways increases your intelligence and creativity, and makes you more effective in getting the results that are most important to you.

Learn to Concentrate Single-Mindedly

First, geniuses have developed the ability to concentrate single-mindedly on *one thing at a time*. The ability to concentrate on a single task seems to go hand in hand with success in any field of endeavor. Every great accomplishment was preceded by a long period of sustained concentration, sometimes for many months, and even years, before the achievement was realized.

When we dealt with the subject of "mastery" a little earlier in this book, I made the point that it takes five to seven years for a person to master a craft or profession. It takes five to seven years to become a good neurosurgeon or a top salesperson. It takes many years of concentrated, focused effort, dedicated to becoming the best in your field, for you to achieve the greatness of which you are capable.

Geniuses have the ability to concentrate on one thing, the most important thing, and persevere without diversion or distraction for as long as it takes to achieve their goal.

A brilliant person who cannot concentrate, or who tries to do too many things at once and does none of them well, will fail miserably over time. An average person who concentrates on one goal or result, and who brings all his or her energy to bear on that one point until it is accomplished, will run circles around a person who cannot.

Take a Systematic Approach

The second characteristic of genius identified by the researchers is that they all seem to use *systematic* approaches to solving problems, investigating questions, and making decisions. Especially, geniuses think on paper. No matter how smart they are, they write everything down so they can see it in front of them. This habit of writing things out in detail enables them to think in far more complex forms and in greater detail, and to come up with better and more workable ideas in a shorter period of time.

All successful people think on paper. They are continually writing and rewriting, planning and replanning. The very act of thinking on paper makes you a sharper and more creative thinker. The habit of thinking on paper makes you more effective at whatever you do. When you gather information, take notes that you can compare with other notes, and write down your ideas, your mind functions with greater precision and clarity then if you try to hold thoughts and information in your mind.

Solving Problems Systematically

An effective way of problem solving and decision making consists of the following seven steps:

Step 1. Define the problem clearly in writing. What exactly are you trying to achieve, avoid, or preserve? What is holding you back? What else might be the problem? Accurate diagnosis is half the cure.

Step 2. Make a list of all the possible *causes* of this problem or difficulty. How did it occur? When did it occur? Where did it occur? Who was involved? Investigate the problem thoroughly before you begin seeking the solution.

Step 3. Identify all the possible *solutions* to the problem. What are all the different things that you could do to solve this problem? What else is a solution? What if you did nothing at all?

Step 4. Select what appears to be the very *best solution* to the problem *at the moment*. Don't strive for perfection. Sometimes a half-solution implemented immediately is better than a more complex solution that may or may not be implemented at a later time.

Step 5. Assign *responsibility* for the problem to a specific person. Who exactly is going to implement the solution?

Step 6. Determine how you will *measure* the success of the solution. How will you know that the solution has been effective? What measures or standards will you apply?

Step 7. Set a specific *deadline* for the implementation of this solution and the achievement of the goal. Set subdeadlines if necessary. At the deadline, evaluate progress and make whatever decisions are necessary to keep moving toward a solution.

Any systematic method of problem solving is better than no method at all. In every area of specialization, there are established, systematic methods of solving the problems and achieving the goals in that area. The more problem-solving methodologies you are familiar with, the faster and easier it will be to come up with excellent solutions that bring the results you desire.

Keep an Open Mind

The third characteristic of geniuses throughout the ages is their ability to keep an open mind on any subject. Open-mindedness requires flexibility in your approach to the problem. This requires the willingness to look at any subject or problem in a variety of different ways.

Mechanical Thinking

Studies conducted over the years have divided people into two categories based on the way they think. The first group, mechanical thinkers, are those who tend to be rigid and inflexible in their thinking. Once they decide on a particular course of action or embrace a particular idea, you cannot get them to change or to consider another approach.

Mechanical thinkers tend to be fearful, doubtful, and insecure. They are afraid that any suggestions that their preferred method of thinking and acting is not the best are a threat to them. They have low self-esteem and low levels of self-confidence. They cling to their tried-and-true ways and become anxious at the thought of trying something new or different.

Adaptive Thinking

The second type of thinkers are adaptive thinkers. These people remain open-minded, flexible, and curious when facing a new problem or difficulty of any kind. Adaptive thinkers work to keep the question open as long as possible, avoiding the natural tendency to jump to conclusions or close off discussion and debate.

Adaptive thinkers believe that every question remains open to new information. They are always willing to consider different possibilities.

From this day forward, you should practice being an adaptive thinker. Keep your mind open and flexible toward any problem or difficulty that you are facing. Always begin with the assumption that there may be a better way to do it, or a better solution to the problem.

Einstein once said, "Every child is born a genius." Probably 95 percent of children test out as highly creative up to the age of five. You are born with the ability for unconventional thinking and abstract thoughts. You have a natural creative capacity to see the world in new, novel, and imaginative ways. When you tap into your inner genius, you will tap into a deep wellspring of ideas that can help you solve every problem you face, and achieve any goal that you set for yourself.

Thinking More Creatively

Three primary ways to stimulate creative thinking are to have intensely desired goals, pressing problems, and focused questions. You should use all three regularly and consistently to generate the ideas that you need to achieve your goals.

Intensely Desired Goals

Intensely desired goals are things you really want and for which you have a burning desire. The more emotionally committed and intense you are about wanting to achieve a particular goal, the more your subconscious mind will bring you ideas and insights necessary to make it a reality.

Many people set goals for themselves because they think other people want them to achieve these goals. But if your goals are not personal they will have little motivational force or power. This is why it is so important that the goals you set for yourself are things that you personally want to achieve.

Pressing Problems

Pressing problems, clearly defined, with specific benefits for solving them, are powerful ways to stimulate your creativity. The more clarity you have regarding the specific problems and obstacles that are holding you back, the more and better ideas that you will trigger to help you to solve them.

Focused Questions

Focused questions that penetrate to the heart of a situation or matter often trigger insights and ideas that lead to breakthroughs in your life or work. "Why are we doing it this way?" "Could there be a better way?" "What are our assumptions in this situation?" "What if our assumptions are wrong?" The more questions you ask about your goal or situation, the more often you will trigger ideas to move forward.

Ways to Get Rich Your Own Way

Here are different ways for you to achieve financial independence.

Keep an Idea Log

Buy a spiral notebook. Carry it with you if you possibly can, and write down every idea that comes to you throughout the day.

Review this idea log on a regular basis. Sometimes, one idea that you have while you are driving along, sitting, reading, watching television, or in a conversation may be the insight that will lead to the start of your fortune.

The rule is, "Catch the idea and write it down." If you don't write it down quickly, you will very often lose it. As the Chinese say, "The palest ink is stronger than the finest memory."

Relax and Reflect

Take regular time-outs to relax and reflect on your goals and the obstacles that are holding you back from achieving them. During these times of relaxation, ideas will often pop into your mind that can save you hours, days, or sometimes years of hard work.

One of the very best creative thinking exercises of all is to practice solitude on a regular basis. This is often called "going into the silence." You sit down quietly for 30 to 60 minutes, with no distractions, and just let your mind flow freely.

In solitude, you deliberately let your mind float. Don't worry about concentrating or thinking about any particular goal or problem. Just relax. While you are sitting there quietly, very often wonderful insights and ideas will come into your mind.

Magic Wand Technique

Practice the exercise of *fantasizing* on a regular basis. Sometimes this is called the "magic wand technique." Imagine that you have a magic wand and you can wave it over your current situation or problem. Imagine that as a result of waving this magic wand all the obstacles are removed from between you and your goal.

What would your situation look like if you had already achieved your goal? What would it look like if you were already there? See yourself as already wealthy. See yourself as already healthy and happy, and living the kind of life you desire. Imagine that your life is ideal in every respect. Describe it on paper.

Here is the key question: "What would have to happen for you to be able to create your ideal lifestyle?" What would be the first step that you would have to take, right now? What would be the second step? What would be the process you would need to go through to create the perfect life that you desire?

Project Forward and Think Back

Imagine that your goal is to build a successful business in a particular field. Project forward three to five years and imagine that you now have a successful business in that field. What would it look like? How big would it be? What kind of people would you be working with? What kind of a reputation would you have in the marketplace? What would be your level of sales and profitability? How would you be running this business? And especially, what could you start doing right now to make this future dream a reality?

Complete the Sentence

Here is a creative thinking exercise you can practice called sentence completion. This is a powerful way to stimulate ideas and insights that you can use immediately to achieve your goals faster and more easily.

In sentence completion, you create a partial sentence and then you think of as many different ways as possible to complete it.

For example, you could say, "We could double our sales over the next 12 months if we . . ." and complete the sentence. Or you could say, "We could double our profits over the next 12 months if we . . ." and complete the sentence.

Sometimes you can do this with a group of people. You can each contribute ideas and ways to finish the sentence. This form of group problem solving often triggers remarkable thoughts and insights.

Generate Personal Answers

On a personal level, you could begin with a sentence, "I could double my income over the next 12 months if I . . ." and complete the sentence with 10 or 20 different answers or ways to double your income. The first time you do this, you might be amazed at the results you get.

Here are some examples of questions that you could complete that might bring you answers that would change your life:

- "I could achieve my goal if I . . ."
- "I could start a business immediately if I . . ."
- "I could turn my business into a success if I . . ."
- "I could solve this problem completely if I . . ."
- "I could get the money I need if I . . ."

You can create a sentence completion exercise for any problem or goal that you are dealing with. Remember, the *quality* of the ideas you generate will be in direct proportion to the *quantity* of ideas you come up with. The more time that you spend generating constructive solutions to your problems and goals, the more ideas will come to you throughout the day.

Practice "Mindstorming" on Every Problem

Perhaps the most powerful method of stimulating creative thinking is called "mindstorming," or the 20-idea method. More people have become wealthy, including myself, using this idea than any other method of creative thinking ever discovered. In fact, if all you learned from this book was this simple method and you applied it consistently, this technique alone could enable you to get rich your own way.

The method is simple. Take any problem or goal that you have and write it at the top of a sheet of paper in the form of a question. For example, if your goal is to double your income over the next 12 months, then you would write, "How can I double my income over the next 12 months?"

You then discipline yourself to write at least 20 answers to that question. You can write more than 20 answers if you like, but you must use your discipline and willpower to write at least 20 answers.

Everything Is Hard Before It Is Easy

You will find that the first three to five answers are fairly easy. The next three to five answers will be harder. But the last several answers will be excruciatingly difficult. Often, your mind will go blank. You will sit there looking at the paper and be completely unable to think of any more answers to the question.

But the good news is that if you force yourself to stay there until you have written out at least 20 answers, your creative juices will begin to flow. One by one, new ideas will pop into your mind and appear on the paper in front of you. And surprisingly enough, it is often the very last answer, the twentieth answer on the page, that is the breakthrough idea that changes the whole direction of your life or work.

From this day forward, whenever you have a question or a problem of any kind, write at the top of the page in the form of a question and discipline yourself to generate at least 20 answers to that question. Do this with every goal you have. Do it with every problem. Do it with every obstacle or difficulty you face. Make the completion of this exercise as normal and natural to you as breathing or brushing your teeth.

The quality and quantity of ideas that you will generate using this mindstorming method will astonish you. And the more often you practice it, the brighter, sharper, and more creative you will become.

If you perform this exercise first thing in the morning, just after writing out your goals, your mind will sparkle with ideas all day long. In every situation, your mind will dance with new ideas and ways to achieve your goals and solve your problems. Soon, people will be bringing you their problems and asking for your ideas. Sometimes you will have more ideas than you can implement, or than other people can handle.

Brainstorm Your Way to Riches

A powerful and popular method for generating creative ideas is called "masterminding," or brainstorming. This incredible method involves sitting down with a group of other people in a spirit of harmony to generate ideas to achieve your goals or solve your problems. When a group of people get together to focus all their minds on a single problem or question, the quality and quantity of answers that emerge can be absolutely amazing.

The key to effective brainstorming is for you to mutually agree on the definition of a problem or question in advance. Write it out on a whiteboard or a flip chart. Make sure everyone knows exactly what the group is going to be focusing on and talking about.

Give yourself a specific time limit, between 15 and 45 minutes. Agree in advance that there will be no ridicule, criticism, or evaluation. The aim is to generate as many answers to the brainstorming question as possible in the amount of time you have. You are racing against the clock.

We conducted brainstorming exercises for a Fortune 500 company a few years ago. The group consisted of senior managers, middlemanagers, several secretaries, and personal assistants. They each sat in their own groups at round tables. We then gave them a common question and encouraged them to compete against each other to see which table could generate the greatest number of ideas to the brainstorming question.

At the end of 20 minutes, we stopped the exercise and counted up the answers. The average number of answers per table made up of senior and midlevel executives was 52 solutions. But the biggest surprise was that the table consisting of five secretaries had generated 177 ideas, many of which were quite good. In a brainstorming session, you can never tell where the great ideas and insights will come from.

Ask "What If?" Questions

You can use the technique of hypothesizing to stimulate your creativity. In the use of hypothesizing, you simply throw off all restraints and ask "what if?" questions. You ask questions such as, "What if we did it this way, or stopped doing it altogether?" You ask "Why?" questions, such as, "Why are we doing it this way?" or "If we weren't doing it this way, would we start this up again?" Remember, most people get into a comfort zone and continue doing things the same way over and over, without ever asking the question, "Could there be a better way?"

Improve Your Personal Life

You can use this method of hypothesizing in your personal life. Write out a clear description of your ideal lifestyle. Describe your ideal work environment. Describe your ideal job or your ideal position. Describe your ideal income and your ideal relationship with the members of your family. Then begin asking yourself why you are doing certain things, and why you aren't doing other things. What if you did things completely differently, or stopped doing things that you have been doing for a long time?

Here is an exercise that I have given to many of my students. I simply say, "If you are not happy with any part of your life, take a few minutes to write out the exact kind of situation with which you would be the happiest."

Once you sit down and begin writing out a clear description of your perfect life and work sometime in the future, you then begin asking questions like, "Why aren't I enjoying this work or this job or lifestyle already?"

You can ask, "What changes do I have to make to begin making my current situation more like my ideal situation?" "What would have to happen for me to start moving closer to creating the kind of life that I desire?"

Clarity Is Essential

The primary reason that people do not accomplish the things they want in life is because they are not even clear about what these things are. If you ask an unhappy person to describe his or her ideal lifestyle, in most cases, the person has no idea. This is the main reason he or she never achieves it.

What would be your ideal lifestyle? What would be your ideal work or business? If you could do anything you want, live anywhere you want, work with whomever you want, or work in whatever kind of occupation, what would they be? What would you have to do, starting today, to make these dreams and goals a reality?

Visualize your ideal goals in as much detail as possible, as though they were already a reality. The act of visualization not only triggers creative thinking, but it activates the law of attraction and starts drawing into your life the people, circumstances, ideas, and opportunities that help to make it a reality.

Project yourself forward into the future as though you were already doing what you want to do and living the life you want to live. Then look back to the present day and from that vantage point, and imagine the steps that you can take, starting today, to reach your ideals.

Project yourself forward three years. Then return to the present and ask, "What would I have done to get from where I am in the moment to where I want to be three years from today?" List every step that you can think of that you can take to begin moving in that direction. Organize the list by priority and select the first thing that you can do. Then, discipline yourself to take that one action immediately. A journey of a thousand miles begins with a single step.

Evaluating Your Ideas

Once you have generated a variety of ideas that you can use to solve your problems and achieve your goals, the next step is for you to evaluate them before you commit time, money, and energy to implementing them. You have to sit down and look at the ideas you have come up with and sort them out, choosing the good ones and discarding the poor ones.

Most ideas are not practical or worthwhile, at least in their original form. Ideas themselves are a dime a dozen. That is why we put an emphasis on continuous creativity, and on generating a large quantity of ideas. Most of them won't work.

Ideas Can Be of No Value

Once you have come up with an idea that you consider valuable, here are three things to keep in mind. First, ideas in and of themselves have no value. They are only the start of the creative process. As Thomas Edison said, "Genius is 1 percent inspiration and 99 percent perspiration." Once you have come up with a good idea, now the real work begins.

Remain Objective

Second, remain objective with regard to your ideas. Ask other knowledgeable people for their opinions of your idea and listen with an open mind. Don't make the mistake of falling in love with the idea just because it is yours and then spend all of your energy defending it. Be prepared to accept the possibility that your idea, no matter how much you like it, may not be workable.

Let Them Cool

Third, let your ideas cool for a while before you launch them. Sometimes an idea that seems brilliant to you today will have lost most of its allure or attractiveness after three days. Practice solitude and reflection. Go and sit quietly for an hour and turn the idea over in your mind. Try to look at it calmly and unemotionally. Be patient. Fast business decisions are often wrong business decisions.

Ask the Right Questions

Here are some questions you can ask to determine whether your idea is a good one:

- Is it effective?
- Would it work?
- Will it do the job?
- Is it good enough to make a meaningful difference?
- Is it efficient?
- Is it an improvement over what people are currently using?
- Can people use it without having to radically alter their behavior?

There is no point in investing in an idea that is not a significant improvement over what is already being done. In addition, a key problem that many entrepreneurs have is that they think customers will change their behavior to use a new product or service just because it is better or cheaper. This is seldom the case.

How People Buy

Not long ago, there were entrepreneurs who were predicting that in the near future everyone would be doing grocery shopping by Internet, television, or telephone. But there are very few people who buy groceries this way. Why is that? It is because people actually enjoy going to the grocery store and personally viewing the various foods that are available before buying them. They would have to radically alter their behavior and cut out the visual pleasure of shopping to order by telephone or Internet.

If a new product or service will cause or require a major change in the way people do things, in their buying habits, it will seldom be successful.

How Badly Do You Want It?

Here is another question: Is this idea compatible with *your* goals? How badly do you want to try it? Many times, you will come up with an idea that may be in a field that doesn't interest you. Can you develop a passion for this idea or for this product or service? Remember, any business that you start is an extension of your personality. It is an extension of your beliefs, your goals, your character, and your ambitions. Therefore, the idea is only good if you can get excited about it, and then get a lot of other people excited about it as well.

Ask the Key Questions

Here are some additional questions you must ask before you launch a new idea:

- Is the timing right?
- Is it practical now?
- Will it be practical when it is implemented?
- Is the idea feasible?
- Can it be done?
- If it can be done, is it worth doing?
- Is it simple?

This last question is often the most important question of all. Simplicity is vital to successful innovation. All successful new ideas are basically quite simple. If it is not simple, it probably won't be successful. It must be simple to explain, simple to sell, simple to understand, and simple to use. The more steps it has, the more complicated it becomes and the less likely it will succeed.

Perhaps the most important point of all is to remember that, for every obstacle or problem that stands between you and your goal of wealth and financial independence, there is a solution of some kind waiting to be found. Your success in life will be in direct proportion to how well you use your creative imagination to achieve your goals and solve your problems. Fortunately, your imagination is like a muscle that grows in capability as it is used and exercised. The more of your creative resources you tap into, the smarter, sharper, more alert and intelligent you become. Get busy. Start using your creative imagination today.

Action Exercises

1. Focused questions stimulate your mind and provoke your creativity. Decide on a goal and then ask yourself, "Why am I not at this goal already?" What is the main reason?

2. Identify the biggest obstacle between yourself and your goal of financial independence. Practice mindstorming on this problem by phrasing it as a question and then developing 20 answers to that question.

3. Take a product or service that you want to offer or that you are having trouble selling, and analyze it by asking some of the questions listed in this chapter. Be sure that your product or service is workable, salable, and profitable.

4. Practice brainstorming with your coworkers and family. Agree on the definition of a problem or obstacle and then challenge yourselves to generate as many different ways of solving it as possible in 15 to 45 minutes.

5. Practice solitude on a regular basis. Go and sit quietly and let your mind float and relax. Be open to flashes of intuition that give you the insights and ideas to achieve your goals.

6. Imagine that you could be completely wrong in your approach to a particular problem or in the way that you are pursuing a goal. If you were wrong, what other course of action could you take?

7. Continually write and rewrite your goals with as much clarity as you can. This exercise works wonders in stimulating your creativity and unlocking your inner genius.

"Imagination is more important than knowledge.
Knowledge is limited.
Imagination encircles the world."

—Albert Einstein

9

Learn from the Best

"Begin to imagine what the desirable outcome would be like. Go over these mental pictures and delineate details and refinements. Play them over and over to yourself, until they become your reality."

—Maxwell Maltz

There are only two ways to learn what you need to learn to become wealthy. You can learn from *your own* mistakes and experience or you can learn from the mistakes and experience of *others*.

The second method, learning from the mistakes and experience of others, is by far the cheapest and easiest. It is also the least used. However, you can greatly accelerate your growth and progress toward financial success by systematically studying and copying the successful men and women who have gone before you.

In this chapter, you will learn what other self-made millionaires have done to become wealthy. You will learn what the most successful businesses have done to rise to the top of their industries. You will learn strategies, techniques, and methods that are used by the most successful individuals and organizations to achieve goals far above the average.

Copy the Best in Your Business

One of the most powerful techniques of personal development known is that of "modeling." This method requires the seeking out of successful men and women, studying their ways of thinking and acting, and then copying them exactly. The top people in every field, from acting through to music, and including sports and business, all began by learning from the very best people in their fields.

The rule is that if you want to be a winner in any area of life, begin to walk, talk, and act like other winners. As a result, you will soon begin to think and feel like a winner, and get the same results that they do. You will begin to believe that you are born to win and that nothing can stop you. Over time, this belief will become your reality.

Qualities of the Great Ones

Some years ago, the Gallup Organization interviewed 1,500 men and women listed in *Who's Who in America*. This book is often called the "social register." It is made up of the most respected, esteemed, and prestigious men and women in the United States.

The Gallup researchers interviewed this cross section of leading Americans and asked them, among other questions, "Why do you feel that you have achieved such great success in the course of your lifetime?"

By combining the results of these interviews, they isolated and identified five qualities of outstanding men and women in every field. These are the qualities that top people give to explain why it is that they do better than their peers in the same fields of endeavor.

Common Sense Is Not So Common

The first quality that they all agreed on was that of common sense. The interviewees said repeatedly that common sense was a fundamental quality that was a key to their success.

The researchers then asked them, "What do you mean by 'common sense'?" The most accurate definition they received was, "Common sense is the ability to have experiences, to reflect upon those experiences, and then to draw from those experiences, general rules, and guidelines that can be applied to subsequent experiences."

In other words, common sense is the ability to *learn from experience* and to develop the wisdom that accompanies that learning. The Greek philosopher Aristotle once said, "Wisdom is an equal measure of experience plus reflection." Men and women who seem to have high levels of common sense are those who not only have had a variety of experiences, but they have taken the time to reflect upon those experiences and learn from them at a deeper level.

Failing to Learn from Mistakes

There are many people who have had many years of experience, but they have never taken the time to sit down and think through their experiences. They have been too busy to reflect upon them and evaluate them so that they could draw general rules and principles that they could apply to the future.

In the twenty-first century, the keys to success are knowledge and know-how. To paraphrase Aristotle, "Wisdom today is a combination of knowledge plus experience plus reflection." Gaining wisdom today requires, first of all, learning what you need to know in your field to be excellent. Wisdom requires applying that information to each subsequent experience, getting feedback, and then reflecting upon what you have learned. Wisdom requires continually adding to your storehouse of knowledge and experience so that you can improve your performance and do your work even better next time.

Intelligence Is As Intelligence Does

The second quality of top Americans identified in the study was intelligence. Virtually all of those people interviewed said that they had achieved at high levels because of their intellectual ability. The researchers then pointed out that many of them had not completed college, and some had dropped out of high school. Of those who had gone on to college, many had not been academically superior. Many of the members of *Who's Who in America* had received average or below-average grades.

It turns out that there are *two* definitions of intelligence. The first definition is the one that most people go by. It is "intelligence quotient," or IQ. Most people estimate their own IQ based on how well they did in school. The average person who did not get good grades in school often thinks of himself or herself as having a below-average IQ. This belief can affect them for the rest of their lives.

Your Grades Do Not Determine Your Future

The fact is that there are many people who did not get good grades in school, but who became very successful in adult life. Some studies show that successful entrepreneurs often have the same characteristics as children with attention deficit disorder. They are curious, impatient, fast moving, and uninterested in the trivia or details of a school subject or, later in life, of the details of a business. But they are nonetheless highly intelligent.

Dr. Howard Gardner of Harvard University has identified what he calls "Multiple Intelligences." These are different forms of intelligence, such as visual-spatial, kinesthetic or physical, and musical intelligence, none of which is measured in school. The standard IQ tests measure only two dimensions of mental activity, verbal and mathematical. What Dr. Gardner has found is that a person could be a genius (such as a Mozart) in musical intelligence and yet do poorly at academic subjects.

Highest-Paid Intelligences

The highest-paid intelligences in the United States today are "social intelligence," defined as the ability to get along well with a wide variety of other people, and "entrepreneurial intelligence," defined as the ability to see opportunities to create products and services that people want and need, and which can be sold at a profit. These two forms of intelligence are never tested in school. You could be a genius in either or both of these intelligences, but if you got poor grades, you might consider yourself to be less intelligent than other people. This is simply not true.

The fact is that the full range of intelligence cannot be measured by standard IQ tests. The best definition of intelligence that I have found is that *intelligence is a way of acting*. If you act intelligently in a given situation, you are, by definition, an intelligent person. If you act foolishly in a particular situation, you are, by this definition, dumb. And it has nothing to do with the grades you got in school.

An Intelligent Act

If you agree that a person who acts intelligently is smart, and a person who acts unintelligently is not, the logical next question is, "What is an intelligent way of acting?"

Here it is: An intelligent way of acting is when you act in a manner consistent with achieving your own self-determined, self-professed goals. Every time you engage in an action that moves you toward the accomplishment of something that is important to you, you are acting intelligently. It is your choice of what you really want that determines whether your actions are intelligent.

Every time you do either something that does *not* move you toward something that is important to you or, even worse, something that moves you *away*, you are behaving *un*intelligently. Holding constant for everything else, you are intelligent to the degree to which you consistently take the steps that move you toward achieving your own goals. If your goals are to be happy, healthy, wealthy, and have a wonderful family life, everything that you do that moves you toward any of these is, by your own definition, a smart way of acting. It is very intelligent.

Do Your Job Well

The third quality of outstanding men and women identified in the survey was expertise. Expertise is defined as "the ability to do the job extremely well." You have expertise when you are recognized as being one of the top performers in your field, having the ability to get the results that are required of your position.

All the people in the study reached their level of prominence in their field only after they had decided to become very good at what they were doing. They became successful only after they had made a total commitment to personal excellence in their profession. Unfortunately, most people have missed this simple insight. You will never find anyone who became successful in any field by performing in an average or mediocre way. Even above-average performance is not sufficient. Only a determined commitment to excellence will propel you to the top of your field.

Resolve to Be the Best

People who become truly successful begin their upward trajectory as a result of dedicating themselves to "be the best" at whatever they are doing. They commit themselves to mastery of their craft.

As I wrote earlier, there have been many studies done over the years on the subject of "mastery." The bottom line of these studies is that it takes five to seven years, and 10,000 hours of application, for you to rise into the top 10 percent of your field. This seems to be equally true for entrepreneurial or sales success as it is for neurosurgery or the practice of law.

There are simply no shortcuts to mastery in your field. Based on thousands of interviews, it takes about two years of work in a given field for you to know if this is the right career for you. In entrepreneurship, it takes about two years of losses before a new business begins to make more money than it costs to keep the doors open.

You require another two years to determine whether you have the desire and the ability to rise to the top of your field. In business, in year three and four you earn enough to pay back the debts that you incurred in the first two years. After four years, if you are in the right field or business, you start to move toward the front of the pack, as the stronger runners do in a marathon. After four years, you will have had sufficient experience to make better and better decisions, and get better and better results.

Seven Years to Greatness

By the seventh year, if you have put your whole heart into doing your work the very best way possible, and have continually upgraded your knowledge and skills, you will break out into the lead. You will move into the top 10 percent and begin to enjoy success and rewards that are many times greater than the average person in your field. When you get into the top 1 or 2 percent in your field or business, you will be earning 20 to 30 times more than people who are content to plod along at average levels of performance.

Sometimes in my seminars, when I explain these principles and the years necessary for mastery, people complain and argue with me. "That's too long!" they say. But then I point something out to them that stops them in their tracks. I simply say, "The time is going to pass anyway."

How much older will you be in five to seven years? The fact is that you will be five to seven years older. The time is going to pass anyway. The only question is, "Are you going to be at the top of your field in five to seven years, with all the rewards that go along with great success, or are you still going to be running along back in the pack with the other average performers?"

But *the time is going to pass anyway*. Whatever field you are in, make sure that it is the right field for you, and then throw your whole heart into becoming absolutely excellent at what you do. Whether it takes five, six, or seven years, it doesn't matter. All that matters is that sometime in the future you reach the top. When you do, all the pain and sacrifice you endured to get there disappears. What is left is a wonderful feeling of pride, personal power, and self-esteem. It is worth every effort you ever make to be the best at what you do. As Frank Sinatra said, "Overwhelming success is the best revenge."

Take Charge of Your Life

The fourth quality of top men and women in the Gallup study was self-reliance, or self-responsibility. Top people always look to themselves as the *primary creative forces* in their own lives. They see themselves as being the person most responsible for their own success. They see themselves as if they were completely in charge of setting and achieving the goals that are important to them.

Top people refuse to make excuses. When they make mistakes, they admit to them quickly, correct them, and carry on. They do not expect other people to do things for them. They refuse to blame or become angry at other people who disappoint them. They don't criticize or condemn. They always look to themselves as being the key actors in the play on the stage of their own lives.

The Giant Step to Maturity

The acceptance of personal responsibility for yourself, for everything you are, and for everything you become, is the giant step to maturity and high performance. Many people sabotage their own lives by continually reminding themselves of unhappy experiences that have happened in the past. They remain angry with their parents, their siblings, their bad marriages, bad bosses, and bad investment experiences. They can't let them go. They continually rehash them to themselves and others. As a result, they actually put their own feet on the brakes of their own potential. They hold themselves back.

One of the marks of outstanding men and women is that they *let the past go*. They refuse to become upset about something that they cannot change or do anything about. And this includes all past events. The very best way to deal with the past is to *learn* from it, developing greater wisdom and understanding, and then to get on with the rest of your life.

If you are still angry with someone who has hurt you, practice the spiritual principle of *forgiveness*, and let the other person go free. Whenever you think of someone in your past with whom you are still upset, immediately say, "I forgive him/her for everything." Then, get so busy working on your own goals that you don't have time to think about what that person did or did not do, or what might have happened in the past.

Short-Circuit Your Negative Emotions

The very best way to short-circuit or cancel out any negative emotion is simply to repeat the affirmation "I am responsible! I am responsible! I am responsible!" Since your conscious mind can hold only one thought at a time, positive or negative, you can use the law of substitution to cancel out a negative feeling by quickly saying, "I am responsible."

Since most negative emotions that hold you back are rooted in *blame* of some kind, whenever you say "I am responsible!" you pull the plug on blaming and put yourself back into the driver's seat of your own life. You immediately feel more powerful, and in control of your emotions and your situation.

As long as you blame anyone else for anything that makes you unhappy, you are positioning yourself as a victim. If it is a parent that you are angry with, you are positioning yourself both as a child and as a victim. When you blame or criticize, you make yourself weak while making the other person (in your own mind) strong. You actually allow other people to control your emotions by long distance. As soon as you think about them, wherever they are, you immediately become angry and unhappy. You fall into the trap of undermining and sabotaging your future by not letting go of unhappy experiences that took place in the past.

Get the Job Done

The fifth quality of outstanding men and women in every study, including studies of peak performance, is "result orientation." Result orientation is the determination that top people have to think about results continually. They focus single-mindedly on getting the job done well, quickly, and dependably.

Result-oriented people set clear goals, objectives, and priorities. They focus on what is relevant and important, and they stay at the task until it is complete. As a result, they produce far more than the average person who fails to practice these behaviors.

In the final analysis, results are everything. You will always be paid for the quality and quantity of the results that you get in your job or position. Keep asking yourself, "What results are expected of me?" Of all the results that are expected of you, which are the most important? How could you organize your life so that you are getting more and more of the most important results that determine your success and your income?

Think Like a Champion

In our private coaching programs, we train entrepreneurs and executives to think in terms of their "hourly rate." This almost always comes as a surprise. The great majority of entrepreneurs and executives think in terms of how much they earn per month or per year. But top people— high performers, successful entrepreneurs and outstanding executives— think in terms of how much they earn *each hour*. As a result, they use their time much better than average people, and achieve far greater results than the people around them.

The Law of Three applied to your work says that there are three things you do in your work that account for 90 percent or more of your results. Your ability to determine these three tasks is the key to peak performance and maximum results.

Here is an exercise for you: Make a list of everything that you do in your work in the course of the week or month. Review this list, asking the question, "If I could only do *one thing* on this list, which one activity would contribute the greatest amount of value to myself and my business?"

The most important thing you do at your work will probably jump out at you from the list. Then you ask the question a second time, "If I could only do *one more thing* on this list, all day long, which one activity would it be?"

Once you have selected your number two task, apply the question once more until you have identified your *top three* tasks. If you want to move to the top of your field, double your income, and become one of the most successful people in your business, from now on focus on those three tasks or activities all day long.

This simple formula will enable you to increase your contribution and your income faster than anything else you could possibly do. By becoming intensely result oriented, you dedicate yourself to doing more and more of those few things that contribute the greatest value, and doing those few things better and better. This is one of the most important parts of getting rich your own way.

Follow the Leaders

We said earlier that *modeling*, or copying the behaviors of others who are achieving the kinds of goals that you want to achieve, is one of the smartest and fastest ways that you can step on the accelerator of your own life. As Albert Schweitzer once said, "You must teach men at the school of example, for they will learn at no other."

The world around you is full of people whose examples are worth emulating. Dr. David McClelland of Harvard, in his book *The Achieving Society*, concluded that your choice of a "reference group," the people with whom you associate and socialize, has an inordinate impact on everything you accomplish in life. Your ability to choose the people that you look up to and admire, and then spend time with them, can have a greater effect on your success than any other factor.

The Qualities of Leadership

Successful entrepreneurs and businesspeople have certain qualities that you can incorporate into your own behavior as the result of learning and practice.

Vision

The first quality of top people seems to be that they have a *clear vision of the ideal future* that they want to create for themselves and their families.

In 3,300 studies of leadership conducted by James Cribben, seeking the qualities that were most common to great leaders, he identified "vision" as the one quality that appeared in every single study, going back to 600 B.C. Leaders have vision. Nonleaders do not. The very act of creating a vision for your life begins to make you into a leader for both yourself and others.

Imagine Your Ideal Future
One way to develop vision for yourself and your business is to practice "idealization." Project forward three to five years in your life and imagine that your life was ideal in every way. What would it look like?

Imagine that your job or career was ideal in every way. What would you be doing? How much would you be earning? Imagine that your financial situation was ideal. How much would you have in the bank? What would be your net worth? Imagine that your family situation was perfect in every way. What kind of lifestyle would you have? How would you spend your time with your family? Imagine that your health was perfect in every way. How much would you weigh? How fit would you be? What would you be doing differently from today?

In the movie *South Pacific*, there is a song that says, "You've got to have a dream if you want to make a dream come true." Napoleon Hill, in *Think and Grow Rich*, says, "Anything the mind of man can conceive and believe, it can achieve." All leaders allow themselves to dream, and then they go to work to make their dreams come true.

Project Forward into the Future

In building your own business or career, take some time to think about how it would look in the future if it turned out perfectly. If you want your business to be the very best in the industry, describe how it would look from the *outside* when you achieved that goal.

When I do strategic planning for corporations, we begin by imagining that the company is the top company in the industry five years in the future. We then go around the table and ask, "How would we be described by others if we were the very best company in this business?"

We will often get 20 or 30 different ideal descriptions covering every aspect of the business. We then ask, "Which of these are more important than any others?"

We then organize the ideal descriptions by priority and discuss the specific actions we could take immediately to begin creating that ideal future. You can do this for yourself, for your business, and for any part of your life. It is a powerful exercise that often changes the entire direction of your life.

Develop a Sense of Mission

Leaders have a sense of mission. They have a passion for what they do, and are totally committed to doing it well. Leaders visualize what their business will look like when it is the best in the industry. They see their goals and objectives as realized long before they actually happen.

One of the most powerful techniques you can practice is called "back from the future" thinking. With this technique, you project forward mentally three to five years and imagine that your life and work are perfect in every way. From that vantage point in the future, you look back to the present and ask, "What would have to happen for me to get from where I am in the present to where I want to be in the future?"

Very often, this exercise gives you greater clarity about the next actions you need to take. By looking back from the future, you can see immediately things that you should start doing or stop doing immediately. You see things that will need to be changed one way or another. You will see things that you need to do more of or less of.

Believe In Your Dreams

Once upon a time, an unknown film director named George Lucas had a vision of a futuristic space adventure movie that would be different from any movie ever made. He spent month after month going from studio to studio trying to get support and backing for his idea. But it was too radical. He was turned down over and over again.

However, George Lucas refused to give up. He persisted and persevered and finally got together enough money to make *Star Wars*, which became one of the most successful movies in history. *Star Wars* began the era of the blockbuster movies that earn more than $100 million each. His company, Lucasfilms, eventually generated billions of dollars in worldwide sales of the *Star Wars* trilogy, the *Star Wars* prequels, and other worldwide best-selling movies. He doesn't have trouble raising capital for his projects anymore.

Be a Complete Optimist

In addition to vision and a sense of mission, another quality of leaders and successful entrepreneurs is that they have high levels of optimism. Because of this optimism, they have "unrealistic expectations" of success. They absolutely believe that, sooner or later, one way or another, they are going to be successful at what they do.

Optimists seem to have two remarkable qualities. First, because they have unrealistic expectations of success, they *try more things*. If something doesn't work, they try something else, and then something else again. They are willing to fail far more times than the average person in order to achieve the success that they believe is absolutely guaranteed.

The law of probabilities says that the more things you *try*, the more likely it is that you will *triumph*. Virtually all successful people have tried and failed countless times before they eventually developed the wisdom and experience that enabled them to try and succeed. They use the law of probabilities in their favor. As Phil Knight of Nike once said, "You only have to succeed the *last* time."

The Iron Quality of Success

The second quality possessed by true optimists is that they *persist longer*. They never give up. They keep trying new and different things, and if something doesn't work, they try something else.

Again, they use the law of probabilities in their favor. If you try more things and you persist longer, the odds are that you will eventually try the right thing at the right time and break through.

Colonel Harland Sanders set off at age 65 to sell his recipe, consisting of a secret blend of herbs and spices, for cooking fried chicken. He called on more than 1,000 restaurants offering to share his recipe with them, and was turned down more than 1,000 times. But he kept on calling, living out of his old car, with his pots and pans around him. He never gave up.

Finally, after traveling up and down the Atlantic Seaboard for many months, he found one restaurant owner who agreed to pay him five cents per chicken cooked using his method. Soon he found another restaurant, and then another. The rest is history. Kentucky Fried Chicken became one of the most successful franchise operations in history, with more than 7,000 outlets worldwide. Harland Sanders became a millionaire many times over, and one of the best-known and most popular figures in business worldwide.

Know Your Business Inside and Out

An important quality of successful entrepreneurs who become millionaires is that they study every detail of the business. They continually examine and reexamine their information to find the unique factors that can lead to great success.

The founders of the first convenience store franchise, Mac's Milk Stores, found that large grocery stores were open only during standard business hours, from 8:00 A.M. until 6:00 P.M. After 6:00 P.M., it was almost impossible to pick up a quart of milk or a pound of butter. They saw that there might be a market opportunity in this situation. They started their detailed research by interviewing shoppers leaving large grocery stores during the five o'clock rush and asking them what they had purchased. They found that 80 percent of the purchases were represented by 346 items, and 90 percent of the purchases were represented by about 700 items.

Based on this information, they opened a convenience store with extended hours, from 7:00 A.M. until 11:00 P.M. They stocked only the most popular 700 items, the most popular brands, and the most popular sizes of those brands. The rest is history.

Within a few years, there were thousands of convenience stores everywhere, generating billions of dollars in sales. Many people who got into the convenience store business became millionaires as a result.

Look for Opportunities Everywhere

Successful entrepreneurs and businesspeople seem to be very good at finding market opportunities in the form of products and services that people want and need, but which are not available. They then design, create, or get the rights to distribute new or better products or services to serve those market needs. They find a need and fill it.

William Kelly saw an increasing need for secretarial staff who could operate office equipment. He began hiring and training these people for businesses, to work on a temporary basis. His company, Kelly Services, now has offices throughout the United States supplying staff of all kinds to businesses everywhere. William Kelly, from one small office in Detroit, became a multimillionaire. He found a need and filled it.

Tom Golisano, an accountant working in Rochester, New York, saw that his small business clients needed help keeping up with payroll and continually changing labor laws. He started Paychex to handle the payroll needs of his clients and built it into one of the most successful companies in the country. Tom Golisano is now rated by *Forbes* magazine as one of the richest men in America with a net worth of more than $1 billion. He found a need and filled it.

Find Your Own "Acres of Diamonds"

There are countless opportunities for you to find or create a new business, and most of them lie right under you own feet. How do you develop the ability to follow the leaders, and to find opportunities that you can take advantage of to get rich in America? There are several steps you can take.

Step 1. Gather Information

First, begin to gather information about people and businesses in a field in which you are interested. Subscribe to all the magazines and trade journals in that field. Send away for the promotional literature of companies and study it, compare it, and analyze it. Talk to employees, customers, and other businesspeople about the industry leaders and the rising companies in your area of interest.

Attend seminars put on by experts in your chosen field. Ask these experts questions at the breaks. Ask them for advice and recommendations for what to do and what to read. Begin to assemble a body of information on your chosen field, and then go over it again and again. Become an expert. Expert power is very valuable.

Step 2. See Yourself As Already Successful

Begin to visualize yourself as a success in that business. Create a clear mental picture of how you would look, walk, dress, talk, act, and live as the success you intend to be in the future. Combine your visualization with action. Do something positive and constructive every day that moves you toward your goal of success in this field.

Psychologists have discovered that you can *act your way* into believing in your ability to succeed by pretending that you are already the success that you want to be. The more you walk, talk, and act like a success, the more you will feel it and believe it, and the faster it will become a part of your personality.

Step 3. Keep Your Eyes Open

Look for moneymaking opportunities everywhere. Opportunities exist in almost every job. For example, Jerry Gordon began as a cook in a Kentucky Fried Chicken franchise. He saw a need for a motor-driven flour sifter because they were still sifting flour by hand. He began to build them in his garage in his spare time.

Within a year, he was able to sell 12 of these flour sifters to Colonel Sanders. Sanders was so impressed that he loaned Gordon $10,000 to start his own business. Jerry Gordon went on to become a millionaire manufacturing food-processing equipment to save time and money for fast-food businesses.

Look in Your Line of Sight

In business and manufacturing there is a concept called "line of sight theory." What this concept says is that each person can see opportunities for improvements in his or her *line of sight*. You should look in your line of sight, right where you are. You can almost always see room for improvement in what you are doing.

You can get big ideas from routine problems. The founder of Coffeematic observed the time lost by employees going down the street for coffee breaks. He showed employers how coffee machines would pay for themselves in working time saved. He installed the machines for nothing and made money on the coffee and the filters he supplied. There is now a Coffeematic machine, or something similar, in almost every single office of any kind throughout the world.

Start Small and Use Customer Financing

You don't need a lot of money to get started. You can start small and get your customers to finance you. Daniel K. Ludwig started with very little money, but with one great idea. He found that if he could enter into a long-term charter deal with an oil company to carry its oil in tankers, he could then take the lease to the bank and borrow the money to build the oil tankers. The lease fees, guaranteed by the big oil companies, paid off the bank loans and generated huge profits. He then repeated this formula over and over, signing shipping leases with oil companies, borrowing the money to build the tankers, and then paying off the loans from the revenues. Within a few years, he became a billionaire and one of the richest men in the world by working with other people's money.

Seek Common Solutions

Look for solutions that can be duplicated for other customers. Look for something that you can do over and over again for other people. Look for problems and solutions for a large number of buyers. Always ask, "Is there a market for this idea? Is the market large enough?" Fish for whales, not minnows. Go after the biggest markets rather than the smallest markets.

Xerox Corporation began with the solution to making multiple copies of a document without using carbon paper. The company developed the patents for xerography and transformed the world of business. The solution Xerox developed was then applicable to every company.

Be Sure It Can Be Sold

Look for a product or service solution that can be sold by ordinary, competent salespeople. Always ask these questions: "Who is going to sell this product or service?" and "How are they going to sell it?"

Remember, since the only kind of salespeople you will find are ordinary salespeople, it has to be a product or service that can be sold by the average person. If it is a product or service that requires a genius to sell it or install it, it is probably not going to be successful.

Use Word-of-Mouth Advertising

Look for a solution to a problem that really works and that can sell itself by word of mouth. Fully 84 percent of sales in the United States, one way or another, are determined by word-of-mouth advertising. If you can find a solution, like lightbulbs that last for 50,000 hours, and you can get people talking about it, that can be your marketing strategy.

Seek Profitable Products and Services

Look for solutions for problems that have an optimum price-cost relationship. The very least you should have is a markup of 3:1. That means that if your product costs \$1 to produce, you should be able to sell it in the marketplace for at least \$3.

It is better, in manufacturing, to have a markup of 4:1 or 5:1 or even 10:1. Many manufactured products, especially imported products, have a markup of as much as 10 to 1 from their manufacturing costs to retail. This amount of markup gives you enough room to get your product through the start-up phases, earn sufficient profit to grow your business, and generate enough profits to introduce new products and services in the future.

Become an Apprentice

Another way to "follow the leader" in any industry is for you to take a part-time or even a full-time job in the field you have chosen. You can gain experience by starting a part-time business in the field that you are thinking of going into. You can find a knowledgeable partner, someone with years of experience in that field, and learn from him or her.

You can piggyback on the knowledge and experience of others by taking special educational courses in your field. Often you can hire someone, like a consultant, with the necessary expertise. You don't have to learn it all yourself.

The rule is that "knowledge is power." One of the main reasons that people fail in business is because they do not know enough of the details of their particular business to succeed. In contrast, one of the primary reasons for business success is that the entrepreneur learns everything he or she needs to know about the business that he or she is going into.

Rent or Buy the Knowledge You Need

One of the smartest things you can do early in your business is to interview or hire an expert in a particular aspect of the business. Be prepared to retain a business consultant, a marketing consultant, an advertising consultant, or a direct mail consultant. You can hire anyone that you need to get the expert knowledge that you require to be successful. Rent their brains the same way you would go to a doctor, a dentist, a lawyer, or an accountant. Go to a consultant who has spent years specializing in a particular field and buy that professional's knowledge and experience.

Take successful people out to lunch and ask them questions. Almost invariably, successful people will help other people to be successful, if you *ask* them. Select the people in your field or community whom you admire the most and invite them out for lunch, or at least invite them for coffee. And be sure to pay the bill when you do. A few minutes with a successful person is often the cheapest investment you can ever make in gaining the critical insights you need for success in that field.

Ask for Advice

If they are too busy for coffee or lunch, ask for 10 minutes of their time to get their advice on the very best ways to succeed in this business. When you meet with them, say, "I really respect the success that you have achieved in this field, and I wonder if you could give me some advice that would help me to be successful like you."

Ask, "What books should I read? What courses should I take? What audio programs should I listen to? Where should I go? What should I do?" A few words from another successful person may save you years of hard work and many thousands of dollars.

Study Successful Companies

Another way to learn by modeling is to study another successful company. You will have to be at least as good as your competition, and usually better, to survive and prosper in any business. Find another successful company, preferably the top company, and copy as many of the things that company does as you can. Then, try to do that company one better; aim to be superior in some way that is important to customers.

How Does the Company Attract Customers?

When you study another successful business, first find out what the company does to attract customers. How does the company promote, advertise, and generate revenues?

How Does the Company Sell?

What selling techniques does it use? What are its most successful selling methods? What does it offer? What kind of warranties or guarantees does it give? What kind of follow-up service does it offer to its customers?

Who Buys the Product or Service?

What type of customers does it sell to? Who are the customers for this particular product or service? Describe them in detail, based on age, income, education, sex, occupation, and financial capability.

How Does the Company Charge?

How much does the company charge for the product, and *how* does it charge? Does it require a down payment? Does it offer monthly payments? Is it all cash? What kind of terms does it give?

What Does the Company Include?

What goes into or is included in its product or service? If you are going to compete with another company, you have to know everything that

that company is doing to attract and keep customers. What does it include in the package?

Where Does the Company Sell?

Where does it sell the most of its product or service? What are the best locations for its stores or offices? What cities? What states? What parts of cities?

What Customer Policies Does It Practice?

What are its customer policies? What are its guarantees, refunds, allowances, service warranties, and so on? In other words, how does it deal with its customers once it has them?

Once you have gathered all this information on your potential competitors, you have to ask yourself, "What can we do to be *superior* to them?"

Twelve Keys to Following the Leaders

Key 1. Find out everything you can about the top people and companies in your chosen area.

Key 2. Copy everything and anything that the others are doing to achieve success. Remember, emulation is one of the highest forms of flattery. If your competitors are the people you admire for doing something successfully, by all means, copy them and use it yourself. When you start to come up with successful ideas and methods, they will surely copy you.

Key 3. Admire your successful competitors. This is very important psychologically. Always think and talk in positive, admiring terms about the top people and the top companies in your industry, and then look for ways to do them one better. Never disparage your competition. Always speak about them in respectful terms. Develop an admiration for successful people.

Key 4. Look for formulas for success that you can transfer or adapt from one industry or business to another.

Perhaps the most famous example of transferring one successful method from one industry to another is that of McDonald's.

What founder Ray Kroc saw was the ability to apply the fast print shop methodology to hamburgers. He saw the rapid production of standardized products from the McDonald brothers of San Bernardino. He wondered if you couldn't standardize that process and repeat it over and over again. That was the beginning of the McDonald's empire, which now includes 30,000 franchises worldwide, each of them using a production line process applied to fast food.

Another example of production methodology that can be transferred from industry to industry would be self-service laundries or self-service car washes. Once they are set up and coin-operated, they can be duplicated over and over again.

Another example of a methodology that has been transferred from one area to another is that used by book clubs such as the Literary Guild. These have now become CD clubs, art clubs, classical music clubs, coin clubs, plate clubs, and now video and DVD clubs.

Key 5. Look for the areas in each field where big profits are being made. Concentrate in those areas. Focus on high-value-added products and services. Remember that 20 percent of the sales in any given field account for 80 percent of the profits. Remember the Mac's Milk Stores, or the 7-Elevens, the convenience store methodology. Always concentrate on selling the highest-profit products or services in your industry.

Key 6. Look at what small businesses are doing successfully and then consider the possibility of building a large organization doing the same thing on a large scale. McDonald's and Century 21 Real Estate each took the methodology that worked for one firm or industry and then multiplied it hundreds and thousands of times. Domino's Pizza took a method of fast-delivery pizza and multiplied it by thousands of outlets. Most successful franchises are examples of duplicating a successful methodology from one field to another.

Key 7. Look at what the established giants are doing, and then provide customers with a less expensive alternative. Big companies have high levels of overhead. Very often, you can observe what they are doing and then provide an equal or better product or service at a lower cost, and offer it locally.

Key 8. Look for an area where you can use speed and flexibility to offer products or services faster, cheaper, or better than the larger companies in that industry. One of the great advantages of a smaller company is that you can move *faster*. You can give more personalized service. You can give more individual attention to customers. This constitutes a real value that people are willing to pay for.

Key 9. Look at the best-selling products in your field and find a way to improve on them. You only have to come up with a product or service that is 10 percent better to start yourself on the way to a successful business.

Robin Cook, the author of the best-selling novel *Coma*, used this type of formula. He sat down and read the last 100 best sellers from the *New York Times* fiction list. In reading these books, he came up with a formula for writing best sellers. He wrote *Coma* based on that formula, and it became a best seller overnight.

Robin Cook has now written a series of best sellers, using the same formula over and over again. Many successful authors, like Harold Robbins, Tom Clancy, and John Grisham, have done the same thing.

Key 10. Always follow the leaders. Don't go in first with a new product or service. Let other, stronger companies go through the trial-and-error process for you. Let them take the risk. Large companies can afford to risk money on new products or services. Small companies cannot. When a business, product, or service is a proven success, then you can enter and look for a way to improve upon it.

Key 11. Remember that no one can patent a good business idea. Borrow generously from others. Anytime you see anyone who has a good business idea, take it and run with it. Sometimes the person who takes the idea and runs with it does far better than the person who came up with it originally.

Key 12. You get on top and stay on top by watching other companies, especially your competition, and then by adopting their *proven success methods*. Never stop learning and applying proven success methods in any field. Learn from the experts, and then do what they do, over and over again, until you get the same results.

Learn by Trial and Error

In every field of human endeavor, you learn to succeed by trial and error. You gradually build up a reservoir of experience that enables you to make more right decisions than wrong ones. You can speed up the necessary learning process by carefully observing other people and businesses, and by copying the very best they have to offer.

You have the ability to achieve financial success in any one of many different areas. At the moment, you may not have an idea of which one is best for you. But the fastest way for you to become a financial success is to make a lifelong habit of studying the leaders in your field, of learning every possible detail of the business you are interested in, and then by staying on top of it all the time.

Sometime in the future, people will study you and your business methods to learn how to become wealthy. In the meantime, continue to learn and grow every day, profiting from the experiences of others and saving yourself countless dollars and many years. And remember, don't lose money!

Action Exercises

1. Select a business, industry, or person you greatly admire and begin studying the most admirable actions and qualities; resolve to learn from the best.

2. Choose a business that interests you and begin to assemble information on how people and companies succeed in that field. Learn from both the successes and failures of others.

3. Pick a role model in business whom you especially admire and respect. Learn everything you can about this person and practice thinking and acting as you imagine he or she would.

4. Investigate before you invest time, money, or emotion into a new business or product; find out what potential competitors are doing in this area to generate sales and profits.

5. Imagine that your business, or some aspect of your life, were ideal sometime in the future. What would it look like? How would it be described?

6. In evaluating a business opportunity, identify the most profitable and popular products and services offered in that area. How could you improve upon them and become the best in the business?

7. Identify the three most important things you do in your work—those three tasks or activities that account for most of the contribution you make; organize your time so that you work in these three areas most of the time.

> *"Employ your time in improving yourself*
> *by other men's writings so that you shall come*
> *easily by what others have labored hard for."*
>
> **—Socrates**

10

Lead the Field

"Don't bunt. Aim out of the ballpark.
Aim for the company of immortals."
—David Ogilvy

In the course of this book, I have focused on the ways that most people become wealthy: They provide a needed product or service of good quality at a fair price. They add value in some way and keep a part of that value. They continually seek better, faster, cheaper ways to do things for more people.

Three Pathways

In this final chapter, I want to introduce you to three other pathways to affluence, to *getting rich your own way*. Each of them has been followed successfully by hundreds of thousands, and even millions, of people to achieve financial independence.

Get a Good Job and Do It Well

The first pathway is simply getting a good job and working your way up in a successful company over the course of your career. About 10 percent of self-made millionaires in the United States have worked for other companies all their lives. They became wealthy by becoming very good at what they did, being paid very well for doing it, and then holding on to the money in the form of savings, investments, and stock options.

Become a Professional

The second way that people become wealthy is by entering a profession such as law, medicine, architecture, or engineering, and then dedicating themselves to getting to the top of their field.

Fully 10 percent of self-made millionaires in the United States are professionals, defined as someone with an advanced degree, who have reached the top 10 percent of their fields. As a result, they are paid very well for what they do. They fall into the 20 percent in any occupational category who earn 80 percent of the money in that category.

Become a Top Salesperson

The third way you can become a self-made millionaire, accounting for some 5 percent of self-made millionaires, is by becoming a top salesperson in your field.

In sales, the 80/20 Rule holds true as well. The top 20 percent of salespeople earn 80 percent of the money. What this means, when you work it out, is that the average income of salespeople in the top 20 percent is 16 times the average income of the people in the bottom 80 percent.

But it gets better. The top 20 percent of the top 20 percent, or the top 4 percent of people in selling, earn 80 percent of the money in the top 20 percent. This means that people in the top 4 percent of sales can be earning 25 times or more than the average of the people in the bottom 80 percent.

Over the years, I have spoken at sales conferences arranged to celebrate the top people in a particular organization. At two of these meetings, in different industries, the average income of the people in attendance was $850,000 per year. The average income of the average salesperson in those same industries was $24,000 per year.

The Common Denominators

It turns out that there are two common denominators of the people at the top of their fields. First, every one of them started at the bottom. At one time, they knew nothing about that field. Everything they ever accomplished they had to learn and do for themselves.

Second, at an early stage in their careers, they made the decision to "be the best" at what they were doing. They started earlier, worked harder, and stayed later. They dedicated themselves to relentless, ongoing, never-ending personal and professional development. They resolved to "pay the price," whatever it was, to achieve great success in their chosen fields.

In each of these different ways of becoming a millionaire, there are three keys to success. First, set a goal to be paid the very most possible in your field. Second, decide to become absolutely excellent at what you do through continuous personal and professional improvement. Third, resolve to save and invest 10 percent to 20 percent of your income throughout your career.

By doing these three things, your financial future will be guaranteed.

Secrets of Health, Wealth, and Happiness

Throughout the ages, and in this book, we have uncovered some of the keys to living and enjoying a wonderful life. Here are some of the rules and practices followed by the happiest, healthiest, and most financially successful people living today. Each is possible for you.

Do What You Love to Do

The common denominator of successful people in every field is that they do what they love to do. They analyze and decide on their natural talents and abilities, and then choose their careers accordingly. They then organize their lives so that they can focus single-mindedly on doing something that they really enjoy, and from which they get an enormous amount of satisfaction and pleasure.

Identify Your Core Competencies

Whatever your field, you must first identify your core competencies, those things that you do especially well, and then organize your life around doing more and more of them better and better. You must identify the area of specialization in your work where you can make the greatest and most valuable contribution doing what you do best.

Throw Your Heart into What You Do

Live with passion! Once you have determined what it is that you can do really well and what you most enjoy, you must throw your whole heart into doing whatever it is. Burn your bridges. Make a total commitment. As Ralph Waldo Emerson said, "Nothing great was ever accomplished without enthusiasm."

Commit to Excellence

There are no shortcuts to personal and professional excellence. The primary reason that people underachieve and "live lives of quiet desperation" is that they are not continually getting *better* at what they do. They fail to dedicate themselves to lifelong learning. They get a basic education, sometimes including a college degree, and then attempt to coast through their careers on their accumulated knowledge. This is a sure prescription for failure. You must resolve to be the best, and then pay whatever price is required for you to achieve it.

Become a Lifelong Student

To be the best, you must read in your field continually. You must listen to audio programs in your car rather than driving around listening to music (chewing gum for the ears). You must attend every seminar and course that you can find that will help you to get ahead in your field. Sometimes one small idea or change in your approach, or way of doing things, can alter the direction of your career and lead you on to great success.

Top people in every field are not necessarily those who are innately smarter than others. They are rather those who have taken the time to learn what they need to know to be superior to their competition.

Earn Superior Rewards

If you want to have a superior life, you have to be better than the other people in your field. The market pays extraordinary rewards only for extraordinary performance. It pays ordinary rewards for ordinary performance, and it pays below-average rewards, insecurity, and unemployment for below-average performance. Resolve to join the top 10 percent of money earners in your field.

Save Your Money

It is quite possible for you to become wealthy working for someone else. Many top professionals, senior executives, and superstar salespeople earn hundreds of thousands of dollars every year. Some earn even more. But even at an income of $50,000 per year, if you save 10 percent off the top, $5,000 per year, and receive an $8^1/_2$ percent to 10 percent return from the age of 25 to the age of 65, you will become a millionaire.

Whatever you earn, even an average salary, if you put 10 percent or more of your income away over the course of your working lifetime and never touch it, you can become a millionaire.

If you start earning $50,000, $60,000, $70,000, and more, and saving 10 percent off the top, your chances of becoming a millionaire or multimillionaire are virtually guaranteed.

Do a Great Job Right Where You Are

Not everyone can or should be an entrepreneur, starting and building their own business. About 90 percent of people working today are more ideally suited to work within the framework of a larger organization where they can use their specialized talents to their very best advantage. You may be perfectly suited to helping to build a corporation. You may be more comfortable within a company environment.

Peter Drucker said, "The purpose of an organization is to maximize strengths and make weaknesses irrelevant." The reason that companies form is because the owners recognize that they need a variety of different people with specialized talents in order to accomplish their goals of producing products and services, and marketing them effectively.

If you have a specialized talent or competence, you can actually be more valuable working within a business than on your own. You can work in an area where your special talent or ability is highly valued and makes a maximum contribution to the results that the company has to achieve to survive and thrive.

Put Your Career onto the Fast Track

There are several strategies that you can implement to put your career onto the fast track, and to assure that you earn the very most possible in the shortest period of time.

Make Yourself Indispensable

First, and perhaps most important, make yourself indispensable. The good news is that this idea has not occurred to very many people. When you begin working to become indispensable, you step on the accelerator of your own career.

The rule is this: You will always be paid in direct proportion to what you do, how well you do it, and the difficulty of replacing you. Your aim must be to focus on becoming so valuable and important to your company that the company cannot do with you. Your contribution should be so essential that even with market downturns and layoffs, you will be one of the last people that the company could do without.

Keep asking yourself, "What does my company need from me?" And "Of all the things that I can do, what are the few things that I do that contribute the most value to my company?"

In our Advanced Coaching Program for successful executives and entrepreneurs, we continually encourage people to ask the question, "*If I could do only one thing all day long, what one thing would that be?*" The answer to this question is almost invariably the one task or activity where you contribute the greatest value to your company and to the people around you.

Work Harder Than Anyone Else

Develop a reputation for hard, hard work. There is nothing that will put your career on to the fast track more rapidly than for you to develop the reputation of being one of the hardest-working people in your organization.

Unfortunately, most people are lazy. Although they will never admit it, they start at the last possible minute, they take every possible lunch and coffee break, and they quit at the earliest possible time. They are always sick enough to take every day of sick leave available to them in a course of a year, and they are adamant about taking vacations, holidays, and personal days. They unconsciously look upon work as a punishment. They seek every way to do as little work as possible and to get away from the workplace as soon as they can.

But this mind-set is not for you. Hard work will bring you to the attention of your superiors faster than any other single quality you can demonstrate. The rule is always, "Start earlier, work harder, and stay later."

People who get to the top of any organization are invariably people who have worked much harder than the average on their way up. These people are alert to and aware of others below them in the organization who are also hard workers. "Birds of a feather flock together." Top people are continually looking for others who can be promoted and pulled up to their levels. Hard workers find doors of opportunity opening for them wherever they go.

Work All the Time You Work

Perhaps the most important rule for success in your job is to work all the time you work! Don't waste time.

Work all the time you work. This simple rule enables you to leap ahead of your competition. When you arrive in the morning, go to work immediately. Don't drink coffee, read the newspaper, chat with your coworkers, or check your personal e-mail. Instead, start on your most important task, the task that your boss considers the most valuable, and work on it single-mindedly until it is complete. Work on it as though your life depended on it.

If someone comes in and asks, "Do you have a moment to chat?" you immediately say, "Not now. Right now, I have to stick to my work!" Suggest that you get together and talk after work. Refuse to treat the workplace like a social club where you spend time in idle chatter with your coworkers. This is the fastest road to failure and underachievement.

Invest the Extra Time

Opportunities for promotion, advancement, greater responsibility, extra training, and more education seem to go to the person who is willing to put in the extra time and the extra hours. Companies are always open to investing in people when they feel that that investment will pay off in increased productivity and performance. This is why training opportunities and greater responsibilities seem to gravitate toward the hard workers, like iron filings are attracted to a magnet.

The average *executive* workweek is approximately 60 hours. Virtually all of the highest-paid people work more hours than the lower-paid people. There are very few people on the fast track in any job or career who work only five days or 40 hours each week. All the top people work longer hours, and they work all the time they work.

If you want to enjoy an executive lifestyle, it is simple: You have to be willing to put in the same number of hours that executives invest in their careers. Because of the law of sowing and reaping, which is inviolable, you have to be willing to put in those hours for a long time. You must be prepared to work for months and even years before you begin to reap the rewards that go with the long hours.

Transform Your Career

Here is a simple strategy that can transform your career. Resolve from now on to *start one hour earlier*. This will require that you turn off the television at night, get up a little bit earlier, and get into the office so that you can start one hour before anyone else. The rule is that one hour of uninterrupted work will give you the same amount of productivity as three hours of interrupted work when people are continually coming in and out.

The second part of the strategy is for you to *work through lunchtime*. Because of childhood conditioning in school and earlier employment, many people think that the lunch hour is a sacrosanct period that must be honored, no matter what else is going on. This is completely false. From now on, resolve to work at lunchtime, when everyone else is away. This will give you another hour of almost completely uninterrupted time, during which you can catch up with your tasks and responsibilities and get ahead of your work.

Finally, resolve to *work one hour longer* than anyone else by staying later in the day. During this time, you can catch up with your work, plan the coming day, answer your correspondence, complete your proposals and reports, and be on top of your job.

Expand Your Workday

By starting one hour earlier, working through lunch, and then staying one hour later, you will only slightly expand the size of your workday. By coming in earlier you will avoid most of the rush hour traffic, and by leaving later you will be going home after the traffic.

If your normal workday is from 8:30 A.M. until 5:00 P.M., resolve from now on to start at 7:30 A.M. and work until 6:00 P.M. You will be absolutely astonished at the difference it makes in your career.

First of all, you will gain three extra hours of productive time each day. Since most of this time will be uninterrupted, you will be able to produce two or three times as much as anyone around you. You will feel more calm and confident. You will feel more positive and in control of your work. And most of all, the people who can help you the most will notice your additional hours, and how productive you are. This will open the doors of promotion to you faster than almost anything else you can do.

Accept 100 Percent Responsibility

One of the best strategies for putting your career onto the fast track is for you to accept complete responsibility for the results of your job. Keep repeating the words to yourself, "I am responsible!" Refuse to make excuses or to blame other people for delays or problems that crop up. Instead, accept complete responsibility and take charge of your work.

There is a direct relationship between the amount of responsibility that you are willing to accept for the results of your organization and the amount of power, influence, status, prestige, and pay that you will achieve in that company.

Determine Your Priorities

There are two key areas of responsibility that you must dedicate yourself to fulfilling. First, be sure that you are crystal clear with your boss regarding the most important things that you do for the company. It does you no good to work hard and do an excellent job on something that your boss does not consider particularly important. But it can help you tremendously to start and complete tasks that your boss considers valuable.

Take Over Tasks from Your Boss

Second, take responsibility for those tasks that your boss does not like. Some years ago, when I was working for a senior executive, he gave me permission to review his correspondence each morning before he came in. I immediately found small problems that I could deal with quickly and efficiently, saving him the time and trouble of doing them himself.

As it happened, no one else who had ever worked for him had voluntarily taken over these little responsibilities. I was amazed to see how much he appreciated being freed from these petty details. The more of these small tasks I took away from him, the more he valued me, and eventually, the more he paid me. I later learned that in the course of my career with that company he had paid me more than any other person who had ever worked for him in any capacity.

Never Be Satisfied

The third strategy with regard to responsibility is perhaps the most important. It is simply this: *Ask for more*. This approach can make your career.

Occasionally, I am invited to speak to graduating classes of business students. The organizers will tell me that these young people are about to embark into the world of work. They are nervous and unsure. They do not know what it is that they need to do to be successful. Could I organize my remarks to address these concerns?

My advice always consists of three parts. First, I tell them that their main job is to become absolutely clear about what their boss wants them to do, and then to do those jobs quickly and well. Set priorities on their time and always work on their most important task, as their boss defines the tasks.

Second, once you are on top of your job, go to your boss and say, "I want more responsibility." From now on, and throughout your career, this will become your mantra: "I want more responsibility."

At first, your boss will thank you for offering and tell you that he or she "will think about it." But each time you meet with your boss, once you are on top of your job, say that you want to make a more valuable contribution to the company, and that you "want more responsibility."

A Lucky Discovery

I stumbled into this strategy some years ago when I started working for a large company. Because I started earlier, worked harder, and stayed later, I was always on top of my job, if not well ahead. I had lots of energy and I wanted more work to do. So I began asking for more responsibility. And eventually, I got it.

This brings us to my fourth recommendation. Once your boss gives you an additional responsibility, grab it like a fumble in a Super Bowl game and run for yards. Throw your whole heart into fulfilling that responsibility quickly and well. Get a reputation for speed.

Whenever my boss gave me an additional responsibility, even if it was on a Friday afternoon, I would immediately plunge in and work nonstop until the job was done. Sometimes, I would end up working all weekend so that the proposal or report was complete by Monday morning. This always amazed my boss, because no one else in the company had the same sense of urgency.

You Can Never Tell

On more than one occasion, when I bent over backward to get a job done quickly, it turned out that the proposal or report was needed far sooner than my boss had originally estimated. But it was always ready. And my boss was delighted. As a result, he gave me more and more responsibility.

Each time you get a new responsibility, you get an opportunity to learn, grow, and become more valuable. Each time you complete a new responsibility quickly, you enhance your reputation for being the "go-to" guy or girl. Soon, whenever your boss needs something important done quickly, you will be the first person who comes to mind. This strategy is so powerful and effective that it can transform your entire career.

Step on Your Own Accelerator

In a survey, 104 chief executive officers were asked what qualities would most help a young person in their organizations to get paid more and promoted faster. Some 86 percent of them agreed on two qualities for rapid advancement. First, they said, was the ability to set priorities. They looked for people who could separate the relevant from the irrelevant. They valued people who could work on those tasks that represented 80 percent of the value of the entire job.

The second quality they looked for was the ability to do the job quickly. They looked for a "sense of urgency." It was not enough to be working on your most important task. What was required was that you got the job done quickly and well. These are the two qualities that most mark a person for rapid promotion, and they are both learnable through practice and repetition.

Develop a Niche Strategy

A powerful method for putting your career onto the fast track is called the "niche strategy." This strategy requires that you work yourself into a job where the results of that job are critical to the success of the business or organization.

No matter what the size, cash flow is almost always the lifeblood of the company or organization. Any interruption of cash flow can threaten the survival of the company. The niche strategy requires that you identify the most important function in the company's operations as it affects cash flow, and then work yourself into a vital position in that area.

There are six areas of operations in most companies, any one of which can be the essential activity that determines the cash flow to the business. Your job is to first understand how your organization operates and where its revenues come from, and then to pinpoint that key area.

Marketing and Sales
The primary source of cash flow for most companies is marketing and sales. Companies depend for their very survival on a continuous flow of sales and revenues. The success of the sales and marketing department is at the heart, or core, of the organization.

If marketing and sales is the key area in your company and you want to get ahead rapidly, you must to work yourself into a position in marketing and sales. You must to learn how to sell, which you can through study and practice. You then must commit yourself to doing your job in an excellent fashion, and become indispensable in that area.

Finance
The second area of importance in a company can be finance. Some companies depend for their survival on the ability to negotiate loans and to raise money in the financial markets. The people in that company who are the most capable of raising money, dealing with financial intermediaries such as banks and venture capitalists, become the most important people within that organization.

Production
Another area that determines cash flow has to do with the production of the product or service. In some cases, the people in charge of production are more important than anyone else in the business.

For example, an established brewery has a unique position in its market. Because of competition, market share for a particular beer is largely fixed. It does not fluctuate very much from month to month. However, if a particular brand of beer is not available for any reason, purchasers will not wait. They will simply buy a competing brand of beer, and often switch their beer buying loyalties permanently.

Therefore, the most important position in a brewery as it relates to cash flow is the chief maintenance engineer. Why is this? It is because the success or failure of the brewery depends on consistent, dependable, steady production that keeps the shelves full. Any interruption to the production of beer at the brewery immediately causes the entire business to grind to a halt. Sales stop, revenues are cut off, and the financial well-being of the brewery can be threatened.

What this means is that the chief maintenance engineer in a brewery is actually more important than the president. The president and other executives can come and go, but if the chief maintenance engineer is not able to assure that all the equipment is in working order, the activities of the brewery can grind to a halt.

Look around your company. Never assume that the critical core competency exists in a particular area. Sometimes you can identify a job or position that is absolutely vital to the survival of the company. By working yourself into that key position, you can dramatically increase your value. You can actually become indispensable.

Distribution Channels
In some organizations the distribution channel for the product or service can provide your niche. The success of the distributors and the

maintenance of the distribution channels can be more important than any other activity.

For example, automobile manufacturers require a dealership network in order to generate continuous cash flow. Virtually all manufactured products, for that matter, are totally dependent on their distributors. The person who exerts the greatest influence over the distribution channels or the dealer networks is often the most important person in the company.

If distribution is the key to your organization's success, this could be the niche that you should work yourself into. By taking the time to work with the people and organizations that distribute your product, you can become vital to assuring the cash flow on which your business depends.

Labor Relations

The niche strategy can be applied in labor relations. Sometimes the success of an organization, especially a unionized organization, is based entirely on its ability to keep its labor force working smoothly. If labor relations are a key part of your business, by becoming excellent in labor management activities you can become indispensable to your business, and as a result be paid at a higher level.

Government Relations

Another area where the niche strategy is applicable has to do with government relations. Some organizations are totally dependent on their ability to get government approvals. They need to maintain high-quality relationships with key government officials who determine and control the activities of the business. If this is the case in your business, one of the most vital positions in your company will be the person who meets and interacts with government officials to assure that the company can continue developing and marketing its products.

For example, pharmaceutical companies today are totally dependent on Food and Drug Administration (FDA) approvals to manufacture and distribute drugs. The process has become so complicated that it now takes 8 to 10 years and costs approximately one billion dollars, plus a moving van full of paper and reports, to get approval for a single drug. The person in the company who can negotiate this process effectively is vital to the success of the organization, and highly paid.

Become Valuable and Then Indispensable

Whatever the niche is in your organization, one of the fastest ways to get ahead in your business is to work yourself into the area of operations that is vital for cash flow and essential for the success of the business. Your job is to become first excellent and then indispensable in that area. You will be amazed at how much more rapidly you will be promoted and paid more money for your work.

Develop Specialized Knowledge

"Knowledge is power." Specialized knowledge or skills in a vital area enhances your promotability. Control of vital information is power, as well.

Here is the rule: *Learn all you can in your chosen job, but never tell all you know.* The more specialized information and knowledge that you have, the more valuable and irreplaceable you become. This does not mean that you hold back information. You share it generously with the people who need it to do their jobs well. The more of your specialized knowledge that you share, the more intelligent and valuable you appear.

Meanwhile, take the time to become extremely knowledgeable about your job, especially in the specialized area in which you work. Give and share the information when it is asked for. But if it is not asked for, keep the information to yourself.

The more proprietary information you have that is vital to the success of your company, the more important you become to the company. The more important you are to the company, the faster you will be promoted and the more you will be paid.

Do Things Faster

Move fast on opportunities. Get the job done quickly. Become known as the person who gets things done fast.

This reputation for *speed*, above almost anything else you can do, will move your career ahead. By doing things quickly, you will increase your chances of being given even more opportunities to take on more responsibilities. When you back these responsibilities with a sense of urgency, and fulfill them quickly and dependably, you will attract the attention of people who can help you.

Today, there is a "need for speed." People who do things *faster* are thought to be smarter and more capable than people who take more time to get the job done. Your decision to move quickly when opportunity knocks, or responsibility demands, can give you the winning edge in your field.

Cast a Wide Net

Make a plan to network continually with other people, both inside and outside of your organization. This can help you more than you can imagine and result in all kinds of doors being opened for you. In a recent study comparing successful, rapidly promoted managers with managers whose careers seemed to be moving more slowly, the researchers found that the habit of networking was the key distinguishing factor between the two groups.

The study concluded that *effective* managers were defined as managers who got the job done. But *successful* managers were defined as those who got promoted more often. In looking at the time usage of both groups, they found that effective managers, those who got the job done, spent only about 14 percent of their time networking and interacting with people inside and outside of their own departments and companies.

However, successful managers, those who got promoted rapidly, spent 54 percent of their time networking. They had breakfast with people inside and outside of their industry. They had lunches with key people in their organization and outside. They went to business meetings in the evenings. They joined professional associations and attended the meetings and seminars put on by them. They fraternized and socialized with people within their business and in other organizations.

Know More People
As a result of this continuous networking, they became known to a great number of people. It turns out that the more people you know, and who know you in a favorable way, the more successful you will be in your career.

People like to do business with people they know. People like to hire and promote people they know. People like to recommend and refer people they know. Sometimes, one referral or recommendation as the result of a contact you have made can change the entire direction of your career. This happens over and over to managers who network continually.

The Networking Strategy

To use the strategy of networking, your first step is to join your professional association. Join your chamber of commerce. Join your local business association and get involved. Don't just pay your dues and attend meetings. Instead, volunteer to serve on a key committee. Look for a way to make a contribution to the organization.

Whenever you join an organization, you will get the directory listing the members and the organization chart. Look at the various committees and the people who sit on those committees. Ask yourself, "Which individuals in this organization or association would it be most helpful for me to know?"

Identify those people and the committees on which they serve, and then join one of those committees and volunteer for responsibility. Whenever something needs to be done, raise your hand. By working with people in voluntary associations, you can bring yourself to the attention of key decision makers in a nonthreatening environment. These are the very people who can help you and open doors for you in the future.

A Success Formula

Here is one of the best formulas for success that I have ever seen. It is simple. "$T \times R = P$." This formula means that "talents multiplied by relationships equals productivity." This formula predicts and determines the amount of money you will eventually be paid, and how high you will rise.

This simple formula explains the success of many people. When you multiply your talents times your relationships, or the number of people whom you know, your productivity, performance, effectiveness, pay, and promo- tions increase.

The more people you can meet, multiplied by the greater talents that you can develop, the more successful you are going to be. The more people whom you meet and know, and who meet and know you, the greater will be the probability that you will meet and know the right person at the right time. This can save you years of hard work.

The quality and the quantity of the people you know, and who know you in a positive way, will largely determine your success in business and in life. Your goal must be to continually expand your network throughout your career.

Learn to Speak on Your Feet

A great way to move ahead more rapidly in your career is to learn how to speak on your feet. This is one of the most valuable and respected skills in business. And the good news is that most people who can speak well today were at one time absolutely terrified of giving a presentation of any kind. But as a result of learning how to do it, they became accomplished speakers.

Join Toastmasters

The best way to learn how to speak on your feet in front of groups is to join Toastmasters International. Toastmasters was formed in 1923 by a businessman who realized that there were a lot of other businesspeople who wanted and needed to learn how to speak competently and confidently in front of others.

He developed a simple process that psychologists call "systematic desensitization." With this process, you repeat a behavior over and over again until you eventually become *desensitized* to the behavior. If you stand up and speak on your feet repeatedly, every week, you eventually lose your fear of public speaking. This is the basic method of Toastmasters International.

Virtually anyone can join; Toastmasters is a voluntary organization. Pick up your Yellow Pages, look for the name and number of a Toastmasters chapter close to you, and then phone and arrange to attend a meeting. If you enjoy the meeting and like the people, they will encourage you to join and begin attending meetings each week. At each meeting, you will have an opportunity to stand up and share some of your thoughts and ideas with other people. Eventually, you will reach the point where you are completely unafraid of speaking in front of groups. This experience can be life transforming.

Take a Dale Carnegie Course

Another way that you can learn to speak on your feet is to take a course from the Dale Carnegie organization, which offers one of the finest crash courses in the country on learning how to speak on your feet. In 12 to 14 weeks, the instructor will help you to become more confident, competent, and outgoing. You will learn how to design and give a speech quickly in front of friends or strangers. Again, the Dale Carnegie organization is listed in any telephone book.

Get Serious about Learning

As you are learning to speak on your feet, read books about public speaking. Listen to audio programs on speaking effectively. Remember, public speaking is a learnable skill. The more that you do, the less fear you have, and the more competent you become.

There is an additional benefit of learning to speak publicly. It is that the more competent you become speaking to a group, the more confident and effective you will become in one-on-one conversations. Being a competent public speaker dramatically increases your effectiveness with others, especially in sales. It can increase your income as well.

Don't Let Fear Hold You Back

If you are a bit shy or uneasy about meeting new people, make a decision to overcome it. The more confident you become, the wider will be your network of relationships. The more you meet and interact with different people, the faster you will move ahead in your life. The very act of learning how to speak confidently to groups can save you 10 to 20 years of hard work in reaching the same levels in your career.

When you can speak well on your feet, your listeners will actually think that you are smarter, more knowledgeable, and more competent than a person who cannot. People think that you are better than you really are by the very fact that you can stand up and speak as opposed to sitting there paralyzed with fear. The payoff for learning to speak to groups can be tremendous.

Be the Best

Make a decision today, as I mentioned earlier, to commit to excellence. Make the decision to be the best at what you do. Make the decision to join the top 10 percent in your field. Here is a rule: *If you don't like what you are doing enough to want to be the best at it, it may mean that you are in the wrong job or the wrong career.*

People who are doing the right work for them are excited about the idea of getting better and better in that field. They are eager to read the books, listen to the audio programs, and take the courses. They are excited about working harder so that they can move ahead faster. If you don't experience this emotion in your current job, it does not mean that there is anything wrong with your job. It just means that there is a mismatch between your special talents and abilities and the requirements of your current position. It may mean that you are in the wrong job or the wrong career.

Identify Your Key Result Areas

In every job there are "key result areas." These are the results that you absolutely, positively have to get in order to do your job well. In sales, management, and business, there are key result areas that are essential in each of those fields. Your first job is to determine the most important results that are required of you, and then to make a plan to become excellent in each of those areas.

Your Slowest Kid

Here is an important discovery. Your *weakest key skill* sets the height of your performance and your income in your job. You can be excellent at every key result area except one in your work. That one weak skill area can hold you back more than any other factor.

Sometimes I ask my audiences, "If a group of children goes for a hike, which child sets the speed at which the entire group must walk?" Without much hesitation, people reply, "The slowest kid."

By the same token, your "slowest kid" is your weakest skill. This is the skill that determines how fast you move ahead in your work. Ask yourself this key question regularly: "What one skill, if I developed and did it consistently in an excellent fashion, would have the greatest positive impact on my career?"

Your answer to that question will likely be your weakest skill. Increasing your competence in this area will have a greater impact on your overall results than anything else you can do. Your job is to identify this one skill area, either by yourself or in discussion with your boss, and then dedicate yourself wholeheartedly to learning and excelling in that particular area.

Mastery Is the Key

Your weakest key skill area is usually something that you don't particularly like to do. You are not comfortable at it. Sometimes you dislike it or fear it. But remember this: The only reason that you are uncomfortable in a particular skill area is because you have not yet mastered that skill. You are not nervous or uneasy in any area where you feel competent and confident.

The good news is that all business skills are *learnable*. Whatever business skill you need to learn in order to move ahead more rapidly in your career, it is possible for you to acquire it. Set it as a goal, make a plan, and then work on becoming a little bit better in that area every single day. In a week, a month, or a year, you will look back and you will be astonished at how good you have become at that task. By this time, your fears and uneasiness over this task area will have disappeared and your career will be on the fast track.

One Skill Away

Here is a final point on becoming excellent. You could be only *one skill away* from doubling your productivity, performance, output, and income. By learning one more key skill, added to your existing skill base, you may become capable of achieving at a vastly higher level than you ever have before. Don't let yourself be held back in your career because of a single learnable skill that you have not yet acquired.

Develop Good Work Habits

To put yourself onto the fast track it is important to become a good time manager and to develop productive work habits.

In life, you will always be paid for the quality and quantity of your contribution. You will always and only be paid for the results that you get, not the hours that you put in.

The focus on contribution is the hallmark of personal effectiveness. Continually ask yourself, "Why am I on the payroll? What have I been hired to accomplish? What results are expected of me?"

You and Only You?

Here is the most important question: "What can I, and only I, do that if done well will make a real difference to my company?" Your answer to this question, and your ability to discipline yourself to work on this answer, can move you ahead more rapidly than anything else you can do. By asking and answering this question, you will be able to stay focused on your key result areas.

Most people in the world of work are poor time managers. According to Robert Half International, the average employee works at 50 percent or less of capacity. People on average spend 37 percent of their time in idle chatter with coworkers. They waste the other 13 percent of their time by coming in later, leaving earlier, taking extended coffee breaks and lunches, reading the newspaper, drinking coffee, and surfing the Internet.

During the 50 percent of their time that they are actually doing something that has to do with their jobs, they tend to work on low-priority tasks that they often fail to complete. They procrastinate, delay, and then complain about being overwhelmed with work.

Working Less Each Year

According to recent studies, the average American workweek has dropped over the years from 44 hours down to about 32 hours today. By the time you take out lunch breaks, coffee breaks, personal days, sick days, tardiness, and a variety of other factors, the average employee works about 32 hours per week. During those 32 hours, he or she wastes about 50 percent of the time. It is no wonder that people complain that their incomes are not increasing with the rate of inflation. It is because no one can afford to pay a person more for working less.

What is even worse is that most people not only waste their own time, but they waste the time of others. In fact, the people around you are the primary source of your own wasted time.

Don't Waste Time

To get on to the fast track in your career, don't waste time. Instead, imagine that you are receiving a specific quantity of money each hour to perform a specific quantity of work. Imagine that you are being watched all the time to make sure that you do the work for which you are being paid. Imagine that you have to *earn* your "hourly rate" every single hour. Work all the time you work.

The best news is that the more you work while you are at work, the more you will get done. The more you get done, the better you feel. The act of task completion releases endorphins in your brain, giving you a sense of happiness, elation, and well-being. These endorphins stimulate and motivate you into doing more work of even greater importance. The biggest payoff of being a hard worker and completing important tasks is that you begin to feel genuinely happy about yourself, your work, and your life.

Develop a Power Base

Begin today to build a power base in your company and in your community. The more powerful you are perceived to be, the more doors will open for you and the more opportunities you will be offered.

There are three basic forms of power in any organization. These are variously referred to as *personal power*, *expert power*, and *position power*. You develop them in order.

Personal Power

Personal power refers to your ability to get along well with other people, to be popular and friendly, and to be liked by your coworkers. The more people who like and enjoy you because you make an effort to get along well with them, the more they will look up to you and value your ideas and your opinions. They will ascribe to you additional characteristics of competence, capability, and efficiency. Because they like you, people will, in effect, support you and want you to do well.

Expert Power

You develop expert power by specializing in your job and doing your work in an excellent fashion. The more you are perceived to be an expert at a key part of the work that your company does, the more people will respect and admire you. The better you become at your job, the more you will come to the attention of the key people in your work who can promote you and pay you more. The development of expertise is absolutely essential if you want to become wealthy over the course of your working career. Money always follows excellent performance.

Position Power

Position power has to do with titles and rank. If you have a particular position in a company, this gives you the authority to hire and fire, to reward and punish, to make decisions, and to determine the outcomes of events. When you achieve position power and do your job in an excellent fashion, money, rewards, and opportunities quickly follow.

The Process of Power Accumulation

Each of these forms of power is essential to your long-term success and to getting rich your own way. First, you develop personal power by being a team player. You work hard and you work well with others. You do and say the things necessary for people to like you and feel comfortable with you.

Meanwhile, you read, listen, study, and take courses to become absolutely excellent at your job. By doing your job well, you develop expert power. As the result of personal power and expert power, you will almost automatically be given position power, which you can use to move more rapidly up the ranks in your organization.

The Law of Reciprocity

Perhaps the most powerful principle of human relations is called the law of reciprocity. This law says that each person has a deep subconscious desire to reciprocate or repay other people for what they have done *to* or *for* them. People want to get even, positively or negatively.

This law of reciprocity says that people will be willing to help you achieve your goals to the degree to which you help them achieve their goals. This is why the best practice you can incorporate into your relationships is the golden rule: *Do unto others as you would have them do unto you.*

Combine the law of reciprocity and the golden rule in all your work activities. Continually look for ways to be of service to people who can help you, by helping them *in advance*. Everything that you do that helps other people to be successful in their work predisposes them to helping you to be successful in your work as well.

List the People Who Can Help You

Here is a simple technique. Make a list of all the people it would be helpful for you to know. Next to their names, write down what you think you could do to help each one of them in some way. What kind of favors could you do for them? How could you put them in your debt? Make a list of all the people who you feel can help you and then begin implementing your strategy of "sowing and reaping."

How could you *sow* favors, kindnesses, help, or assistance in such a way that, should the time come, they would be predisposed to helping you? This is both a selfish and an unselfish strategy. It is unselfish in that you look for ways to help others *in advance* of them helping you. The rule is that whenever you do something nice for another person without expectation of return, rewards will come back to you in the most unexpected ways.

Ask other people, "Is there anything that I can do for you?" Continually look for ways to help people in their work and personal lives. Be willing to sow before you reap. Be willing to put in before you get out. Make a habit of sowing the seeds of appreciation so that, sooner or later, you will reap the harvest of gratitude.

Guard Your Integrity as a Sacred Thing

To put yourself onto the fast track, practice impeccable integrity in everything you do. As Ralph Waldo Emerson wrote, "Guard your integrity as a sacred thing; nothing is at last sacred but the integrity of your own soul."

Integrity is perhaps the most important quality for success and leadership, for several reasons. First, *trust* is the basis of all relationships. Trust is the basis of your relationships with your coworkers and superiors at work. Trust is the basis of your relationships with your family. Trust is the basis of your relationships with your friends, with your bankers, suppliers, customers, subordinates, and so on.

Trust is the glue that holds all relationships together, and trust is very fragile. It is based on absolute, dependable, consistent, and predictable integrity on your part. The key to building trust is to be trustworthy. People must know in their hearts that they can absolutely trust you to keep your word and rely on you to do what you say you will do when you say you will do it.

Trust Yourself

The key to developing trust with others is to trust yourself. And the key to trusting yourself is to be true to yourself, in all things, large and small.

Shakespeare wrote, "To thine own self be true, and then it must follow, as the night the day, thou canst not be false to any man."

Being true to yourself means being true to the very best that is in you. It means to keep your word. Building trust requires that you always follow through on your promises. Trust means that you do what you say you will do, when you say you will, whether you feel like it or not.

It is said that the strength of a man's word is measured when it costs him money to fulfill his promises. Talk is cheap. It is only when you have to back up your words with actions and assets that you demonstrate to yourself, and to others, how much your word is really worth.

Practice the Universal Maxim

Live your life in a way that is consistent with your innermost values and convictions. Practice the *universal maxim* of the philosopher Immanuel Kant: "Live your life as though your every act were to become universal law."

Virtually all the problems we have in relationships and society exist because people do not ask themselves this question. They habitually engage in behaviors which, if everyone engaged in those behaviors, would cause society to collapse. Here are four questions that you can ask your-self to keep yourself on track throughout your life:

1. *Your world.* First, ask yourself, "What kind of a *world* would my world be if everyone in it were just like me?"

   What kind of a world would this world be if everybody in it lived their lives the way you do? What kind of a world would it be if everyone treated other people, and their responsibilities to their work and families, exactly the way you do? If you are honest, you will probably admit that there are some areas in which you could improve.

2. *Your country.* Ask yourself, "What kind of a *country* would my country be if everyone in it were just like me?"

   If everyone in the country behaved exactly the way you do with regard to civic and social responsibilities, obeying the laws, working and investing, paying bills, and even driving through traffic, would this be a better country or not? If you are honest, you will admit that there are some areas where you could improve.

3. *Your company.* The third question you can ask yourself is, "What kind of a *company* would my company be if everybody in it were just like me?"

   If everybody at your company came to work, did their jobs, and treated everyone else exactly the way you do every day, would your company be a better company or not? If you ask and answer this question honestly, you will probably come up with some ideas where improvements are possible. Resolve to be a role model from now on.

4. *Your family.* Finally ask yourself, "What kind of a *family* would my family be if everyone in it were just like me?"

   If everyone in your family treated everyone else exactly the way you do, would your family be a wonderful, warm, loving, and secure place to live and grow up in? Are there improvements that you could make in the way that you deal with your family members that would improve and enhance the quality of your family life?

If you ask these questions regularly and set them as your standards for your behavior and conduct, you will find your entire life improving.

You will not only move onto the fast track in your career, but you will begin to become an outstanding human being.

Honesty Is the Best Policy

All good leaders were once good followers. They became leaders because other people wanted them to be in leadership positions. And the primary qualities we look for in our leaders are honesty, competence, integrity, and character. As you develop in character, by becoming a completely honest person, and in competence, by becoming excellent at what you do, every door will open for you.

Focus on the Future

One of the rules for success is that *it doesn't matter where you're coming from; all that matters is where you're going.* Almost everyone has the uneasy feeling that they have wasted a good deal of their time and their potential in the past. If they had it to do over again, they would do it differently. Unfortunately, many people use these feelings of regret as brakes that they set on their own lives. Instead of rededicating themselves to the exciting months and years ahead, they allow themselves to be overwhelmed with the mistakes that they may have made in the past. Don't let this happen to you.

Instead, think about the future and where you are going. Think about what you can do right now to create the kind of future you imagine for yourself. Learn what you can from past mistakes and forget the rest. Your resolve to be future-oriented will give you energy and enthusiasm. And your future is limited only by your imagination.

Work on Your Talents

In the parable of the talents in the Bible, there is a line that says, "Oh good and faithful servant, ye have been faithful over small things. I will make you master over large things."

There is a great life lesson in that parable. It says that if you are faithful over small things, you will become master over large things. If you do your job well, right where you are, you will very soon get opportunities to do bigger, better, and more important jobs.

Every leader, every great success in business, was once a young follower who was faithful over small things. People who are at the top today started at the bottom. When they started at the bottom, they went to work on their talents, abilities, gifts, and opportunities and developed them day by day and month by month. Over time, as they became better and better, they rose gradually to positions of greater responsibility, and eventually, to positions of leadership. As a result, they were paid well and promoted faster. They became rich their own way. And so can you. There are no limits.

Start Where You Are

The fact is that you can become wealthy, just like millions of others. You can start right where you are, right now, and go to work on yourself.

You can start saving 10 percent of your income, get your costs of living under control, and pay off your debts. You can start putting your whole heart into what you are doing right now. You can commit yourself to becoming excellent in your chosen field. You can resolve to go the extra mile and always do more than you are paid for. You can dedicate yourself to making any effort, any sacrifice, to achieve your dreams.

You can become wealthy during the course of your working lifetime by studying what others have done to become wealthy before you. You can then commit yourself to doing the same things, over and over, until you get the same results.

If a mentally retarded boy repairing furniture in a group home and saving $100 each month can become a millionaire, then surely you can do at least as well, if not much, much better. But you must get started.

Develop a Prosperity Consciousness

The starting point of all financial success is for you to develop a prosperity consciousness. Think of yourself as a wealthy person in training, as a work in progress.

Write and rewrite your goals over and over. Make detailed plans of action and work on your plans one day at a time. Visualize yourself as the great success you will someday be. See yourself and feel yourself experiencing the joy and pleasure of great achievement. What you *see* in your own mind is what you will eventually *be* in your reality.

The greatest minds of history have concluded that your outer life is merely the reflection of your inner life. What you experience in your reality is the outward expression of your beliefs and your inner-most thoughts. There are no real obstacles to success *outside* of you. All barriers to accomplishment exist only on the *inside* in the forms of fear and ignorance. You can overcome these mental obstacles by de-ciding right now, today, this minute, to do something wonderful with your life.

Become a No-Limit Person

It is just as easy to achieve financial success, and to get rich your own way, as it is to struggle and remain poor. And it takes just as long. By working a little harder at the beginning, you will enjoy vastly greater re-wards later on. When you begin practicing some of the ideas in this book, you will launch yourself, like a rocket, toward financial indepen-dence. You will eventually become one of most important people in your community. You will have the house, the car, the lifestyle, the bank ac-count, the inner satisfaction, the pride, and the self-esteem that accom-pany great success.

It's all up to you. Get going and keep going. Never give up. You can do it!

What to Do Now

1. Decide exactly what you want! Make a list of 10 goals that you would like to achieve in the next 12 months. Which one of these goals would have the greatest positive impact on your life? Write it down at the top of a separate sheet of paper.

2. Set a deadline on your goal. Set subdeadlines as well. A specific date acts as a "forcing system" on your subconscious and conscious minds, triggering them into action on your behalf.

3. Identify all the obstacles that stand between you and your goal. Why haven't you achieved it already? Select the biggest single obstacle and concentrate on removing that before anything else.

4. Identify the additional knowledge and skills you will need to achieve your biggest goal. Make a plan to acquire them, starting today.

5. Identify the people, groups, and organizations whose cooperation and assistance you will need to achieve your goal. Determine what you will have to offer them for their support, and give it to them, in advance.

6. Make a detailed plan of accomplishment, organized by sequence and priority (what you have to do before you do something else). Take action on your plan immediately.

7. Do something every day that moves you toward the accomplishment of your most important goal. Resolve in advance that, no matter what happens, you will never give up. You will persist until you succeed.

"Nothing in the world can take the place of persistence. Talent will not; nothing is more common than unsuccessful men with talent. Genius will not; unrewarded genius is almost a proverb. Education will not; the world is full of educated derelicts. Persistence and determination alone are omnipotent."

—**Calvin Coolidge**

Focal Point Advanced
Coaching and Mentoring Program

This intensive one-year program is ideal for ambitious, successful men and women who want to achieve better results and greater balance in their lives.

If you are already earning more than $100,000 per year and if you have a large degree of control over your time, in four full days with me in San Diego—one day every three months—you will learn how to double your productivity and income and double your time off with your family at the same time.

Every 90 days, you work with me and an elite group of successful entrepreneurs, self-employed professionals, and top salespeople for an entire day. During this time together, you form a "mastermind alliance" from which you gain ideas and insights that you can apply immediately to your work and personal life.

The Focal Point Advanced Coaching and Mentoring Program is based on four areas of effectiveness: **Clarification, Simplification, Maximization, and Multiplication.** You learn a series of methods and strategies to incorporate these principles into everything you do.

Clarification. You learn how to develop absolute clarity about who you really are and what you really want in each of seven key areas of life. You determine your values, vision, mission, purpose, and goals for yourself, your family, and your work.

Simplification. You learn how to dramatically simplify your life, getting rid of all the little tasks and activities that contribute little

275

to the achievement of your real goals of high income, excellent family relationships, superb health and fitness, and financial independence. You learn how to streamline, delegate, outsource, minimize, and eliminate all those activities that are of little value.

Maximization. You learn how to get the very most out of yourself by implementing the best time and personal management tools and techniques. You learn how to get more done in less time, how to increase your income rapidly, and how to have even more time for your personal life.

Multiplication. You learn how to leverage your special strengths to accomplish vastly more than you could by relying on your own efforts and resources. You learn how to use other people's money, other people's efforts, other people's ideas, and other people's customers and contacts to increase your personal productivity and earn more money.

Brian Tracy gives the Focal Point Advanced Coaching and Mentoring Program personally four times each year in San Diego. Each session includes complete pre-work, detailed exercises, and instruction, all materials, plus meals and refreshments during the day. At the end of each session, you emerge with a complete blueprint for the next 90 days.

If you are interested in attending this program, visit our web site at www. briantracy.com, or phone our Vice President, Victor Risling, at 1-800-542-4252 (ext. 17) to request an application form or more information. We look forward to hearing from you.

Index

About the Author

Brian Tracy—Keynote Speaker, Consultant, Seminar Leader

Brian Tracy is a successful businessman and one of the top professional speakers in the world. He has started, built, managed, or turned around 22 different businesses. He addresses more than 250,000 people each year throughout the United States, Canada, Europe, Australia and Asia.

Brian's keynote speeches, talks and seminars are customized and tailored for each audience. They are described as "inspiring, entertaining, informative, and motivational." He has worked with more than 500 corporations, given more than 2,000 talks, and addressed over 2,000,000 people.

Some of his talks and seminars include:

Leadership in the New Millennium—How to be a more effective leader in every area of business life. Learn the most powerful, practical leadership strategies ever discovered to manage, motivate, and get better results than ever before.

21st Century Thinking—How to outthink, outplan, and outperform your competition. Learn how to get superior results in a fast-moving, fast-changing business environment.

The Psychology of Peak Performance—How the top people think and act in every area of personal and business life. You learn a series of practical, proven methods and strategies for maximum achievement.

Superior Sales Strategies—How to sell more, faster, and easier to demanding customers in highly competitive markets. Learn how to sell higher-priced products and services against lower-priced competitors.

Brian will carefully customize his talk for you and your audience. Call today for full information on booking Brian to speak at your next meeting or conference. Visit www.briantracy.com, phone 858-481-2977, or write Brian Tracy International, 462 Stevens Avenue, Suite 202, Solana Beach, CA 92075.